D0209355

ENGLISH LANGUAGE SERIES

TITLE NO 1

Investigating English Style

ENGLISH LANGUAGE SERIES
General Editor: Randolph Quirk

Investigating English Style

DAVID CRYSTAL

Professor in Linguistic Science: University of Reading

DEREK DAVY

Lecturer in English: University College London

LONGMAN

LONGMAN GROUP LIMITED
Longman House, Burnt Mill,
Harlow, Essex CM20 2JE, England
Associated companies throughout the world

Published in the United States of America
by Longman Inc. New York

© Longman Group Ltd 1969
All rights reserved; no part of this publication
may be reproduced, stored in a retrieval system,
or transmitted in any form or by any means,
electronic, mechanical, photocopying, recording,
or otherwise, without the prior written permission
of the Publishers.

First published 1969
Tenth impression 1986

ISBN 0-582-55011-4

Produced by Longman Group (FE) Ltd
Printed in Hong Kong

Foreword

The theory and practice of stylistics have been much bedevilled by the multiplicity of sharply different emphases that have been given to the notion of style itself. There are two that have clashed with what seem to be particularly detrimental effect: style as an evaluative index ('The style is poor' or even 'This has no style') and style as an intimate, individuating index ('Le style est l'homme même'). Shaw, in his preface to *Man and Superman*, may be taken as typifying the first of these. 'He who has nothing to assert has no style and can have none: he who has something to assert will go as far in power of style as its momentousness and his conviction will carry him.' As equally typical of the second, we may add Pascal to Buffon; in his *Pensées*, he speaks of the delight experienced on encountering a 'natural style', a delight springing from the consciousness not that we are in the presence of a writer and artist but that 'on trouve un homme'.

The authors of the present book might not deny that in the last resort Pascal is right: the whole 'gestalt' of a person's use of language is as individual as his finger prints – and much more obviously so to the ordinary observer; but they are concerned to establish a theory of textual comparison which will explain our recognition of other, broader and socially more generalisable varieties of language than what is referable to the individual. Nor, surely, would they claim that all examples of language use are equally pleasing; but they are concerned to give us analytic tools with which we can dissect and identify those features that any of us is free to like or dislike according to his taste and sense of literary values, if literary evaluation is his purpose.

Style is thus placed squarely (as is shown in the theoretical discussion of Part One) within the framework of general language variation and it follows that no reader should expect to find the field of inquiry even tending to be limited to poetry and belles lettres. Rather, the authors scrutinise the linguistic differences to be observed primarily within the repertoire of English used in everyday life, and they divide their attention fairly evenly between spoken and written language – the former largely neglected by analysts of style in modern times. One additional feature should here be stressed. Again and again, the authors insist on confronting us with specimens of current English as it really works in actual situations, giving us not merely the experience of examining language (such as spontaneous conversation and broadcast sports commentary) that we have probably never had within our grasp before, but also the discipline of subjecting it to a kind of analysis which clearly isolates the most relevant features.

The importance of such work to students of literary style will be obvious, but of course its importance goes further. As English has increasingly come into world-wide use, there has arisen an acute need for more information on the language and the ways in which it is used. The present book has a welcome place in the English Language Series, which seeks to meet this need and to play a part in further stimulating the study and teaching of English by providing up-to-date and scholarly treatments of topics most relevant to present-day English – including its history and traditions, its sound patterns, its grammar, its lexicology, its rich and functionally orientated variety in speech and writing, and its standards in Britain, the USA, and the other principal areas where the language is used.

University College London   RANDOLPH QUIRK
June, 1969

Preface

It is always dangerous to write an introductory book about a developing and controversial field of study, but in the case of stylistics, such a book is very necessary at the present time. A great deal has been published in and about the subject over the past few years, but there has been no attempt to provide a meaningful guide to the subject for the general reader. This deficiency is all the more unfortunate as so much of what has been published is extremely technical, provides but a partial account of the subject, and bears witness to a substantial amount of disagreement among those most prominent in the field; and while some of this disagreement centres upon the relatively unimportant (though nonetheless confusing) problems posed by choice of terminology, much of it concerns fundamental issues of theory and procedure. There has been a similar lack of attempts to balance the practical and theoretical sides of the subject: most work has involved either theoretical discussion with little illustration, or detailed analysis with no explicit theoretical perspective. Much work in stylistics is vitiated because of analytical methods whose bases have not been stated clearly enough to allow evaluation and comparative study.

By dividing this book into two parts, we have tried to give due weight to the various tasks which stylistics tries to do. In Part One, after giving a general idea of what stylistics involves, we outline a set of techniques for describing any piece of language, and the various theoretical concepts which are needed to classify the varieties of language into types. We are using English as the language of exemplification, but of course the same techniques and procedures could be used for the stylistic analysis of other languages. In Part Two, we illustrate our approach by describing in detail various extracts of English. We have tried to maintain a balance between spoken and written materials, to present a range of usage running from the most to the least familiar and to concentrate our attention on those varieties of English which have hitherto been largely or completely ignored. The first extract, the language of conversation, seemed an appropriate choice with which to begin, because it is the variety which is most familiar to most speakers – a familiarity which must, moreover, form an important part, both consciously and unconsciously, of one's ability to identify other, less common varieties. We then move on via spoken commentary, which provides a clear illustration of the wide range of vocal effect available in English, to the language of religion, where both speech and writing have their own distinctive parts to play. The news reporting which follows presents a kind of written language which the majority of people come into regular contact with, and which in some form or other is relatively familiar; and we conclude this, the most detailed, part of our analysis by looking at a form of written language – that of legal documents – which is probably further removed from conversation than any other. This is a selection which was bound to remain to some extent arbitrary, but we hope to have done something towards achieving a balance by committing ourselves to a choice of several other varieties and collecting convenient specimens of them in Chapter 9, where we make suggestions for further study and analysis. Our reasons for excluding the discussion of literary language are presented in Chapter 3. After each chapter, there are exercises designed to raise some of the points which, for reasons of space, could not be dealt with in the main part of our discussion, and to allow lines of investigation which were only briefly mentioned there to be followed up. In both parts, we emphasise the exploratory nature of our approach: we are *investigating* English style, and quite expect that many of our suggestions will have to be modified as more material is examined.

We hope that this book will be particularly useful to students just embarking on college and university studies. We hope too that readers will let us have comments on our method, and suggestions for improvement (particularly of our descriptive terminology, which we are anxious to make as clear as possible); and we should be glad for opinions on the usefulness for study purposes of the transcribed specimens of spoken English – material which is much less easily come by than printed language. We welcome criticisms along these lines, particularly from those who, like ourselves, have the job of encouraging in their students a greater awareness of the wide range of English usage. Work for this book was supported in part by the Research Board of the University of Reading and by a grant from

the Department of Education and Science to the Survey of English
Usage. We are also fortunate in having had free access to the files of
the Survey, housed in University College London.

We are of course greatly indebted to all those listed in the ac-
knowledgments who have given us permission to reproduce the illustrative material in this book, but it seems appropriate at this point to
express our gratitude for being able to use spoken material, most of
which has never had a written existence. In particular we should like
to thank Mr Arlott, the Reverend I. Gillan, Professor Hough,
Mr Mittler, Mr Mishcon and our anonymous conversationalists for
personally allowing us to use specimens of their language; Mr
Thesiger for arranging permission to quote from Mr Justice Roskill;
and the BBC for their many acts of helpfulness, including permission
to make use of extracts from broadcasts of the Speech from the
Throne, from Mr Baxter's commentary on the funeral of Sir Winston
Churchill, and from the news bulletin read by Mr Kingsbury.

Finally, we should like to thank the many people who have provided us with helpful advice and criticism during the long period in
which this book was being written. We are particularly grateful to the
general editor of this series, Randolph Quirk, for his help at all stages;
and also to Frank Palmer, Peter Matthews, and present and past
colleagues on the Survey of English Usage at University College
London. Needless to say, we have only ourselves to blame for those
inadequacies which are still present.

University of Reading   DC
University College London   DD
June, 1969

Acknowledgments

We are grateful to the following for permission to reproduce copyright material:

Beecham Group Ltd for the text of 'Body Mist Lemon Bouquet' television commercial; The British Motor Corporation Ltd and Colman, Prentis & Varley Ltd for an advertisement for *Austin 1800*; Burns & Oates Ltd for extracts from *The Rite of Low Mass*; Crawford, Manley & des Tombe, Mr Derek Rayner, Letts Brothers, Cooper & Sibson Ltd, Mrs Davies, Mr Ellis and Mr Fitch for various personal 'small ads' from *The Evening Standard*; The Proprietors of *Daily Express* for a photonews extract from issue dated 3 November 1965; Andre Deutsch Ltd Publishers for an extract from *Swift's Polite Conversation* by Eric Partridge; Eyre & Spottiswoode (Publishers) Ltd for prayers from the text of the *1662 Book of Common Prayer*, and extracts taken from the *Authorised Version of the Bible – Matthew XIII*; Gibbs Proprietaries Ltd for the text of 'Sea Witch' television commercial; The Controller of Her Majesty's Stationery Office for an extract from *The Queen's Speech at the Opening of Parliament*, an extract from an *Inland Revenue Tax Return Instruction Form*, and an extract from *The Highway Code*; The Controller of Her Majesty's Stationery Office and Mr Graham M. Wilson for an extract from *The Royal Warrant appointing a Member of the Royal Commission on Medical Education*; Hoover Ltd for the text of their 'cleaner' television commercial; F. Hughes-Freeland of Hughes-Freeland Ltd for an advertisement for *H.A.G. Caffeine-free Coffee*; S.C. Johnson & Son Ltd for the text of 'Pledge' television commercial; The Estate of the late Mrs Frieda Lawrence, author's agents, William Heinemann Ltd and The Viking Press Inc for an extract from *The Lost Girl* by D.H. Lawrence, Copyright © 1921 by Thomas B. Seltzer, 1949 by Frieda Lawrence; Liverpool Victoria Friendly Society for an extract from an *Endowment Assurance Policy*; Longmans, Green & Co Ltd and Indiana University Press for an extract from *The Movement of English Prose* by Ian A. Gordon, Copyright © 1966 by Ian A. Gordon; Nicholas Products Ltd and Masius, Wynne-Williams Ltd for the text of 'Aspro' television commercial; The Proprietors of *The Observer* for two recipes from 'Cook-Hostess in Action' by Shirley Conran from *The Observer Colour Supplement* dated 7 November 1965; Patons & Baldwins Ltd for an extract from *Quickerknit matinee coat, No 464*; Penguin Books Ltd and Gregson & Wigan Ltd for an extract from 'Everything in the Garden' by Giles Cooper from *New English Dramatists 7*; Pergamon Press Ltd for extracts from *Homolytic Aromatic Substitution* by G.H. Williams (International Series of Monographs on Organic Chemistry, Vol 4), Copyright © 1960 by Pergamon Press; Philips Electrical Ltd for an extract from *Washing Machine Directions*; The Phillips, Scott & Turner Co for an extract from a 'Sona' television commercial; The Postmaster General for an extract 'How to make a Call' from *G.P.O. Telephone Directory*; The Roman Catholic Hierarchy of England and Wales for 'The Credo' from *The Rite of Low Mass*; the Solicitors' Law Stationery Society Ltd for clauses 7 and 8 of *Hire Purchase Agreement 13A (2)*; and The Proprietors of *The Times* for an article 'Weather Forecasting by Numbers' from issue dated 3 November 1965.

Contents

Contents

Part One Theoretical Preliminaries

Chapter 1

Introduction

THE NEED FOR STYLISTICS

When we talk about 'a language' – in our case, 'the English language' – we must not be misled into thinking that the label should in some way refer to a readily identifiable object in reality, which we can isolate and examine in a classroom as we might a test-tube mixture, a piece of rock, or a poem. There is no such object. The label 'the English language' is in fact only a shorthand way of referring to something which is not, as the name may seem to imply, a single homogeneous phenomenon at all, but rather a complex of many different 'varieties' of language in use in all kinds of situation in many parts of the world. Naturally, all these varieties have much more in common than differentiates them – they are all clearly varieties of one language, English. But at the same time, each variety is definably distinct from all the others.

One of the clearest examples of this is the difference between spoken English on the one hand, and written English on the other. Another example would be the range of varieties which we would distinguish as regional dialects: a person speaks differently depending on where he is from. No one is likely to confuse the types of English current in New York with those current throughout the London area, for instance; and we readily apply labels of origin to people with accents different from our own – 'Cockney', 'Scouser', 'Geordie', and so on. Again, there are noticeable, though dissimilar, differences between varieties, which are due to the sort of person who is talking or writing and the kind of social situation he is in. To take some examples from spoken English, most people would have little difficulty in recognising whether a dialogue they overheard (without seeing the participants) was taking place between a mother and her baby, between two scientists 'talking shop', or between two businessmen over a telephone. We would also distinguish quite easily a BBC announcer reading the news from a lawyer defending his client in court, and both these from a clergyman giving a sermon, even if all we had to go by (and this is the important point) was evidence in a tape-recorded extract, with no clues, other than the language used, as to the status and role of the participants.

These are just a few examples of the varieties of English that are used around us: each of us can immediately add many more from his own experience. We may not be able to say precisely what a variety is, what differentiates it from another, what types exist, how many there are or whether they are all as clearly distinguishable as the examples given above; these are things a stylistic theory should tell us. But once the matter is brought to our notice, we are at least aware that there are differences. In the normal process of living, of course, we tend to take these differences completely for granted, recognising and discriminating between the varieties in a largely unconscious way. Only when the differences become so great as to interfere with our understanding, or when someone else's mode of expression is so strange that we remark about it (and, frequently, complain to the daily press in the process!) do we begin to discuss this situation in a more conscious way. But we should recognise that the issues are much larger than these. Each of us, as an educated speaker of English, is, in a sense, multilingual; for in the course of developing our command of language we have encountered a large number of varieties, and, to a certain extent, have learned how to use them. A particular social situation makes us respond with an appropriate variety of language, and, as we move through the day, so the type of language we are using changes fairly instinctively with the situation. We use one variety of English at home, another with our friends, a third at work, and so on. We usually take this ability for granted; but what are the implications of doing this, how far does the ability extend, and how can we begin to study it?

Unfortunately we do not always appreciate sufficiently the potential of language for making communication successful and establishing social togetherness – ends which language may help us to achieve if used well. But if we choose to disregard the rules of language, or fail, through ignorance, to obey them, then language can become instead a barrier to successful communication and integration. This is where the danger lies: it is necessary to replace, by a more controlled, sensitive, and responsible reaction, our hazy awareness of how language should be used in the less familiar situations in which we find ourselves. One test of a successful education is whether it has brought us to a position whereby we can communicate, on a range of subjects, with people in various walks of life, and gain their understanding as well as understand them. But to be in such a position requires a sharpened consciousness of the form and function of language, its place in society, and its power.

It is not difficult to think of examples where a failure to achieve this desirable fluency is evident. There are many varieties of English which we have not mastered fully, which we have difficulty being at home in – and this involves just as much reacting appropriately to others' use of English as being able to use English ourselves. How often do we speak or write without knowing that what we are doing is causing a bad impression on other people, because of our poor command or inadequate social awareness of our language? There are many occasions when we may unwittingly or carelessly fail to reach social standards of acceptability: obvious examples would be errors like spelling mistakes, breaking the conventions of letter-writing (such as beginning a letter with 'Dear Sir' and ending with 'Yours sincerely') or badly used punctuation; or, at a more sophisticated level, using slang on a relatively formal occasion, making improper use of technical terms in a specialist context, or using language which 'goes over the head' of an audience in making a speech or delivering a lecture. Clearly there are appropriate linguistic 'manners' for the different types of situation in which language is used, which we are expected (and usually want) to show. To remain unaware of the full extent and power of these conventions when entering into one of these situations, and insensitively to carry on using language habits which we find come most easily to us is liable to produce general confusion, and probably criticism and embarrassment as well – a state of affairs which many business firms, and advertising courses in speech-training or word-power improvement are well aware of.

The native speaker of English of course has a great deal of intuitive knowledge about linguistic appropriateness and correctness – when to use one variety of language rather than another – which he has amassed over the years. He will probably have little difficulty in using and responding to the most 'ordinary' uses of language, such as the everyday conversation (described in Chapter 4) which occupies most of our speaking and writing lifetime. Normally, in such a context, mistakes, if they occur, pass by unnoticed or are discounted as unimportant. It is with the relatively infrequently occurring, more specialised uses of language that the average English user may find difficulty. The experience of each of us is limited, and there will always remain a range of linguistic habits, of whose nature and conventional use we will be largely or totally unaware, but which we may nonetheless from time to time meet. One such range has been approached in a very interesting way by Lewis, Horabin, and Gane,[1] who examine the increasing complexity and unintelligibility of rules and regulations in society, and who point out that when people come up against such language, in many cases the reaction is one of despair.

> 'To judge from innumerable press reports, many people no longer even try to understand complex rules and regulations. They enter into hire purchase agreements, and into highly dubious contracts that they patently do not understand. If they suffer personal damage or injury, they tend to miss out on their legal rights. They pay income tax and similar demands without knowing whether they are right or wrong. And they pay their gas bills without enquiring whether a different tariff might be more favourable . . . To some extent, the man in the street has habituated to the difficulties posed by present-day rules and regulations . . . obscurely-worded rules and regulations and instructions are tolerated simply because they are so familiar. Although their obscurity engenders feelings of helplessness and frustration, there is an over-riding assumption that nothing of moment can be done to improve matters' (*p* 3).

There is thus a strong case for saying that this lack of (primarily linguistic) understanding is an important gap in a general education, and should be remedied, particularly in those cases where the gap is at all wide, and where a person has a minimal amount of linguistic adaptability. (At the extreme end of the scale, there are people who are not able to read and write, or who have difficulty in speaking and understanding anything: at this point, the lack of a relatively subtle stylistic awareness has become a more general lack of linguistic awareness in its most fundamental forms.)

The foreign learner of English is one of those most at a loss in this matter. He too needs to be made aware of the difference between common and rare types of language behaviour, and of the alternatives available in particular situations; he too needs to react appropriately to language, if he wants to be accepted – and the same applies to the native speaker of English when he learns another language. The extra difficulty for the foreigner, however, is that he has no intuitive sense of linguistic appropriateness in English at all: he has no awareness of conventions of conformity, because he has not grown up in the relevant linguistic climate. He knows only what he has been taught in language lessons. Hence it is important that the syllabus for foreign language teaching should be so ordered that it includes instruction in those varieties of English that he will be likely to meet and need most frequently. Some courses attempt to do this, for example those which aim to provide a 'tourist' English, and no more, or a 'written English for scientists'; but the process can be carried much further and done more systematically. If a foreigner hopes to come to an English-speaking culture, then, he should not be in the position of having to make use of one variety of English in all situations, as so often happens. He needs to be fluent, and fluency should here be measured by his ability to conform in the approved manner to many disparate socio-linguistic situations. He needs to develop a 'sense of style', as it is often called – a semi-instinctive knowledge of linguistic appropriateness and (more important) taboo, which corresponds as closely as possible to the fluent native speaker's. But this ability does not come easily, and in many language-teaching institutions there is insufficient training for it ever to be gained at all.

Both the foreign student of English and the native speaker, we have argued, need to develop an awareness of differing varieties of the language, if they do not have it already; and the natural process of habit-formation in this respect may be reinforced, supplemented, and speeded up by a more rational approach. We can learn to analyse our speaking and writing habits and those of others, to discover and describe the patterns which differentiate varieties of language from each other, to explain as far as possible why people speak in a certain way, and to determine what alternative forms of expression they choose to use or to ignore in particular situations.

These are some of the reasons why the study of the varieties of English ought to be put on a more systematic basis and extended. But there remains another situation which should not be overlooked in this connection: the familiar case of a dispute over linguistic interpretation – of a textbook, an official form, or a poem, for example. Whether a particular effect or meaning has been expressed in an utterance is a question which will not receive a very clear or convincing answer unless the arguments are based on something other than the personal feelings and impressions of the participants. A wholly intuitive response is perfectly satisfactory and adequate until someone else comes along with an equally intuitive but different response: then, if personal opinion is the only basis, an argument will quickly reach stalemate. Disparate opinions can only be resolved by reference to the data in which the conflict originated, and hence, once again, there is the need for some kind of linguistic analysis, and an awareness of the internal characteristics of the variety of language in question. It may seem to be stating the obvious to say that the source of linguistic effect lies in language usage; but very often the problem is not phrased in such clear terms, the obvious is missed, and irrelevant reasons are brought to bear on what is, at bottom, a matter of language. It is very significant when a literary critic finds it necessary to begin her book on poetic language with the following remark: 'In considering the language of poetry it is prudent to begin with what is "there" in the poem – "there" in the sense that it can be described and referred to as unarguably given by the words.'[2] The fact that such a comment needs to be made at all implies a sharp criticism of much that goes on under the heading of literary stylistics. In the sense described below, stylistic analysis and description is a necessary part of clarifying linguistic problems of interpretation, or at least pointing to where the source of an ambiguity lies. It is a supplement to, not a replacement for the intuitive response – as we shall have cause to repeat later, in connection with the language of literature in particular.

To accumulate a store of information about varieties of language is, of course, an end in itself for many people who are interested primarily in finding out more about how language works, and the nature of the overall relation between language and society, man and his environment. The main part of the study of language varieties is in fact entered into for its own sake, as part of the academic discipline of Linguistics, regardless of the large number of potential applications, some of which we have already briefly discussed. The aim of a linguistically orientated, *stylistic* approach is clear: the varieties of a language need to be studied in as much detail as possible, so that we can point to the formal linguistic features which characterise them, and understand the restrictions on their use. To do this, however, we need systematic training and experience in describing the range of linguistic patterns which exist in English and the kinds of relationship which occur between language and society. So far, there has been hardly any attempt to supply the insistent demand for knowledge of this nature, even for fairly common uses of language. In general, schools only scratch at the surface of the problem: they provide a certain amount of tuition in letter-writing and essay-composition, as these are normally part of the syllabus for O-level examinations, but other uses of language are almost completely ignored. And while there *has* been a great increase of attention to this study at higher levels of education, particularly in universities, little progress has been made in providing methods which could be more widely used to help inculcate a critical and sensitive response to language in use. This is as much true of Linguistics as of other subjects. It is partly due to the absence of text-books in the field; but this in turn results from the lack of reliable descriptive information about the facts. What *are* the linguistic features which characterise the main varieties of English? If these were known, and information (even of an elementary sort) available, people could then make use of the material for their individual pur-poses. This book, then, aims to provide an introduction to the answer-ing of this question, in an attempt to suggest an effective approach to what is an extremely complex problem.

THE CONCERN OF STYLISTICS

Linguistics is the academic discipline which studies language scientific-ally. Stylistics, studying certain aspects of language variation, is therefore essentially a part of this discipline. Some scholars have called the object of study 'style', without further qualification. 'Style' is certainly a familiar word to most of us; but unfortunately to say simply that stylistics studies style does not clarify matters greatly, be-cause of the multiplicity of definitions that the word 'style' has. For clear thinking on the subject, as well as to explain the title of this book, we must say what we consider to come within the purview of stylistics. In this connection, at least four commonly occurring senses of the term 'style' need to be distinguished.

Style may refer to some or all of the language habits of one person – as when we talk of Shakespeare's style (or styles), or the style of James Joyce, or when we discuss questions of disputed authorship. (In this sense, it can be confused and identified with an individual's personality: style is mistakenly said to *be* a man, or *be* his thought.) More often, it refers in this way to a selection of language habits, the occasional linguistic idiosyncrasies which characterise an indivi-dual's uniqueness. It is usually impracticable to try and discuss *all* a person's speech and writing habits (even for a defined and very limited period of time or body of text), hence the concentration on those features in a person's expression which are particularly unusual or original.

In a similar way, style may refer to some or all of the language habits shared by a group of people at one time, or over a period of time, as when we talk about the style of the Augustan poets, the style of Old English 'heroic' poetry, the style in which civil service forms are written, or styles of public-speaking. Again, the more widely we generalise a situation, the more selective in describing the language habits of the participants in that situation we must become.

Style is given a more restricted meaning when it is used in an evaluative sense, referring to the effectiveness of a mode of expression. This is implied by such popular definitions of style as 'saying the right thing in the most effective way' or as 'good manners'. When we talk of a 'clear' or 'refined' style, then we are making a value judgment, consciously or otherwise, on the overall effect of the language on ourselves: there is no primary reference to the formal characteristics of the language used, and hence this sense is in no way descriptive and objective, as in the first two senses described above.

Partly overlapping with the three senses just outlined is the widespread use of the word 'style' to refer solely to literary language. Style has long been associated primarily or exclusively with literature, as a characteristic of 'good', 'effective', or 'beautiful' writing, for example, and the focus of the literary critic's attention alone. This sense is partially evaluative, partially descriptive, and stylistics here would not concern itself with uses of language outside that of literature.

With this background in mind, a linguistic approach to style, such as that presented here, is more readily definable: of the above four senses, the first and second come nearest to what we ourselves mean by 'style'. As a starting-point, we would say that the aim of stylistics is to analyse language habits with the main purpose of identifying, from the general mass of linguistic features common to English as used on every conceivable occasion, those features which are restricted to certain kinds of social context; to explain, where possible, why such features have been used, as opposed to other alternatives; and to classify these features into categories based upon a view of their function in the social context. By 'features' here, we mean *any* bit of speech or writing which a person can single out from the general flow of language and discuss – a particular word, part of a word, sequence of words, or way of uttering a word. A feature, when it is restricted in its occurrence to a limited number of social contexts, we shall call a *stylistically significant* or *stylistically distinctive* feature – phrases which will be explained in more detail in Chapter 3.

To make any progress at all in this neglected field of study, we have had to make one major assumption as a basis for investigation: we have assumed that any (linguistically untrained) adult has an ability to identify, in a purely intuitive way, certain features of his language with certain non-linguistic aspects of his experience. We shall refer to these aspects of experience as the *situation*. (It is important to note that we are here using the term *situation* to mean only *that sub-set of non-linguistic events which are clearly relevant to the identification of the linguistic feature(s).*[3] It provides us with a convenient label which covers all categories of such events; these categories, which are referred to for the time being as *situational variables*, are defined in Chapter 3. It should also be noted that in this narrow sense *situation* is not intended to include *everything non-linguistic which exists at the time of using the linguistic feature(s).* Our term for this will be *extra-linguistic context.*) People may not express their sense of identification very clearly, of course – for example, they may talk vaguely about 'thou' having religious 'associations' – but we have never come across anyone who could not consistently identify features to some degree, and accordingly we do not feel it necessary to accumulate experimental evidence to justify the assumption. What does need to be investigated systematically is the precise nature and extent of this identification. Most people are consciously aware of only some of the correlations between language and extra-linguistic context: they vary in the degree of confidence with which they posit that a linguistic feature is stylistically significant (if asked to comment on a piece of language, someone may be more sure of feature X having a certain range of extra-linguistic associations than feature Y), and people differ in their assessment of the obviousness of a correlation between language and extra-linguistic context (person A may note feature X as being associated with context P, whereas person B may not, or may associate it with context Q, or with no context at all, and so on). But there is sufficient agreement over this question of identification to justify our setting up as a hypothesis that *any use of language displays certain linguistic features which allow it to be identified with one or more extra-linguistic contexts.*

Our task is, accordingly, threefold:

We must identify the entire range of linguistic features which people intuitively feel to be stylistically significant, and specify a precise way of talking about them (a metalanguage).

We must outline a method of analysis which will allow us to organise these features in such a way as to facilitate comparison of any one use of language with any other.

We must decide on the function of these features, by classifying them into categories based on the kind of extra-linguistic purpose they have.

In this book, we shall suggest an approach to all three tasks. In Chapter 2 we shall outline the kind of metalanguage which we propose to use in order to discuss varieties of English at all. In Chapter 3 we shall discuss the various categories which any adequate stylistic theory would have to specify in order to account for all the features we have observed, and define more precisely what we mean by a 'variety' of language – a term which we are using rather loosely at the moment. In Chapters 4 to 9 we shall provide a number of samples of spoken and written English, which we shall examine in order to identify the stylistically significant features.

It is perhaps worth emphasising right away that the first step in any stylistic analysis must be an intuitive one. The stylistician is on precisely the same footing as anyone else here: he notices a linguistic feature which he feels to be stylistically significant. The difference between his approach and that of the untrained observer is that he will have a clearer idea of what is likely to be significant, and will know what to do with his observations once they are made. This last point is the stylistician's main competence: he is able to interrelate his observations within the framework of some theory, and thus piece together any general pattern of linguistic variation which may exist. This is where the objectivity claimed for stylistics comes in, not in the initial step, which is a wholly subjective (though, one trusts, informed) decision. The stylistician is able to *talk* objectively about language events. He cannot of course perceive them objectively, although some critics of the subject have seemed to accuse stylisticians of claiming to do just this. The stylistician, ideally, knows three things which linguistically untrained people do not: he is aware of the kind of structure language has, and thus the kind of feature which might be expected to be of stylistic significance; he is aware of the kind of social variation which linguistic features tend to be identified with; and he has a technique of putting these features down on paper in a systematic way in order to display their internal patterning to maximal effect.

But of course we must remember that at the moment stylistics – as indeed linguistics as a whole – is still a relatively undeveloped discipline. A definitive book on English stylistics would provide a specification of the entire range of linguistic features entering into the definition of what we have been calling a variety of language, as well as a theoretical framework capable of accounting for them. As will become obvious in the course of this book, we have by no means reached this final stage of study, though at least we are aware of what has to be done. All we can do is systematically point to certain significant facts in the language being analysed, suggest some theoretical principles which will account for the occurrence of these facts, emphasise the need for further analysis to validate or refute these preliminary soundings, and illustrate a procedure which will allow people to do this.

The view of stylistics which we adopt in this book is therefore essentially an operational one; that is, we are trying to provide a methodology of analysis, so that others interested in this corner of language behaviour can go about studying it in their own time in order to obtain relevant descriptive information within a single theoretical framework, without having to look for guidance at every turn from some teacher. We shall use one approach which we have found to be particularly helpful, though it must not be thought from our concentration on this that other methods of analysis currently being developed are not also enlightening. The methodological emphasis is, we feel, crucial, as it is the lack of an explicit procedure of analysis which has been the major deficiency in stylistic publications hitherto. The student is expected, after reading largely discursive articles on the subject, to work out an analytic procedure for himself; but different authors hint at such different procedures (never working one out in detail), have such different theoretical standpoints, and spend so much of their time arguing points of theory and not working through sample texts in a systematic way, that it becomes in fact impossible for the student to launch out on his own. The central requirement of any linguistically orientated approach to the clarification of stylistic effect is that it should provide a single, clear technique of description which will allow the student to cope with *any* piece of language he wants to study – one procedure which, if carefully followed, will focus the attention on *all* that is interesting in a piece of language and ensure that no item of potential significance is overlooked. Hitherto, stylistic analysis has been rather haphazard: scholars have been attracted to the study of the more obvious eccentricities of a use of language, and have ignored much that is less obvious (though not necessarily less important). It is this largely impressionistic approach, with its over-reliance on intuitive ability, that linguistics seeks to avoid.

Our aim is therefore to replace a sporadic approach with a systematic one; to minimise – we can never remove – the intuitive element in criteria of analysis. In this way we hope that our method will be of assistance to those students of language – the majority – who need some help in understanding relatively subtle linguistic usage (everything from textbooks and income-tax forms to poetry). It is valuable, we would argue, to put the examination of language on more well-defined, coherent, and systematic lines. When faced with a text of some kind – what appears to be a mass of uncoordinated data – a starting-point for analysis is often difficult to choose. The method proposed here suggests a place to start, out of the many possible, and a place to finish; it also suggests some paths for the analyst to take in getting from the one point to the other. It is essentially a research procedure, which we hope others will use, so that more and more material will come to be analysed within the same descriptive framework, and thus be readily comparable. Once and for all, however, it must be stressed that as soon as a student is sufficiently aware of the different types of organisation present in language, the method's rigidity is dispensable: he may 'so to speak throw away the ladder, after he has climbed up on it'.[4]

Notes

1 B. N. LEWIS, I. S. HORABIN, C. P. GANE, 'Flow Charts, Logical Trees and Algorithms for Rules and Regulations', *CAS Occasional Papers*, 2, H.M.S.O., 1967 (*cf p* 3).

2 W. NOWOTTNY, *The Language Poets Use*, Athlone Press, 1962, *p* 1.

3 A similar use of this term is to be found in the work of J. R. Firth.

4 L. WITTGENSTEIN, *Tractatus Logico-Philosophicus*, Routledge and Kegan Paul, 1961, §6.54.

Chapter 2

Linguistic Description

LEVELS OF ANALYSIS

The ordered approach which seems most satisfactory in realising the general aims of stylistic analysis involves taking the object of study – a particular piece of language, or *text* – and discussing it in terms of a number of interrelated *levels* of description. At each level, we are studying one aspect of the way in which language is organised: we shall be distinguishing phonetic/graphetic, phonological/graphological, grammatical, lexical, and semantic levels, and we shall explain what we mean by these terms below. The number and nature of the levels is dictated by convenience for the job in hand, variety analysis: interesting, stylistically relevant variations occur frequently at each of the levels distinguished, and need to be discussed in their own terms. Other levels might have been brought in (what linguists have referred to as *morphophonology*, for example), or we might have distinguished further levels within those already mentioned (*eg lexis, cf p* 58; but the little information found to be relevant in these areas for our discussion was more economically incorporated into the levels distinguished below.

The levels are studied as independently as possible to begin with, using whatever techniques have been developed in linguistics elsewhere; whatever cross-reference between levels is essential, we make; and we conclude by attempting a synthesis of the information made available, in terms of a set of quantitatively based descriptive statements. The order in which the levels are studied is not significant. Syntactic rules may form the starting-point, as they do in generative grammar, phonological and semantic information being built in as interpretative components of the grammar. Alternatively, it is possible to begin with phonetic and phonological information, as do scholars using a more traditional linguistic model, proceeding to grammar and vocabulary and thence to semantics; or one might begin with semantics, and proceed in the opposite direction. In this book, we shall in fact be following an order which moves from sounds, through grammar and vocabulary to semantics, but only for procedural and pedagogical reasons: it seems easier to introduce students to practical stylistic analysis if they begin with the comparatively simple matters of phonetics and phonology, which involve a relatively finite and stable set of contrasts, rather than with the theoretical complexities of grammar, vocabulary or semantics.

In our investigation of any level, we begin by bearing in mind what is already known about the kind of information generally present: at all points the stylistic description of the actual linguistic features used is identical with that made for any other (non-stylistic) purpose. Stylistic considerations only enter in when we begin to select features from the language as a whole and relate these to situational variables via various techniques of quantification, this process of selection being, for most other linguistic purposes, irrelevant. Thus, for example, we know that any variety which is identifiable in terms of phonological features (such as through extra frequency of certain phonemic or non-segmental contrasts, or through a specific set of idiosyncratic distributions) can be described in terms of any general phonological description. The description of the features will not go outside the frame of reference implicit in any study of English phonology: the same frame of reference is simply being used for a different, wider purpose. It is the frequency and distribution within one overall configuration which is the focus of the stylistician's interest.

The first level which may be isolated relates to the actual substance, or raw material of language. This material may be of two kinds: the expression of language involves a primary choice between two media, speech and writing (see *p* 69), and these have a fundamental difference in substance – sound waves for speech, marks on a surface for writing. *Phonetics* studies the characteristics and potential utility of human vocal noise. The study of written or printed shapes has hardly been developed at all compared with this, but we shall find it useful to refer to the visual analogue of phonetics in similar terms, hence *graphetics*. An examination of sounds and shapes in themselves, of course, will not provide a great deal of stylistic information, being as such pre-linguistic phenomena. But at this level, certain facts do emerge which are of relevance for a complete understanding of stylistic effect; for example, that isolated sounds and shapes may have a definite aesthetic appeal, may be interpreted as reflecting aspects of reality (as in onomatopoeia) or conveying a meaning residing wholly in the intrinsic properties of the spoken or written physical event (*cf* the general notion of sound symbolism). Such matters as the choice of type-size or colour in a text are essentially non-linguistic, but they too may have clear linguistic implications, perhaps relating to the semantic structure of the utterance (as in advertising or newspaper articles) or even to its grammatical structure (there are non-random correlations between type-size and grammar in posters, for instance). For further illustration of this point, one could refer to the graphetic flexibility of informal letters (such as the use of irregular spacing or line direction) as compared with the regularity of formal letters, invitations, and so on; or the organisation of utterances into symbolic visual shapes (a kind of 'graphic onomatopoeia') found in such various fields as the poems of George Herbert and Dylan Thomas, and in *Winnie the Pooh*.

A further clear example of distinctiveness operating at this level may be found in spoken language, where voice quality, the permanently present 'background' feature of a person's speech, against which linguistic contrasts can be heard, may at times be used in a semi-conventional way to relate an utterance to a specific situation, such as the tone of voice associated with a sermon, spoken legal language, or certain kinds of television advertisement. The basis of many kinds of humorous or literary effect is the motivated switch from one kind of voice quality to another. Such information is clearly important for a full understanding of the meaning of a text, though it has been little studied. The type of contrast involved at this level is very different from that found at the phonological/graphological level discussed below, however: contrasts at the former level are not so discrete, identifiable or systematic; they have more of a direct, naturalistic link with non-linguistic features, and do not display the arbitrariness of other aspects of language organisation; moreover they frequently transcend language boundaries – type-size, like shouting, has a fairly universal range of function.

Phonetics and graphetics study the basic phonic and graphic substance of language, respectively. The second level studies the organisation of this substance within the framework of a particular language or language group. Human language is clearly more than isolated sounds and shapes: it displays pattern. Out of all the sounds and shapes available, each language selects only a few (*cf* the very small range of shapes out of which the English alphabet is constituted, for instance), and these are used in a predictable and limited number of combinations to build up larger units, such as words and sentences. The sounds and letters of English have a clearly definable form and function, and their systematicness may be formalised in rules (of pronunciation and spelling respectively). *Phonology* (also referred to as *phonemics*, though not in this book) studies the sound system of a given language; *graphology* (or *graphemics*, which again we do not use) is the analogous study of a language's writing system, or orthography, as seen in the various kinds of handwriting and typography. In this area, stylistics describes patterns of sound or writing that distinguish, or assist in distinguishing, varieties of English – repetition of segmental sounds in a specific distribution, patterns of rhythm, intonation and other non-segmental varia (which we describe below, *pp* 24–40), distinctive uses of punctuation, capitalisation, spacing, and so on. These features are well illustrated in Chapters 4 to 9, so we shall not discuss them further here, but simply say that at this level, we are laying stress on the contrasts that can be made within the linguistic system, rather than on the physical characteristics of the system itself, which was studied at the first level of analysis.

At the third level, the result of phonological and graphological organisation is studied. Sounds and letters are used to build up larger and more complex units, some aspects of which are the subject matter of *grammar*, other aspects of which we shall refer to under the general heading of *vocabulary*. From the grammatical point of view, the main aim is to analyse the internal structure of the units called sentences in a language, and the way these function in sequences. To do this adequately, of course, many other kinds of unit and category need to be distinguished, and we shall be reviewing our use of such necessary concepts as words, clauses, nouns, verbs, and so on, later in this chapter: we shall not therefore discuss it further at this point, apart from emphasising that grammar is the central part of a linguistic statement. The traditional division of grammar into morphology, which studies the internal structure of words or classes of words, and syntax, which studies their external relationships, moreover has some relevance for stylistics.

As opposed to abstract statements about word classes and sentence structures, there are also stylistically relevant things to be said about the way *individual* words and idioms tend to pattern in different linguistic contexts, and it seems useful to study separately the attributes of single 'lexical items' (a term which covers idiomatic word-sequences, as well as single words) regardless of their grammatical form and function. We shall refer to this as the study of vocabulary (using *lexical* as the corresponding adjective); observations in this area will be made independently of grammatical considerations, though we shall not of course ignore the existence of any grammatical–lexical interdependence. Under the heading of vocabulary we shall thus give information about the choice of specific lexical items in a text (a choice which will of course be closely related to subject matter), their distribution in relation to one another,[1] and their meaning (for example, if a word was being used uniquely by an author, or was being related to other words in a consistent and stylistically interesting way). It is sometimes more convenient to bring a certain amount of information about word structure into an exposition of a text at this point. Vocabulary in our sense is thus partly a formal and partly a notional concept (*cf* the traditional sense of 'diction' in literary criticism). There seems to be very little gained by separating the formal and semantic aspects of the study of individual lexical items, as long as we are allowed when necessary to talk about the formal aspects of word distribution without any reference to meaning and *vice versa*. In this sense, of course, the situation is no different from the form–meaning relationship to be found in grammar: nowadays, linguists no longer feel it necessary, desirable, nor even possible, to exclude considerations of meaning from grammatical analysis.

We set up a separate level – *semantics* – in order to study the meaning of stretches longer than the single lexical item. The term 'semantics' is thus being used in an idiosyncratic way in this book: semantics for us studies the linguistic meaning of a text over and above the meaning of the lexical items taken singly. Patterns of thematic development, the distribution of concepts in a text as a whole, the use of characteristic figures of speech, semantic ingenuity (such as in the linguistic correlates of wit), and so forth would be studied descriptively here. It seems useful to distinguish such issues from those covered by vocabulary, in that the nature of the 'meaning' being expressed at the semantic level is very different: vocabulary contrasts are relatively discrete, finite, and localised; semantic contrasts tend to be less systematic and definable, and are all-inclusive. Of course, if one could show a regular paradigmatic relationship of some kind existing between the meaning of lexical items and that of longer stretches, then one would not be justified in separating them so clearly; but there does not seem to be any clear way of explicating the meaning of grammatical units such as the clause or sentence in terms of the meaning of their constituent lexical items. It is not normally an additive process.

As stylisticians, then, we approach a text with various levels in mind, and try to organise our material in their terms. We work systematically through the material, allocating points we feel to be of stylistic significance to one level or another. But while it is the case that we are approaching the study of the language of a text using a model wherein the levels are kept apart, it must not be thought that this precludes cross-referencing between the levels, or forces us to ignore significant inter-level linguistic relationships. The analysis into levels is simply a device to help organise our material and focus attention more closely on a particular aspect of language organisation. Whenever features occur which cannot be explained by reference to one level only, then the relevance of all the levels involved must be pointed out. Features at one level may reinforce or explain features at another, and a text may be characterised stylistically as much by the way inter-level features exist as by the features which operate within levels.

Cross-referencing does involve some procedural difficulties, however. A feature which demands reference to a number of levels simultaneously must either be described at each of the levels involved (which is uneconomic), or treated at one of the levels only, with a reference under the others (which gives undue prominence to the level chosen), or treated as a 'bundle' feature, described separately at the end of an analysis, after the levels have been gone through independently of one another (which is rather cumbersome). Not all the multi-level features which occur (and there are relatively few of them, hence there is no real case for dispensing with levels altogether) pose the problem to the same degree. Sometimes it is clear that, although two levels are involved in the explanation of a feature, one of the two is dominant. For example, a text which uses large numbers of foreign words, printing all these in italics, is distinctive at both graphological and lexical levels; but clearly the latter is more important, so that any discussion of this point could be carried on under the heading of vocabulary without any misrepresentation of the text, as long as there was a note under graphology saying that the significance of the italics would be dealt with later. The problem becomes extreme only when it is impossible to determine priorities between the levels involved. For example, when the rhythm and word-order of a text are both stylistically significant, it is very often impossible to say whether the description should be primarily carried out at the phonological or grammatical level.

In this book, bundle features are described as follows: graphetic, graphological, phonetic, and phonological features are described at any of the other levels which are relevant; if grammatical and lexical features co-occur with semantic features, they are described at the semantic level; if grammatical and lexical features co-occur, the description is made at the grammatical level.

Once we have been through a text in this way, we must assess the descriptive statements made in terms of their stylistic importance. Features which are stylistically significant display different kinds and degrees of distinctiveness in a text: of two features, one may occur only twice in a text, the other may occur thirty times; or a feature might be uniquely identifying in the language, only ever occurring in one variety, as opposed to a feature which is distributed throughout many or all varieties in different frequencies. Such differences must be noted, as otherwise there is no way of showing a gradation in stylistic significance or predictability within the features of a text. We must remember that the aim to show *all* the stylistically important features of a text is a rather academic one, and usually involves too much detailed analysis for it to be a task that most people interested in the subject could reasonably be expected to carry out. It is more normal for people to want to select, say, 'the twenty most important' stylistic features in a text, to make a fairly rapid comparison with some other text, or to be able to fit this approach in with the requirements of some school or college syllabus.

We have yet to establish the details of any such process of scaling the importance of stylistic features, but two basic principles are already clear: the more important stylistic feature in a text will be (*a*) that which occurs more frequently within the variety in question, and (*b*) that which is shared less by other varieties. For example, the use of the passive in some types of scientific English is a distinctive feature of this variety, as it has a greater frequency of occurrence than in most other varieties; but within scientific English it is also a very important feature because it is one of the most frequently occurring features of this variety. Again, the use of 'hereinbefore' in legal English is a distinctive feature of a unique kind, not occurring in any other variety of English. It does not occur very frequently in legal texts, but when it does, it assumes a very great stylistic importance, because of its uniqueness. A different unique feature which occurred more frequently in such a text would be graded higher on this informal stylistic scale.

Adopting an approach of this kind enables us to quantify the use of language in a text, grading the stylistic features in terms of the extent to which they characterise a variety as a whole, and attempting to make descriptive and explanatory statements of a more general nature. Our statements about frequency may of course be expressed in either or both of two main ways. First, we may present precise statistical information, using techniques such as the χ^2 test of statistical significance in order to compare distributions between texts and determine the extent to which two texts might be considered samples of the same population (instances of the same variety, in our terms) in respect of certain criteria. Such a method would be prerequisite for any serious research work, but it is too detailed for our present purposes. Consequently we make use of the alternative method of expression, making our statements of frequency in more informal terms, using such quantifiers as 'rarely', 'commonly', 'often', 'very often', and so on. This range of adverbials in English cuts up a continuum of frequency very clearly, with very little overlap, and is readily intelligible. It should not be forgotten, however, that any statements of relative frequency in these terms can be referred if necessary to the precise statistical situation which underlies them. They are not simply impressions: the distinction between 'often' and 'very often', for example, has ultimately an objective numerical basis.

Once we have quantified our texts, and expressed our results using either method, we are in a position to make statements about the overall stylistic 'picture' of a text, prior to comparing it with others. This is the end the stylistician is seeking – to compose a single linguistic picture of a text as a whole, to make a synthesis of the information he has discovered from his earlier analysis into levels. Once he has done this, the descriptive aspect of the linguist's role is complete. The tasks which then follow – critical interpretation and evaluation – are not his concern.

MODELS OF DESCRIPTION

Not all the levels we have distinguished above have been equally studied by descriptive linguistics. There are established techniques for discussing certain contrasts at the phonological and grammatical levels, and for talking about phonetic features; but there is no agreed terminology for the discussion of graphic and graphological contrasts; the theory of non-segmental phonological contrasts used here is of recent devising; many parts of the grammar of English have not been studied in depth and there are many incompatible theories from which a choice has to be made; the linguistic study of vocabulary has not progressed very far; and semantics in our sense is still only studied as part of traditional literary criticism. Our analysis at times will therefore seem somewhat patchy, to say the least; but one must remember that this is not a limitation of the stylistic method as such. Stylistics simply applies available descriptive categories and research findings to a further end: if these categories or findings are not available, it is not the job of the stylistician, *qua* stylistician, to remedy the deficiency – though many try to do so (*cf* our attempt to fill the non-segmental phonological gap, below).

In view of the fluid state of theoretical and descriptive linguistics at the present time, then, it is impossible to take much for granted in stylistic or linguistic analysis, and it is incumbent on the stylistician to illustrate the salient points of the model he is going to use, as a preamble to his actual description. What he must avoid is having to spend time during his stylistic analysis explaining the meaning of the terms he happens to be using; this is irrelevant and distracting. What we have done here, accordingly, is explain at one convenient place all the terms we cannot take for granted which we are going to use in the description of our texts. We shall not be repeating any of our exposition in Part Two of this book. We would also point out that inadequacies in the linguistic model of analysis we use do not necessarily imply inadequacies in the stylistic analysis, and *vice versa*. The model can and should be criticised in its own terms, for what it is, a theory which will account for certain linguistic contrasts in the language: the way in which this model is applied to show stylistic effects involves a quite different set of criteria, which also can and should be criticised in their own terms. It would be wrong to criticise the stylistic descriptions for unclear grammatical terminology, as this is a deficiency in the grammatical model. In evaluating stylistic analysis, it is important to keep the two kinds of criticism apart: we emphasise this at such length because in the past they frequently have not been so separated.

We primarily need to explain the models of non-segmental phonology and grammar used in this book. Phonetics and segmental phonology are sufficiently well established to be taken for granted: in our case, the segmental analysis of English presupposed is that of Gimson.[2] There are few technical terms arising in connection with the lexical and semantic description: terms which do occur will be discussed below.

NON-SEGMENTAL PHONOLOGY

The analysis used in this book for the transcription of the spoken texts is explained in more detail elsewhere.[3] The original transcription, which was devised to suit a typewriter keyboard, has been modified for printing, as the greater range of printing symbols allows for more immediately interpretable shapes to be introduced. The transcription has a complex look about it, but we find from experience with students that it can be mastered quite rapidly. There is certainly no desire on our part to defend its complexity: in order to specify adequately the non-segmental variety markers of spoken English, whose importance is usually underestimated, an analysis of this type is essential. To omit any of the transcription used here in order to achieve greater ease of reading would simply be to introduce distortion of the material which would ultimately preclude any satisfactory comparative statements. Varieties of spoken English tend to be primarily differentiated through non-segmental features of this kind, and it would be unscientific to reduce the transcription. We have nonetheless tried to devise a system whereby the content of the discourse can be understood and read relatively easily, ignoring the marks. This is why we have not put the spoken texts in a phonetic transcription. Our aim, then, is simply to allow people to be able to deduce from the symbolisation the way in which the discourse was spoken. We hope that the transcription is adequate to stand in place of the original tape-recordings, and the following remarks are aimed at producing a sufficient familiarity with the transcription to allow an accurate reading of the text.

The transcription records those features of English which display a clear linguistic contrast of some kind, that is, each feature communicates a meaning which is different from the meaning of any other feature. If one feature were to be substituted for any other, there would be a change in the meaning of the utterance which any native speaker of the language would be able to perceive, whether he had been trained in linguistics or not – though this does not mean he would be able to explain the basis of his perception. Not all these features are of the same degree of obviousness, however; not all carry the same amount of linguistic meaning. For example, it is more important to know whether an utterance ends in a falling or a rising tone than whether the beginning point of the fall is high or low: the first contrast might carry a critical distinction between a statement or a question, whereas the second simply distinguishes between, say, two kinds of statement. From the point of view of the information being transmitted, the first distinction is more important than the second. And it may be argued thus for the whole system, that there is a gradation of linguistic significance, some non-segmental features being more important than others. Our transcription tries to reflect this gradation through the size and darkness of the symbols used; for example, the most noticeable features of the transcription are the tone-unit boundary markers and the nuclear syllables with their tones, which we believe to be the primary features to note in any analysis of connected speech.

The tone-unit may be recognised by a combination of features which occur at its boundary, and by its characteristic internal structure: boundary features may comprise a marked shift in pitch, various types of pause, and modifications to the final phonetic segments in the unit; the internal structure must be one of a finite range of types, which are given below. The following conventions are used to show the structure of the tone-unit:

| indicates the end of a tone-unit, eg

... an at'tempt at "BRÌbery|

SMALL CAPITALS mark the syllable upon which the nuclear tone – the most prominent pitch-movement in the tone-unit – falls, eg

GRÀSS CLÓser

Where nuclear syllables begin or end with a double consonant in the spelling, both consonants are printed in small capitals so as to avoid the typographical clash of putting one in capitals and the other in lower case. For instance, APPROACHes is preferred to apPROACHes, and CUTTer to CUTter. If a non-nuclear syllable which begins with a double consonant is preceded by one of the symbols used in the transcription, it has been our practice to place the symbol between the consonants, so that we print oc'casions, and ef|fective rather than o'ccasions, and e|ffective. In the case of nuclear syllables beginning with a double consonant and preceded by a transcription symbol, we have compromised between the two procedures just outlined, printing the first consonant in lower case and the second as a small capital, with the symbol in between: at+TEMPT, ef|FECTive. Our purpose here is purely aesthetic, and has no implications for any theory of syllable division. Normally, when making decisions on syllable divisions, there is no difficulty in reconciling morphological and phonetic considerations. Occasionally, however, there is a clash between the two. When this happens we allow morphology to take precedence over phonetics, as in the case of a word such as TENdency. Following phonetic criteria in this instance would compel us to transcribe the word as TENdency, and this, it seems to us, is undesirable in that it suggests to the reader another lexical item – *ten* – and distracts attention from the word he should be seeing. The only exceptions to this rule are those instances in which following the morphology would have resulted in too strong a suggestion of an alternative pronunciation; we have, for instance, preferred CHILdren, to CHILDren (/tʃaildrən/).

The location of the nuclear syllable within the tone-unit will be referred to by the term *tonicity*. Usually this syllable occurs at or towards the end of the tone-unit. In cases where it is introduced earlier, for purposes of emphasis or contrast, as in an utterance like: she was a |VERY nice girl|, we shall use the term *contrastive tone*. The direction of pitch-movement in each tone is indicated by a mark over the vowel of the tonic syllable, *eg*

GRÀSS, GRÁSS, *etc*

Further syllables between the tonic syllable and the end of the tone-unit which continue the general direction of pitch-movement are referred to as the *tail* of the nucleus. The following tones are distinguished in the analysis:

Simple tones: ` (falling), ´ (rising), ¯ (level)
Complex tones: ^ (rise-fall), ˇ (fall-rise), ᷉ (fall-rise-fall), ˜ (rise-fall-rise).
Compound tones: ` + ´, ´ + `, ^ + ´, ˇ + `, ` + ¯.

The first prominent syllable of the tone-unit (made prominent either by a marked pitch-movement away from the pitch-level of the preceding syllables plus an increase in loudness, or by an increase in loudness alone) is referred to as the *onset* of the tone-unit, and is indicated by |, *eg*

and the |score goes +up . . .

Unless otherwise marked, with *h* if higher, and *l* if lower than the norm, all onset syllables tend to be at about the same pitch-level for each speaker.

We may now look at the tone-unit in terms of the sections delimited by these points, and label them accordingly (*cf* the example below):

prehead |onset ⌣ NUCLEAR SYLLABLE tail|
           head

Prehead syllables are always unstressed (*ie* are perceived as having a minimal degree of loudness) by definition. Head and tail syllables may be stressed or unstressed. We indicate three contrasts in syllable stress in the transcription:

   strong stress ", ordinary stress ', weak stress (unmarked), *eg*

   the |three 'people are ↗"definitely còming to'morrow|

All the marked pitch features we shall discuss below involve a loudness equivalent to a stressed syllable, as do onset and nuclear syllables. Strong stress may of course occur on any syllable.

The syllables in the tone-unit, whether stressed or not, can occur on quite a wide range of pitches. For this book, we have slightly simplified the total number of possibilities, and make use of the following system. We shall outline pitch contrasts for stressed syllables first, then for unstressed syllables, as the range of contrasts differs.

STRESSED SYLLABLES

A syllable may be slightly lower in pitch than the preceding syllable. This is in fact the most frequently occurring type, and we do not give this a mark in the transcription. When a stressed syllable has no accompanying pitch mark, therefore, we mean it to be interpreted as follows:

   the 'man

A syllable may be on the same pitch-level as the preceding syllable, in which case it is notated with a raised dot, thus:

the ˙man
‾‾‾‾‾‾
‧‐ ‐ ‐ ‐ ‧

‾‾‾‾‾‾‾

Such syllables are relatively rare, and none occurred in the spoken materials used for this book.

A syllable may be higher than the preceding syllable, but *not* higher than a preceding marked step-up in pitch, such as an onset. This is indicated by a short upwards-pointing vertical arrow, ↑, *eg*

I |think the ↑man . . .
‾‾‾‾‾‾‾‾‾‾‾‾‾
  ‧   ‐ ‐ ‐ ‐ ‧
‧   ‧

‾‾‾‾‾‾‾‾‾‾‾

A syllable may be higher than the preceding syllable, and *higher* than the preceding marked step-up in pitch, in which case it is shown by a long upwards-pointing vertical arrow, ↑, *eg*

I |think the ↑man . . .
‾‾‾‾‾‾‾‾‾‾‾‾‾
  ‧ ‐ ‐ ‐ ‐ ‐ ‐ ‐ ‐ ‧
‧   ‧

‾‾‾‾‾‾‾‾‾‾‾

A syllable may be a good deal lower than the pitch-level of the preceding syllable (*ie* a lower drop than in the case of the unmarked syllable mentioned above), in which case it is shown by a short downwards-pointing arrow, ↓, *eg*

I |think the ↓man . . .
‾‾‾‾‾‾‾‾‾‾‾‾‾
  ‧   ‧
‧   ‐ ‐ ‐ ‐ ‧

‾‾‾‾‾‾‾‾‾‾‾

Finally, a syllable may be distinctly lower than this last drop in pitch, producing a very low drop indeed, usually at or near the bottom of a speaker's voice-range, in which case it is indicated by a long downwards-pointing arrow, ↓, *eg*

I |think the ↓man . . .

These features only apply to the head of the tone-unit. In the tail, there is no such pitch contrastivity: the pitch-level of the syllables continues the direction of the nuclear tone, either downwards or upwards depending on whether the tone is falling or rising respectively (the stressed syllables being indicated by '). Occasionally the tail narrows or levels off in pitch, in which case the stressed syllables are indicated by a raised dot.

UNSTRESSED SYLLABLES

We show two kinds of unstressed syllable pitch-heights in our transcription, high *v* low (though there is some evidence to suggest that further degrees of height exist in English). A high syllable in the head is higher in pitch than the preceding (stressed or unstressed) syllable; in the prehead, it is higher than the onset. High syllables are indicated by a small vertical arrow, ↑; low syllables, being the most frequent, are unmarked, *eg*

the 'man ↑who   the 'man who

We may illustrate the above features in combination, along with an interlinear tonetic transcription, using the following sentences taken from Chapter 5, other features not yet explained being ignored.

mc|KÈNzie| |scrubs it ↑FÙriously on his FLÁNNels| and |starts ↓ÒFF|

on |that ↑rather "↑BUÒYant| |"BÒUNCing 'run of his| |up ↑aGÀIN|

|comes mc↑kènzie| |bówls| and |barrington ↑edges ↑thát|

and it's |through the ↑slīps| |and he's ↑going to 'get ↓four 'runs

↓and a lĭfe|

It should be noted that we do not force this material into any classification of nuclear tones in terms of high *v* low. The beginning point of a nuclear tone may be at many different heights, *eg*

    cóme ↑cóme ↓cóme *etc*

this partly depending on the length of the tone-unit, and it would be misleading in a descriptive exercise of the type presented here to adopt such a dichotomy when very little work has been done to specify precisely the kind of contrasts involved and which of them display the greatest similarity.

As well as patterns of pitch within tone-units, there are also significant contrasts between tone-units, but very little research has been done into this matter. This is unfortunate, since many varieties are partly distinguished by the way tone-units tend to cluster into specific patterns. One kind of tone-unit sequence that we do indicate, however, is the phenomenon which we refer to as *subordination*. Usually the pitch range of a tone-unit is not dependent on its neighbours, but occasionally one tone-unit's range tends to fall within the general range of an adjacent unit, so that it becomes formally 'subordinated' to it . If we compare

it's |jòhn on the 'phone| with   it's |jòhn| on the |phòne|

and arbitrarily assign values to both, it would be generally agreed that the second utterance has two central items of information, both equally important, whereas the first has only one. But both these utterances are distinct from

it's |JÒHN [on the |PHÒNE]||

which seems to fall midway between the first and the second examples. The central information still concerns 'John', but extra information is added, perhaps as an 'afterthought' – there is an implication that John's whereabouts cannot be taken for granted. This 'echo' effect between tone-units is characteristic of tonal subordination. Only tone-units that have nuclear tones of the same basic type may enter into a relationship involving subordination: that is, the nuclei in question must both end in a falling pitch movement (*eg* ` + `, ^ + `, *etc*); or they must both end in a rising movement (*eg* ´ + ´, ˇ + ´, *etc*), a level tone being a permissible exponent of subordination in either case. One of the nuclei must be wider (in the case of level, more prominent) than the other: this is regarded as the *superordinate* member of the pair. The other, *subordinate*, member is, of course, the narrower of the two. Where tones of different basic types follow each other they are treated either as a compound nucleus (types of which have already been described) or as belonging to a sequence of two separate tone-units: |´| |`|. Tone-units which are subordinated are enclosed in square brackets, and the boundary mark is placed at the end of the major tone-unit:

the |whole QUÈSTION [of de|FÈNCE]||

It is possible for subordinate tone-units to occur either before or after the nucleus of the superordinate tone-unit; but premodifying subordination is both rarer and systematically less important than postmodifying subordination. It is also, as far as we can see, stylistically insignificant. Accordingly we ignore it and incorporate only the latter in our description.

OTHER FEATURES

There are other variations in pitch and loudness, besides those we have just discussed, which are capable of carrying meaningful distinctions in speech, and these also figure in the system of transcription used in this book, along with a number of features related to speed, rhythm, and characteristic configurations of the vocal organs. We use the term *prosodic and paralinguistic features* to cover the whole range of non-segmental effects that we distinguish as being in some way systematic in speech, and we will now explain briefly those which appear in our transcription.

OTHER VARIATIONS IN PITCH

Here we are concerned mainly with variations in pitch-range. Apart from level tone, which is an obvious exception, the pitch-range of all nuclear syllables may be widened or narrowed with respect to its normal width. For instance, instead of ⟍ we may find ⟍ or ⟍, instead of ⋁ we may find ⋁ or ⋁, and so on. Variations of this kind are indicated by a small italic letter (*n* for narrowed, *w* for widened) in front of the nuclear syllable concerned; – ₙGRÓUND, ₙSHǍDOW, *etc* – but where the nucleus is not on the first syllable, following this procedure would lead to reading difficulties – contriₙBÚtion, etc. Therefore, in such cases we have shown narrowing and widening by means of inverted commas with a marginal gloss (see the next paragraph).

The pitch-range of a stretch of utterance comprising more than one syllable may be widened or narrowed in a similar way. We distinguish the following categories:

Normal pitch-range (*ie* the pitch jumps between syllables made use of by a speaker for the vast majority of his speaking time): this is not marked in the transcription.

Widened pitch-range: here the pitch interval between syllables is noticeably increased, as in some excited speech. This is indicated by the word *wide* in the margin, in inverted commas. The stretch of utterance affected in this way is also singled out by the use of identical inverted commas. *This is the procedure used for all marginalia.*

Narrowed pitch-range: the pitch interval between the syllables is substantially reduced. The word *narrow* is placed in the margin, and the appropriate part of the text put within inverted commas as explained above.

Monotone pitch-range: there is no pitch-range variation between syllables; all are articulated at the same level. The indication *monot* is placed in the margin.

In addition, there is in English a kind of pitch-range variation which is of a different order, involving the distance in pitch between stretches of utterance as wholes (as opposed to single syllables).

In *high* pitch-range (*high* in margin), the pitch-level of the utterance is distinctively above normal.

In *low* pitch-range (*low* in margin), the pitch-level of the utterance is distinctively below normal.

In *ascending* pitch-range (*ascend* in margin), the pitch-level of an utterance gradually ascends in a series of polysyllabic stretches, as in certain kinds of rhetorical climax in public speaking.

In *descending* pitch-range (*descend* in margin), the pitch-level of an utterance gradually descends in a series of polysyllabic stretches, as is found in the 'speech-paragraphs' used by radio news-readers.

The stretches of utterance involved in both these effects usually coincide with tone-units.

OTHER VARIATIONS IN LOUDNESS

Apart from the contrasts in syllabic loudness, discussed under the heading of *stress* above, the relative loudness of a whole stretch of utterance may vary. Everyone has some norm of loudness of speech which is used on most occasions; but one may depart from this norm; and each departure has some effect on meaning. We distinguish in our transcription two degrees of loudness contrast on either side of this norm: there may be an increase in loudness (referred to as *forte* and *fortissimo* articulation) or a decrease in loudness (*piano*, *pianissimo*). The musical terms (as others below) are here being used exactly as in their musical senses; but for our linguistic purposes we are postulating that they carry different, conventionalised ranges of meaning in English, which produce, along with other non-segmental features, complex vocal effects which would be intuitively labelled as 'angry', 'surprised', and so on. We are only specifying four marked degrees of loudness, but the extreme pair are best regarded as ranges of loudness beyond a given point, the outer limits depending on non-linguistic considerations, such as the strength of a speaker's lungs. Similarly, there are non-linguistic restrictions for the extremes of speed discussed below.

There are two other largely self-explanatory features noted in the transcription: *crescendo* (in which a stretch of utterance gets noticeably louder), and *diminuendo* where it does the opposite.

All loudness contrasts are indicated in the margin, within inverted commas, by the following labels *piano*, *forte*, *pianiss*, *fortiss*, *cresc*, *dimin*.

VARIATIONS IN SPEED

In most situations, one tends to speak at an approximately constant rate; but both syllables and longer stretches may be uttered with distinctive changes in tempo to produce different meanings. In the transcription, we note the following contrasts:

Clipped syllables: when a syllable is spoken very rapidly, or abruptly, this is indicated by a dot over the vowel, *eg* bůt.

Drawled syllables: when some part of a syllable is slowed down, the lengthened segment (or segments) is indicated by ⁼ , *eg* rēally, fīne, wēll.

Held syllables: these are indicated by ₌, *eg* b̰ackwards, ungraceful, jab; they occur when one makes ready to articulate a syllable but delays the release of its initial segment. The delay produces a 'bottling up' of the air for the articulation, which results in an anticipatory silence, perhaps also some audible vocal cord vibration, and greater emphasis on what follows. For example, in the phrase 'and he ̰BOWLS', the closure for the /b/ can be heard at the end of 'he', but the plosive stays unreleased for an instant.

Over longer stretches of utterance, the following speed variations have been noted: two degrees faster than the norm, *allegro* and *allegrissimo* (*alleg* and *allegriss* in the margin); and two degrees slower, *lento* and *lentissimo* (*lento* and *lentiss* in the margin); and as with loudness, we also recognise a gradual increase in speed, *accelerando* (*accel* in the margin); and a gradual decrease in speed, *rallentando* (*rall* in the margin).

PAUSE VARIATIONS

Pause features are not really non-segmental at all: they occur in sequence with the 'verbal' side of utterance, and not simultaneously with it. But, on the other hand, they are functionally similar to other prosodic and paralinguistic features, and are equally difficult to define; they enter into the definitions of such systems as speed and rhythmicality; and they have to be taken into account in the definition of the tone-unit, because they co-occur so frequently with other boundary markers. Consequently, it seems best to deal with pause features under the non-segmental heading, and next to speed variation, in view of the complementary roles of speed and pause in any overall measurement of utterance duration.

We indicate in the transcription both silent and voiced pause. Three degrees of silent pause are shown: the *unit* pause (indicated by –) equivalent in length to one beat or cycle of a person's normal rhythm of speech (it seems best to relate a speaker's pauses to his own speech rhythm rather than to some absolute measure); a *brief* pause (indicated by a dot ·), which is perceptibly less than a unit pause; a *double* pause (indicated by – –), which is approximately twice as long as the unit; and a *treble* pause (indicated by – – –), approximately three times as long as the unit. Longer pauses we feel to be no more distinctive than treble pauses, and they are accordingly given the same marking (– – –) on the rare occasions on which they occur in connected speech.

Voiced pauses, usually of the quality of a central vowel in English (shown by ə), with or without accompanying nasalisation, are rare compared with silent pauses, but when they occur, they also show length differences as follows: ə(m), əː(m), which are the voiced equivalents of · and – respectively. These may of course occur in sequences to produce longer periods of pause. They may also be accompanied by different qualities of voice (*eg* some huskiness in the throat) but we do not indicate these differences separately in the transcription.

We do not use the term 'hesitation' to refer to these phenomena, because this may be more usefully used to refer to a much wider range of features, going beyond pause in our sense, for example, false starts to words. When hesitation affects the structure of a word, we show this in the normal orthography, *eg* I thi think that . . .

VARIATIONS IN RHYTHMICALITY

Rhythm in English is a composite matter, a complex of features of pitch, stress, and speed (including pause). Each speaker has his own rhythmic norm, but we are not, in this book, concerned to define or notate this – we assume that it is non-contrastive for each speaker. Under the general heading of rhythmicality, however, we do distinguish three main kinds of departure from the norm. Each of these is linguistically contrastive, and involves a different kind of inter-action between the features of pitch, stress, and speed. The three are:

Rhythmic v arhythmic utterance. An utterance is rhythmic (*rhythmic* in the margin) when the stressed syllables are heard to occur at very regular intervals, that is, they approach the condition of 'subjective isochrony'. The stressed syllables are not clipped and the pitch of the unstressed syllables is either level with that of the stressed or shows the normal amount of pitch drop (see *p* 27). Arhythmic (*arhythmic* in the margin) is the opposite effect: normal speech rhythm is distorted by the introduction of various pause, pitch, and stress features with no apparent pattern to produce an overall effect of disjointedness in a stretch of utterance.

Spiky v glissando utterance. An utterance is spiky when there is an unexpectedly sharp, regular pitch contrast between the stressed and unstressed syllables. The stressed syllables are often clipped, and the unstressed syllables may be either high with respect to them (*spiky´* in the margin), or they may be low (*spiky`* in the margin) as in the following example:

|what on +earth do you +think you're +DÒing|

Glissando rhythm is similar to *spiky*, but the stressed syllables are often drawled and on each there is a pitch glide which may be either up towards the unstressed syllable (*gliss´* in the margin) or down (*gliss`* in the margin) as in this example:

I |really +think you +ought to +GÒ|

Staccato v legato utterance. An utterance is staccato (*stac* in the margin) when there is a rhythmic series of clipped syllables lacking the pitch variation which characterises spikiness; legato utterance (*leg* in the margin) involves a series of drawled syllables with similar characteristics.

TENSION VARIATIONS

This system of vocal effects is primarily produced by different degrees of muscular tension in the regions above the vocal cords. There are four distinct types. The first two, tense – the 'harsh metallic' effect – (*tense* in the margin) and lax (*lax* in the margin) involve respectively an increase or decrease in tension away from a speaker's norm, but there is no accompanying distortion of the individual segments of speech. These fluctuations in tension affect the whole supraglottal area, but especially the larynx and pharynx. The second pair, *precise* and *slurred* utterance (*precise* and *slurred* in the margin) also involve a change in muscular tension, but concentrated in the oral region and affecting the actual manner of articulation of the segments of speech. In precise utterance, all the segments in a stretch of utterance are distinctly articulated, final plosives being released, aspiration and friction being carefully controlled, vowels being slightly clipped, and so on; in slurred utterance, the consonant transitions become blurred, vowels centralised, *etc* (as in drunken speech). Speed and loudness play an important part in the production of these effects.

PARALINGUISTIC FEATURES

The remaining features, as opposed to all the others indicated in the transcription, have no dependence on pitch, loudness or speed for their contrastivity: they are vocal effects caused by different configurations of the glottal and supraglottal organs. They are few and far between in most varieties of English, and it may well be that others exist which do not occur in the data analysed so far. The following contrasts have been found:

> *whispery* voice: utterance without any vocal cord vibration at all; (*whisper* in the margin);
>
> *breathy* voice: utterance where there is too much breath for the needs of the articulation, the effect being one of mild 'puffing and blowing'; (*breathy* in the margin);
>
> *husky* voice: tension in the pharynx produces a hoarse effect; (*husky* in the margin);
>
> *creaky* voice: a slow crackle of vocal cord vibrations at a low pitch, like a stick being run along a fence; (*creak* in the margin);
>
> *falsetto* voice: a switch of the voice from one vocal register to

a higher one, as in yodelling; (*fals* in the margin); usually found only in males;

resonant voice: the whole vocal area is opened wider during articulation, giving a characteristically 'booming' effect; (*reson* in the margin);

spread voice: the lips are kept in a broad 'smiling' position throughout articulation; (*spread* in the margin).

The remaining paralinguistic features are fairly self-evident, comprising various vocal effects, simultaneous with speech, and involving pulses of breath which are irregularly distributed over a series of syllables, *eg* laughing, giggling, sobbing, or crying while speaking. There is also a tremulous articulation which can be introduced into the voice, a kind of 'catch' in the throat, which has been noted whenever it occurred. Only laugh, giggle, and tremulousness occurred in our data, and these are indicated in the margin as *laugh*, *giggle*, and *trem*.

The above is the range of non-segmental linguistic contrasts which we have observed occurring in English, and have accordingly recognised in our system of notation. In one or two cases, we have explained a feature which is not in fact exemplified in any of our materials, in order to show the systemic relationship which exists between many groups of features. Most of the prosodic and paralinguistic features can co-occur, unless they are opposed within the same system (*eg allegro* and *lento* are obviously incompatible); and some co-occurrences are very frequent indeed, *eg* '*low, piano, allegro*', which are a regular accompaniment of grammatical parenthesis. In the transcription, when two features occur over the same stretch of utterance, they are glossed together within one set of inverted commas. When two features (or sets of features) overlap, the commas need to overlap also, and hence double inverted commas have had to be introduced, *eg* ' " ' ". This can sometimes cause a complex looking margin, but by working through a text systematically, and matching each pair of inverted commas in the text with the corresponding marginal label – which will always be arranged strictly in its order of occurrence – there should be no confusion.

We shall now summarise the range of non-segmental contrasts noted in the transcription, giving symbols and abbreviations, for ease of cross-reference:

FEATURES NOTED IN THE TEXT

Tone-unit boundary: |
Nuclear syllable: SMALL CAPITALS
Onset syllable: |; higher than normal: |ₕ; lower than normal: |ₗ
Tone types, Simple: ` , ´ , ‾
          Complex: ^ , ˇ , ˄ , ˜
          Compound: ` + ´ , ´ + ` , ˄ + ´ , ˇ + ` , ` + ‾
Stress, weak: not marked; other stress: '; strong: "
Pitch-range, stressed syllables
        slight step-down: not marked
        marked step-down: ↓
        very marked step-down: ⬇
        level with preceding syllable: · , (eg that ·man)
        step-up higher than preceding syllable: ⬆
        step-up higher than preceding step-up: ↑
      unstressed syllables
        high: ˙ (eg in˙advertent)
        low: not marked
Subordination: [ ]
Nuclear syllable pitch-range, narrow: ₙ; wide: ᵥ
Syllabic clipping: ˘ (eg lŏt); drawling: ‾(eg ānd); held: ₌(eg b̲ut)

Pause	Silent	Voiced
unit:	–	əː (m)
double:	– –	əː əː
treble:	– – –	əː əː əː
brief:	·	ə (m)

FEATURES IN THE MARGIN

Pitch-range: *narrow, wide, monot(one), high, low, ascend(ing), descend(ing)*

Loudness: *forte, fortiss(imo), piano, pianiss(imo), cresc(endo), dimin(uendo)*

Speed: *alleg(ro), allegriss(imo), lento, lentiss(imo), accel(erando), rall(entando)*

Rhythmicality: *rhythmic, arhythmic, spiky* ` or ´, *gliss(ando)* ` or ´, *stac(cato), leg(ato)*

Tension: *tense, lax, precise, slurred*

Paralinguistic features: *whisper, breathy, husky, creak, fals(etto), reson(ant), spread, laugh, giggle, trem(ulousness), sob, cry*

Traditional orthography is used throughout, with the exception that proper nouns are not begun with capital letters: this was to avoid drawing too much attention to a linguistically insignificant feature of the text. The only traditional capital, retained to avoid giving *too* alien an impression, is 'I'.

We have not made any attempt to transcribe the voice-quality, the permanent individual 'background' to a person's voice. In most varieties, the specific nature of the voice-quality is irrelevant, but in some the background quality does enter into the identification of the variety at the phonetic level. Some varieties are regularly character-ised by a specific kind of voice-quality, such as is found in sermons; and reliance on types of voice-quality is probably one of the most important features of the language of television advertising. When necessary, we shall point to such qualities, and give them an im-pressionistic description which we hope will guide the reader. This may be in the margin (as on *p* 99), or it may be mentioned in the preamble to the textual discussion. We are under no delusion about the inadequacy of such an approach; but research on the description of voice-quality has progressed so slowly that it would be premature to adopt any one method for use here.[4]

GRAMMAR

In this section we shall draw attention to certain features which we feel to be important characteristics of our analysis, and explain the terminology which we make use of in the discussion of our texts. Our choice of grammatical model has been dictated by the requirements of stylistic analysis, and any assessment of its value should bear this in mind. We want a method of defining and interrelating those stylistic-ally relevant grammatical contrasts which we have noted in the data; a method which will (*a*) allow easy recognition of where in a grammar the stylistic distinctiveness of a text may be said to lie, and (*b*) facilitate grammatical comparative statement. We feel that in the present state of knowledge, with many crucial grammatical questions inexplicit or unanswered, it is wise to adopt a slightly conservative position, and we have thus decided on a model which sees grammar in terms of a series of interrelated components, each of which deals with a par-ticular aspect of grammatical structure, *eg* the sentence, the clause, the word. We wish to make use of such a framework without involving ourselves too much in theoretical discussion: we are not concerned to establish the precise nature of the relationship between the components (*eg* we do not feel it necessary to decide whether the components exist in a hierarchical relationship of any particular type), nor do we insist that there is one theoretically most satisfactory method of working through the components in carrying out any analysis. We do not wish to deny the importance of such issues, but merely to point out that any adequate discussion of such points would take us so far afield that we would never get back to stylistics, and that in any case we can carry out our stylistic task without going into them. All we want to do is talk clearly and consistently about those grammatical contrasts we have noted: to do this, we need a minimum of theoretical discussion.

Nor do we need a complete grammar of English. This is the second main feature of our grammar, namely, that it is unfinished, as all others; but, unlike others, there is no theoretical obligation to finish it before commencing analysis. We do not need a comprehensive grammatical description in order to be able to begin stylistic analysis, for the simple reason that not all grammatical contrasts in English are involved in the specification of stylistic contrast (*cf* below, *p* 65). Of course ultimately all such partial grammars will have to be evaluated against some more adequate grammar, but as a basis of investigation we can proceed without this latter grammar, which in any case does not exist. It would be nice if we could simply refer our stylistic points to a generally agreed body of grammatical information, in much the same way as we can for phonetics; but this stage is still some way off. Meanwhile, therefore, the stylistician must proceed by making use of what information is available, adding to it where he can, and being aware of the fact that he is probably leaving out a great deal that is of potential relevance. For example, we feel sure that there is much to be said about the way different varieties make use of types of inter-sentence linkage, or adjective order, or predeterminer contrasts (see below), but in view of the fact that hardly any work has been done on such matters, and that we are not clear as to what the general state of affairs is in English, all we can do is make tentative observations about some of the patterns which strike us as obvious. It must not be thought that we have noticed everything that is grammatically relevant in the texts analysed here. We have simply gone as far as our experience of English grammar as a whole has let us go; and as more information accumulates about the structure of English, so our stylistic analysis will have to be further supplemented. The grammatical part of our description is, then, in the nature of things, very 'open-ended' and incomplete. We hope that, by stressing this point, people hitherto unaware of the extent of the inadequacy of available descriptions will do something to help remedy the deficiency.

A further point which has to be decided is where stylistic information should be incorporated into the complete grammar of English which we hope one day to have. For such a grammar to be descriptively adequate, it would have to include any such situationally restricted features as those described in this book. The question is how the stylistic information should be related to the non-stylistic parts of the grammar. There are essentially three choices open to us. First, it would be possible to make the first rules in the grammar stylistic rules, generating a set of varieties which are then described, each in its own terms. This is really to write a separate grammar for each variety, a case which has been argued for substantially deviant uses of language (*eg* extreme cases of literary idiosyncrasy).[5] It is doubtful, however, whether this approach is useful: it is highly uneconomical, in that much of the information which has to be generated separately for each variety is the same (common-core); it makes comparative study difficult; and it poses great theoretical problems, such as how to deal with differences in the ordering of rules between varieties. It is of course useful as a research procedure, when one wishes to examine a variety purely in its own terms, and we shall make use of it ourselves later in this book; but its ultimate value is very limited.

Second, we can deal with our stylistic contrasts at the end of a grammar of the common-core features or of some norm (*cf note* 8, *p* 91). This involves assuming a 'variety-less' or 'normal' or 'unmarked' set of grammatical structures which accounts for features which occur with similar frequency and distribution in all varieties of the language, and then bringing in uniquely restricted and distributionally marked features as a kind of appendix. This arrangement, too, we find uneconomical, since it entails, if a deviation is to be fully described, reference to or repetition of the appropriate point in the common-core grammar: for example, a stylistic point about order of adverbials requires consideration of some 'unmarked' order of adverbials described already. In view of the amount of cross-referencing which would have to take place to relate the whole range of stylistic contrasts to their unmarked counterparts, it is clear that such a grammar could become very complex.

We therefore prefer the third choice, which has the advantage of allowing easy comparative statement without the complexity just described. This is to have only one grammar for the language, and to integrate stylistic information at all relevant points. Thus when the grammar defines the notion of sentence, all stylistically interesting points about sentence-types, distribution, *etc*, are described; when the grammar goes on to discuss adjectives in nominal groups, all significant stylistic points about adjectives are described, and so on. Such an approach means that in order to obtain a complete description of any one variety a description has to be pieced together by working through the grammar in some predetermined way, and noting points about a variety as they arise; but this is no objection to the approach, as it would in any case be necessary to work through the grammar in this way in order to specify the common-core information. In other words, the entire range of stylistic contrasts appropriate for any given point in the grammar must be specified before going on to any other point.

This is therefore another reason for looking at grammar as if it were a series of components which can be described reasonably independently of each other. It allows attention to be focused more strongly on the contrasts operating within a particular component, without fear of distraction from the others. This flexibility is ultimately undesirable, as any final theory would have to be more explicit in specifying the relationships between the components, but procedurally it is invaluable.

We isolate five components in all, chosen on a strictly pragmatic basis, in the sense that stylistic contrasts seem to be satisfactorily organised if they are described in terms of one or other of these components. We shall begin with the most general kind of contrast and proceed to the least, though this is only one possible order among many. The components are: I inter-sentence relationships; II sentence typology; III clause typology; IV group typology; V word typology. We shall now briefly describe the linguistic features operating at each of these places within the grammar, and explain what we mean by these labels.

I INTER-SENTENCE RELATIONSHIPS

Like most people, we shall begin with the sentence, since this is generally agreed to be the most convenient point of departure for grammatical investigation, not requiring the prior specification of any other grammatical unit, being semantically more self-contained than any other unit, and being also relatively easy to identify in both speech and writing – especially printed writing. But it must not be assumed because of this that everything that is of stylistic interest in grammar is to be found within this notion of sentence. It is clear that there are important restrictions on the ways in which we can group sentences together in connected speech – either in conversation or monologue – and many varieties are characterised partly by the way in which their sentences tend to cluster together. Features traditionally discussed under the heading of 'paragraph formation' would be relevant here, though the concept of a 'paragraph' is usually reserved for the written medium only (whereas there is evidence for the existence of speech 'paragraphs' also), and is moreover difficult to define in precise grammatical terms because of its notional basis (*cf* the semantic status of such traditional concepts as 'topic sentence'). The sequential patterns into which sentences fall have not been clearly defined as yet, but some patterns (for instance, the question-response pattern) are familiar; certain sequences of sentence-types can be described without difficulty (see below); and certain features which link sentence-types can be recognised.

We ought therefore to mention what these sentence-linking features are, since they are not dealt with by most grammars which concentrate on the analysis of sentences.[6] They cover such features as ellipsis, anaphora (especially the use of the definite article, the demonstratives, the personal pronouns), the use of concord (in number, or tense, for example), lexical features (such as word repetitions), adverbial contrasts (especially sentence initiators like 'however', which always imply a preceding sentence), and prosodic features (such as contrastive tone, 'listing' intonation patterns). We can expect a variety to be characterised by features of this kind, and any grammar should therefore be able to account for them, though at present the way in which this is done cannot be expected to be very systematic. Examples of distinctiveness in inter-sentence linkage would be the frequent use of anaphora (as in conversation), or its absence (as in legal writing, see *p* 202), the use of specific patterns of paragraphing, and so on. Various types of utterance, such as indirect speech, and language produced by the 'stream-of-consciousness' technique, would be identified primarily at this level.[7]

II SENTENCE TYPOLOGY AND STRUCTURE

By contrast, the description of sentence-types in English is well advanced, though there remains the problem of identification. In writing, this problem is very slight, as there are graphological indications of the beginning and end of the sentence (except when normal sentence punctuation is absent, as is occasionally the case with writers like Cummings or Joyce). In speech, however, it is not possible to make a comparably unambiguous use of intonation, and it is sometimes difficult to say exactly where a sentence ends. We mention this since we have found difficulty in dividing our spoken texts into sentences on a number of occasions. This is the case, for example, when two main clauses, the first concluding with a falling tone, are separated by *and*, but without a pause; or when there are complex sequences of major and minor sentences (see below, *p* 110), so that a structure could be interpreted as either a separate sentence or perhaps an adverbial element of clause structure only; or when there is a sequence of clauses ending in rising tones, each clause being an item in a list. It is not our task to solve this problem; but by drawing attention to it we can point out that some varieties are characterised by many problems of this kind, whereas in others such problems never occur.

On the whole, however, we find little difficulty in recognising a sentence and placing it in a category. It may be noted at this point that we also make use of the notion of *utterance*. For us, utterance is an *ad hoc* term for a stretch of (spoken or written) language, used by one person, that is capable of being formally characterised in some way: this provides a convenient means of breaking down certain texts into more readily discussable units – which may, of course, be of different lengths.

We make a primary division of our non-dependent structures into two types: *complete sentences* (ie formally complete) and *incomplete sentences*, in which for some reason – perhaps interruption – the speaker never reached the end of what he was intending to say. Some varieties are characterised by a relatively high proportion of the latter (for example, conversation and commentary). Of the formally complete sentences, we make a division into MAJOR and MINOR types (note that the term 'minor' is not to be taken as being in any way equivalent to 'unimportant').

1 Major sentences

A major sentence may be one of a number of types, and in the first instance a breakdown into four categories seems useful, the labels at least being familiar from traditional grammar: [a] simple, [b] compound, [c] complex, and [d] mixed.

[a] A simple major sentence consists of a *Subject* and a *Predicator*,[8] with or without a *Complement*, depending on the class of verb occurring as Predicator, with or without one or more *Adverbials*, and with or without a *Vocative*. (These terms will be explained below; they will normally be referred to by the abbreviations s, p, c, a and voc. There are restrictions on the order in which they may occur, which correlate with such semantic categories as 'statement', 'question', and so on (*eg* SP *versus* PS); and there are various other transformational possibilities which may delete or rearrange some of these elements – such as the passive or imperative transformations – which we do not describe separately here as they do not affect the definition of the basic elements of structure.)

Examples

SP: you 're |KNÌTTing| (*see p* 98, *l* 34)

SPC: One of the Bracknell experts glanced at Mr Comet's current prediction of the weather to come. (*p* 175, *l* 76)

SPCA: |I 'll be all'right in a ₙMÍNute| (*p* 97, *l* 11)

PS: ⁺do ⁺you |sĔw| (*p* 99, *l* 53)

For convenience, we shall be referring to all the structures covered by this basic type as SPCA-type structures.

Before explaining and illustrating the other types of major sentence (compound, complex, and mixed), it is necessary to distinguish between the fundamental concepts of *sentence* and *clause*. The difference may be clearly seen by comparing two such sentences as:

John asked a question yesterday.

John asked me as I was leaving.

Both these utterances are sentences, and both have a SPCA structure; but in the case of the second sentence, the A is expounded by a further SPC structure, which itself is not a sentence. Consequently it is useful to have two descriptive labels, so as not to confuse the two functions which a SPCA-type structure is capable of performing. Whenever a SPCA-type structure is overtly linked with another SPCA-type structure to form a single sentence, therefore, we refer to the co-occurring structures as *clauses*. The term clause is only used by us in the description of combinations of SPCA-type structures within a single sentence.

In any combination of clauses, one clause is always *main*, the others are always *dependent* in some way.

A main clause is a SPCA-type structure which is not syntactically dependent upon any other SPCA-type structure.

A dependent clause is a SPCA-type structure which requires another SPCA-type structure, to which it is overtly related, to co-occur. The linkage is marked by: (*a*) one of the sequence-determining conjunctions (*eg and*, *or*), which are usually referred to as coordinating conjunctions[9]; (*b*) a subordinating conjunction (in the case of clauses introduced by *that*, the subordinator may be omitted); (*c*) by the dependent clause being a *non-finite* construction. The concept of finiteness is important for the description of English, and we distinguish between non-finite and finite clauses. Clauses are non-finite when the only Predicator is an infinitival or participial form of the verb, and where the S is usually absent or optional; they are finite where the P is any other form of the verb, and where the S is obligatory (optional in imperative structures). In major sentence-types, whereas finite clauses may be either main or dependent, non-finite clauses are always dependent.

[**b**] A compound major sentence may be one of two types:

1. It consists of a simple main clause and one or more simple dependent clauses, linked by one of the sequence-determining ('coordinating') conjunctions, or, in writing, by one of a range of coordinating punctuation devices (for instance, a semi-colon).

Example

MAIN	COORDINATE DEPENDENT
his |foot is ↑"r̄ight 'down 'the ↓ₙLÍNE|	· and he |pushes ↓back

↑down to the BÒWLer\| (*p* 127, *l* 40)

MAIN	COORDINATE DEPENDENT
Move the machine into position ,	remove the tabletop and

wash tub lid. (*p* 237)

Certain ellipses of elements of clause structure are permissible in all clauses in a compound sentence apart from the first, *eg* 'He came and went'.

2. It consists of a simple main clause plus a clause of the 'parenthetic' type (such as 'you know', 'I mean'), which may be embedded in the main clause, or may occur in sequence with it.

Example

PARENTHETIC	MAIN
'you |KNÓW|	|that's „MỲ sort of 'knitting| (*p* 99, *l* 47)

[c] A complex major sentence consists of one main clause of the simple type, with the Adverbial element of its structure expounded by at least one dependent clause.

Example

MAIN	DEPENDENT
The operator will demonstrate the tones	if you are

uncertain. (*p* 240)

We do not, however, regard as complex those sentences in which a clause replaces or occurs as part of s or c. That is, we exclude noun clauses, relative clauses and non-finite clauses functioning in this way. Noun clauses and non-finite clauses operating as s or c, if omitted, would not leave a complete main clause, and cannot therefore be considered dependent in the same sense as that outlined above. Relative clauses, and non-finite clauses operating as postmodifiers in a nominal group (see below) do not constitute an element of sentence structure, but only part of some such element. Only an exponent of the optional A element is directly referable to sentence structure. Without this decision, we should be forced to say that:

S	P	C
kicking the ball	was	easy

is as 'complicated' a sentence as:

S   P   C   A

I saw John when he was kicking the ball

and more 'complicated' than:

                              S   P   C

the bright red ball near the tree in the garden was pretty.

This does not seem useful for stylistic analysis.

[d] A mixed major sentence consists of a compound sentence in which at least one of the clauses has a dependent clause, introduced by a subordinating conjunction.

Example

MAIN

Give the proper signal before moving out

DEPENDENT

COORDINATE DEPENDENT[10]

, and only move off when you can do so safely . . . (*cf p* 238)

DEPENDENT

2 Minor sentences

A minor sentence is defined as any structure other than those outlined above which displays functional characteristics normally associated with a major sentence – in particular, non-dependence and graphological or prosodic features of sentence-ness.

Minimally, a minor sentence may display any of the following structures (which will be referred to under the general heading of *minor constructions* – the term 'clause' only being used in the context of minor sentences when it is necessary to refer to a structure of the kind already described which happens to form part of a compound, complex, or mixed minor sentence):

[a] A subordinate SP(CA) structure

Example

Drink X. Because it's good for you.

[b] An element of clause structure (s, p, c, a, voc) or some partial.[11]

Examples

s |sèa 'witch| – – (it's sup|pŏsed to be| · |just a ↑hàir 'colourant|) (*p* 220)

p (John's working.) |wŏrking|

c |sŏrry| (*p* 117, *l* 31)

a |same tíme| (*p* 118, *l* 47)

voc |"vălerie| (*p* 116, *l* 4)

[c] A combination of elements of clause structure other than those allowed for in major sentences, *eg* sc, sp (where p would normally require a c), pc, pa, aa.

Examples

sc $\overline{\text{|everything}}$ $\overline{\text{'all ríght|}}$ (*p* 118, *l* 61)

pc $\overline{\text{|didn't gét}}$ $\overline{\text{'that|}}$ (*p* 117, *l* 31)

sa $\overline{\text{|england}}$ $\overline{\text{↑nòw}}$ $\overline{\text{[of |còurse]|}}$ · · · $\overline{\text{|on the 'back ↓fòot|}}$ (*cf p* 126, *l* 5)

[d] A non-finite construction.

Example

|m̄icrofined| (to |b̄eat the ab↑sorption ↓barrier ↑fàster|) (*p* 221)

As with major sentences, we find simple, compound, complex and mixed types of minor sentence.

Examples

(*a*) Simple: The Nation's priorities (*p* 224)

(*b*) Compound: $\overline{\text{in |}_n\text{óther words| mc|kénzie's| – |}_1\text{off}}$

$\overline{\text{↑"cŭtter|}}$ |or the ↓one that he moves ↑in off 'the

$\overline{\text{↓séam|}}$ (*p* 128, *l* 54)

(c) Complex: |worth ↑"ĒvĒry "penny| · be|cause it

↑CLÉANS| · |and ↑SHÍNES| · |as you ↑DÙST| (p 222)

(d) Mixed: |goes óUT| and − |sweeps a↓wĀY a| − |little

· ↑loose ↓ₙGRÁSS| or per|haps ↑sweeps away 'nothing

'at ↓ÀLL| · |while he TRÌES to| · |"ₙSÈTTle| · |those

↑ever 'present ↑BŬTTer 'flies| (p 127, l 42)

We prefer not to refer to minor sentences as 'ellipses' of major sentence-types, as frequently there is no intuitively clear relationship between a minor sentence and a corresponding major version, and in many cases it is impossible to say what in fact was the form of the major sentence from which the minor sentence is supposed to have been derived.

At the level of sentence, then, in stylistic analysis, we would expect to be told such things as whether a variety made use of a particular type of sentence to the exclusion of others – for instance, if it consisted solely of simple sentences; whether it had a high proportion of minor sentences; whether it showed a preference for a particular kind of complex sentence pattern; and so on. We would also deal here with particular categories of a given sentence-type, for instance, whether such sentences as commands or questions could occur in a text; with such matters as the 'poetic syntax' in which sentence form has to be considered in the light of its relation to verse structure;[12] with the placement of clauses within a sentence – whether adverbials are initial, medial, or final, for instance; and with contrastive tone (see p 26).

III CLAUSE TYPOLOGY AND STRUCTURE

We must now examine the notion of clause as such, to see what kind of information is contained here. We postulate five elements of clause structure for our analysis:

Subject, Predicator, Complement, Adverbial, Vocative.

We do not describe as separate elements of structure cases where there is 'overlapping' or 'conflation' of elements; for example, the way in which the word *him* in the sentence 'I saw *him* go' functions both as c of 'saw' and s of 'go'; or the way in which nominal groups, when they occur without a Predicator as part of a minor sentence, may be construed as either s or c, as in:

and |Nŏw| · a|GĂIN| – the |TĬNkle| · of the |CĂvalry| (*p* 128, *l* 65)

Structurally, Subject and Complement have a great deal in common. Both may be a nominal group, or sequence of nominal groups (see below, *pp* 53–4), a personal, interrogative or indefinite pronoun, or a noun clause (*ie* a SPCA-type structure introduced by *what, whether, that, etc* – *that* being optional when the clause occurs as c):

Pron. as s   Nominal group as c

He   can scan   half a million weather reports . . . (*p* 175, *l* 22)

Clause as s

|what 'I wanted to say to you ↑RĚALLy| was əm –

Clause as c

I |didn't know 'whether you were 'going to say · that you ↑could come or you ↑CÒULDn't| (*p* 117, *l* 17)

The c element, according to the type of verb, allows various expansions which are not to be found in s – for instance, the indirect object/direct object relationship:

      I.O.   D.O.
He gave the boy a bun

the occurrence of an agent after the passive:

|when – his ↑BÍcycle| – |was ↑STRŬCK| · by a |MÒtorcycle| (*cf p* 245)

and the intensive–extensive relationship, as in:

They called the boy a fool. (intensive)

They called the boy a taxi. (extensive)

The predicator is always a verbal group (see below, *p* 55):

and he was |having TRÓuble| · with his |african ↓CÀRRiers| (*p* 228)

The Adverbial may be a single word (an adverb), *eg*

Revolutions can begin ⌐quietly.⌐ (*p* 176, *l* 87)

on an adverbial construction such as a non-finite clause, or a prepositional phrase (for which see below, *p* 54), *eg*

Heat the chocolate and water . . . ⌐stirring to a creamy

‾ ‾ ‾ ‾ ‾ ‾ ‾ ‾ ‾
    consistency.⌐ (*p* 241)

the tax office will supply details ⌐on request.⌐ (*p* 243)

or an adverbial clause (that is, a finite SPCA-type structure introduced by a subordinating conjunction):

. . . there would be |no ˈkind of interFÉrence| with their

|ₙFĂMilies| – ⌐|while they were in reˈTÌREment|⌐ (*p* 248)

The Vocative is a nominal, usually a proper noun, which is used in direct address:

|ˈˈhave you ᵥNÒticed ⌐ₙPRÍNcipal|⌐ (*p* 99, *l* 60)

It is not preceded by an article, but it may have other premodifiers (*eg* 'Dear Sir').

At clause level, we are looking for distinctiveness in a given variety which relates to the way in which elements of structure are realised, for instance, the proportion of nouns to verbs, the frequency of pronouns as opposed to nominal groups, how often clauses operate as complement, or whether nominal groups tend to occur in clusters, as in apposition.[13] We are also concerned with the ordering of elements of structure in relation to one another, *eg* whether the order SP, which is usually expected in statements, may be reversed, as in journalism; with the position in which the Adverbial tends to occur in a clause – initially, medially, or finally; and with how many Adverbials there are in a variety.

IV GROUP TYPOLOGY AND STRUCTURE

The group may be defined as an 'endocentric' construction, that is, a construction with a 'head' word, which performs the same syntactic function as the whole and may stand in place of it. In the case of a nominal group the head word is a noun, and in the case of a verbal group a verb.

The structure of the nominal group, briefly, consists of an obligatory head which may be optionally premodified:

PREMODIFICATION　　　HEAD

this |dreadful sui↑cidal wáll| (p 233)

or postmodified:

HEAD　　　POSTMODIFICATION

the |plùmes| · |of the ↑cǎvalry| (p 129, l 85)

or both:

the |delicate 'water colour ↓mǎnner| that we as|sòciate

with ↓máx| (p 250)

Premodification involves three main slots, as follows:

Predeterminer　Determiner　Adjectival　Head

|just　　　　　a　　　quick　　wìpe| (cf p 222)

At the determiner position function the articles, demonstratives (*this, that, these, those*), and possessive pronouns (*my, your, etc*); preceding this occur words like *all, both, just*.

Adjectivals may contain a premodifying genitive (*eg* 'John's'), one or more adjectives (with certain restrictions on their order), and an adjunct noun, (*eg* '*garden* fence'). Adjectives may be preceded by one of the set of adverbial intensifiers (*eg very, awfully*).

Postmodification can be one of four types: a preposition with a further nominal group (what we call a prepositional phrase):

the de|"fence of the ↓free ↓ₙwórld| (p 234)

a non-finite clause:

the diazo- and azo-compounds discussed above (p 253)

a dependent clause, which may be introduced by a relative pronoun or simply attached directly to the nominal it modifies:

Thou who takest away the sins of the world (p 155, l 35)

The man ⌐I know⌐

or, occasionally, an adjective:

God the Father ⌐almighty⌐ (*p* 155, *l* 46)

With these possibilities, and the further possibility of sequences of such items within a single nominal group, it is easy to see the potentiality of nominal groups for making stylistic contrasts in terms of complexity. Varieties are to be found which, characteristically, have hardly any premodification or postmodification at all (*eg* conversation); some are typified by complex premodification (*eg* journalism and science); and others by complex postmodification (*eg* legal language). The use of adverbial intensifiers is at times distinctive; and so is the placing of adjectives when they occur after the noun.

In the verbal group, there is less potential for stylistic contrast. Verbal groups may be non-finite (*cf p* 47) or finite. Essentially, the finite verbal group consists of a lexical verb operating as head, with or without one or more auxiliaries preceding it. The various restrictions on coordination of lexical verbs, sequence of auxiliaries, *etc*, have not been classified here.

AUXILIARIES   LEXICAL VERB

⌐I shall have to⌐ ⌐go through⌐ this (*p* 231)

Here we would point to various features of the verb to indicate which were relevant from a stylistic angle, for instance, whether a variety was restricted in the tense forms it used (as in commentary); whether it was restricted in its use of aspectual contrasts (that is, the distinction between, for example, *I go* and *I am going*); whether passive forms were frequent (as in some types of scientific writing); and whether contracted forms of the verb were used (as in conversation).

V WORD TYPOLOGY AND STRUCTURE

Finally, word structure is straightforwardly discussable in terms of traditional morphology: root, prefix, and suffix (as in *compose*, *de*compose, decompos*ition* respectively). Under this heading would be noted distinctive categories and types of word formation, such as frequent compounds, complex affixation involving elements from classical Latin or Greek, and also any deviant forms that might occur, including portmanteau words, nonce formations, word–class changes (such as *he pillar-boxed the letter*), puns, and so on.

The distribution of individual words is described under the general heading of *Vocabulary*, but it is convenient to explain here that when we speak of 'collocation' of lexical items, we are referring to regular patterns of co-occurrence in which items may be found in a given stylistic context, as seen independently of the phonetic, phonological, grammatical or semantic roles being fulfilled by these items; for example, *goods*, in legal English (*cf* Chapter 8) regularly co-occurs (or 'collocates') with *chattels* to produce a relatively fixed phrase in which the component items have a powerful mutual predictability.

SUMMARY

We may now summarise what has been said in this section in the following display, whose resemblance to the symbology of generative grammar is purely superficial. The arrow should be read as meaning simply 'must be a'. Round brackets enclose elements that are optional; a plus sign following a symbol within brackets indicates that an element may in principle recur any number of times; braces indicate that one of the enclosed range of structures must be selected. Combinational possibilities (the various types of transformation, recursion, sequence restrictions, *etc* mentioned above) have been ignored in this table, which is designed to show the main hierarchical relationships between the grammatical categories recognised in the description. Categories which are not further sub-classified here are followed by an asterisk.

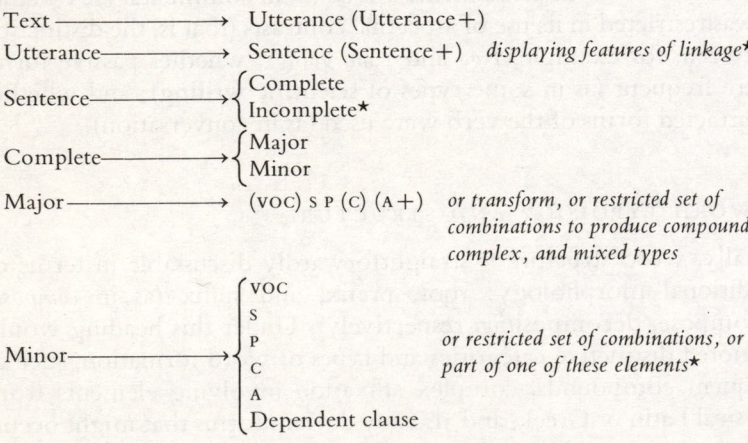

Text ⟶ Utterance (Utterance +)

Utterance ⟶ Sentence (Sentence +) *displaying features of linkage*★

Sentence ⟶ { Complete / Incomplete★ }

Complete ⟶ { Major / Minor }

Major ⟶ (VOC) S P (C) (A +) *or transform, or restricted set of combinations to produce compound, complex, and mixed types*

Minor ⟶ { VOC / S / P / C / A / Dependent clause } *or restricted set of combinations, or part of one of these elements*★

S ⟶ { Nominal group / Pronoun / Dependent [noun] clause }   *or restricted set of combinations★*

C ⟶ { Nominal group / Pronoun / Dependent [noun] clause / Other complement structures★ }   *or restricted set of combinations★*

A ⟶ { Adverb / Adverbial construction / Dependent [adverbial] clause }   *or restricted set of combinations★*

VOC ⟶ { Proper noun / Sub-set of nominal groups★ }

Dependent clause ⟶ { Conjunction★ (VOC) S P (C) (A +) / Non-finite clause }

Non-finite clause ⟶ P_n (C) (A +)

P ⟶ (Premodification$_v$) Lexical Verb

P_n ⟶ (Auxiliary verb★) + { Infinitive / Participial } form of Lexical Verb

Premodification$_v$ ⟶ Auxiliary verb★ (Auxiliary verb★) (*not*)

Nominal group ⟶ (Premodification$_n$) Noun (Postmodification)

Premodification$_n$ ⟶ (Predeterminer) (Determiner) (Adjectival)

Determiner ⟶ { Article / Demonstrative / Possessive }

Predeterminer ⟶ *all, both, quite . . .   or restricted combination★*

Adjectival ⟶ (Premodifying genitive) ((Intensifier)(Adjective +)) (Adjunct noun)

Intensifier ⟶ *very, awfully . . .*

Article ⟶ *a, the, no*

Demonstrative ⟶ *this, that, these, those*

Possessive ⟶ *my, your . . .*

Postmodification ⟶ { Preposition★ + Nominal group / Non-finite construction / Dependent clause [relative type] / Adjective }   *or restricted combination★*

Pronoun ⟶ { Personal / Interrogative / Indefinite }

Personal ⟶ *I, you . . .*

Interrogative ⟶ *who, what, where . . .*

Indefinite ⟶ *one, someone . . .*

This grammatical framework is clearly extremely crude, and is intended simply as a perspective for the kind of analyses made in the course of this book. We have not defined terms which are generally unambiguous (such as 'adjective', 'relative'), and we readily admit that the ordering of the above rules is to a certain extent arbitrary. We ought also to emphasise that the choices we have listed are not in all instances completely free (indicated by the phrase 'restricted combination'): there are many restrictions on the ability of structures to co-occur and further restrictions on the order they may adopt when they do co-occur. However, it is not our purpose here to attempt to specify all these restrictions, even if sufficient information were available to allow us to do so: any such restrictions and any further sub-classification which have particular stylistic relevance will be pointed out in the sections in which they happen to turn up. The display which we have just presented has as its only object the indication of the main interrelationships between the central descriptive categories which we use.

Notes

·1 Vocabulary for us thus subsumes the purely formal information about lexis in the sense of Halliday and others, *cf* M. A. K. HALLIDAY, 'Lexis as a linguistic level' in *In Memory of J. R. Firth*, ed. C. E. BAZELL, *et al*, Longmans, 1966, *pp* 148–62. We do not distinguish lexis as a separate level of formal study because (*a*) the theoretical distinction between grammar and lexis is by no means clear, nor are there recognised procedures of analysis for the latter; (*b*) lexical study in this sense has hardly begun, and there is no body of results that stylistic judgments can be referred to (apart from intuition, which is usually perfectly clear on any important lexical co-occurrences); and (*c*) it is uneconomic to set up a separate level for lexical analysis, as in almost all cases information about formal distribution of lexical items does not differ from semantic information about the distribution of the same items.

2 A. C. GIMSON, *An Introduction to the Pronunciation of English*, Arnold, 1962.

3 See D. CRYSTAL, *Prosodic Systems and Intonation in English*, C.U.P., 1969.

4 For further study of voice-quality, see the review of the field made in D. CRYSTAL, *op cit*, Chapter 3.

5 See J. P. THORNE, 'Stylistics and Generative Grammars', *Journal of Linguistics*, 1, 1965, *pp* 49–59. *Cf* also the initial rule of the grammars described by M. W. BLOOMFIELD and L. NEWMARK, *A Linguistic Introduction to the History of English*, Knopf, 1963, *p* 245.

6 But *cf* R. KARLSEN, *Studies in the Connection of Clauses in Current English*, Eides, Bergen, 1959.

7 *Cf* J. SPENCER, 'A Note on the "Steady Monologuy of the Interiors"', *Review of English Studies*, VI, 2 (April 1965), *pp* 32–41; M. GREGORY, 'Old Bailey Speech in "A Tale of Two Cities"', *ibid*, 42–55.

8 The term *Predicator* is not to be confused with *Predicate* in its traditional sense of the whole of the sentence except the Subject.

9 Traditionally, a structure introduced by one of these conjunctions has been regarded as a coordinate main clause in a compound sentence. This, however, seems to ignore the fact that in almost all cases the coordinated component is functionally as much dependent on the preceding clause as a subordinate clause in the same position. While admitting that there are some exceptions to this statement (*eg* of the 'Do this and I'll shoot' type) and recognising the existence of important functional differences between coordinating and subordinating conjunctions, we do not feel that the coordinate/subordinate distinction, as far as the clause is concerned, is as clear as has been traditionally implied – especially if formal considerations are primary. We shall refer to such structures as coordinate dependent.

10 *Cf* [**b**] on *p* 47, and *note* 9.

11 It is sometimes difficult to decide whether an utterance is to be regarded as s or c. See *pp* 51–2, where this problem is mentioned.

12 See R. QUIRK, *The Use of English*, Longmans, 1962, *pp* 249 *f*; W. NOWOTTNY, *The Language Poets Use*, Athlone Press, 1962, Chapter 1.

13 We restrict the term *apposition* to sequences of identically functioning nominal groups, excluding contiguous structures of any other kind which may be appositional in some notional sense.

Example

The second stage – the translation of forecast pressure distribution into

forecast weather . . . (*p* 176, *l* 104)

Chapter 3

Stylistic Analysis

PRESUPPOSITIONS

We have outlined in Chapter 2 the methodology we use in describing the linguistic features of any text. In the first instance, the procedures for approaching stylistic analysis are no different from those made use of in any descriptive linguistic exercise: the primary task is to catalogue and classify features within the framework of some general linguistic theory. Our aim is to produce, initially, an inventory of interrelated contrasts. Ultimately, we would expect any descriptively adequate grammar to incorporate, as part of its rules, all stylistically significant information. We are not concerned, as has been pointed out, with the description of everything that goes on within a text, but only with that which can be shown to be of stylistic importance in the sense discussed in Chapter 2. To study everything would produce an undesirable conflation of the notions of stylistics and linguistics. We now have to go a stage further and discuss how we link our linguistic analysis with the stylistic purpose of the exercise. What are the theoretical notions that need to be established in order to bridge the gap between the description of a language, on the one hand, and the description of a variety of that language, on the other?

A first impression of the theoretical problem may be gained in the following way. We have hypothesised (*cf p* 11) that any utterance, spoken or written, displays features which simultaneously identify it from a number of different points of view. Some features may provide information about the speaker's regional background, or his place on a social scale of some kind, for example; other features may reveal aspects of the social situation in which he is speaking, the kind of person to whom he is speaking, the capacity in which he is speaking, and so on; and further features (often the majority in an utterance) will tell us nothing about a situation at all – apart, that is, from the fact that the speaker is using English, as opposed to some other language. The question is, basically, what types of feature are there?

Into how many categories can these features be classified, and how are the categories to be defined?

Stylistic analysis, in the sense implied by these questions, is something new; and much of the early work which has taken place, while valuable for its stimulus and initiative, is suspect. There are a number of reasons for this. In the first place, the categories which have been set up to account for the features, or sets of features, in the language data are frequently inconsistently used, are incomplete, and usually have no adequate formal basis. The criticism of inconsistency can best be illustrated from the use of the term *register* (which is a fundamental notion in 'Neo-Firthian' stylistics). This term has been applied to varieties of language in an almost indiscriminate manner, as if it could be usefully applied to situationally distinctive pieces of language of any kind. The language of newspaper headlines, church services, sports commentaries, popular songs, advertising, and football, amongst others, have all been referred to as registers in one work.[1] We shall however see below that there are very great differences in the nature of the situational variables involved in these uses of English, and that it is inconsistent, unrealistic, and confusing to obscure these differences by grouping everything under the same heading, as well as an unnecessary trivialisation of what is a potentially useful concept. The criticism of incompleteness is readily illustrated by the fact that at least one central theoretical variable (*modality* in our sense, see *p* 74 *ff*) has been ignored, and that there are many aspects of the way in which English is used which no one has tried to account for, and which cannot be handled adequately by such categories as *register, tenor, field, mode*, and so on in any of their current senses. And while it is impossible to achieve completeness in the present 'state of the art' (*cf p* 85), the extent to which stylistic theories are at the moment inadequate should at least be admitted and the difficulties outlined. The lack of large-scale formal empirical analysis is well displayed when situational categories such as 'newspaper reporting' are set up, and assumed to have a predictable linguistic identity. It takes only a little analysis of texts to show that many such generalisations are of very little descriptive value (*cf* Chapter 7). In fact the majority of the situations claimed to be stylistically distinctive have hardly been studied at all from the linguistic point of view, and many of the labels used are vague in the extreme (*eg* 'science', 'literature').

Further, in the published work on the subject, there seem to be many hidden assumptions that can be seriously questioned, for example, that there is a one-for-one correlation between linguistic features and situation, or that the language can be predicted from the situation and the situation from the language with the same degree of certainty. Such assumptions are not valid in our experience; we shall discuss them further below. Finally, we find a great deal of difficulty in understanding the use of such terms as 'restricted language', 'norm' (or 'normal'), 'discourse', 'standard', and 'situation' in the literature. Often a word is used in both an everyday and a specialist sense, without the difference being explicitly recognised.

We cannot but conclude that stylistic theory, at the time of writing, has reached a stage where it would do well to wait for practical analysis to catch up, so that the theoretical categories may be tested against a wide range of data, and more detailed analyses of texts carried out. Consequently, further theorising in this book is kept to a minimum: we are mainly concerned to established certain central notions that do not seem to have been sufficiently rigorously defined and verified hitherto.

The main procedural difficulty, which we have already had cause to refer to, arises from the fact that linguistic features do not usually correlate in any neat one-for-one way with the situational variables in an extra-linguistic context. It is of course possible to find examples in most utterances from which predictions can be made with confidence about the situation, or some aspect of the situation – utterances from religious or legal English are particularly clear in this respect. But even here a linguistic feature is frequently ambiguous as to its situational function, indicating more than one variable simultaneously: much of the grammatical idiosyncrasy of written legal and religious English, for example, has a double function, contributing both to *province* and to *status* in the senses described below (*pp* 71, 73). As all the analyses in Chapters 4 to 8 show, any piece of discourse contains a large number of features which are difficult to relate to specific variables in the original extra-linguistic context, even though they may be felt to have some kind of stylistic value. The majority of linguistic features in English have little or no predictive power, that is, they are ambiguous indications of the situational variables in the extra-linguistic contexts in which they are used. This state of affairs must be recognised by any adequate theory of language variation. And if, working the other way round, one specifies a situation and tries to predict its linguistic features, it is impossible to make reliable predictions about any but a small number of features.

It may, of course, be convenient to posit a one-for-one correlation between a set of linguistic forms and a situation, but while this relation does sometimes genuinely exist, it would be a mistake to assume that it always exists, and to talk rigidly in terms of 'one language – one situation'. It is more meaningful instead to talk of *ranges* of appropriateness and acceptability of various uses of language to given situations. Thus, in situation X, feature Y will be highly probable, but one must allow for the possibility of feature Z occurring, other things being equal – for instance, the introduction of informality where on all other occasions one has experienced formality. Situations in which positively only one set of stylistic features is permitted, with no variation allowed (or, to put it another way, where it is possible to state confidently that 'the following features will never occur here . . .'), are far outnumbered by those situations where alternative sets of features are possible, though not usually equiprobable.

It is, then, unreasonable to expect that all situational variables are equally predictable from the language data. The number of constraints influencing the use of language varies from one situation to another: some situations are very clearly predictable, with many constraints; others are vague. Therefore we prefer to see this notion of language-situation predictability as a scale, with linguistic features which are to all intents and purposes totally predictable at one end, features which are entirely unpredictable within the English speech community at the other, and, in between, features showing many different degrees of predictability, some very restricted, some less so. This of course is the interesting area for study. The totally predictable cases, which are those usually cited in the literature on this subject, are relatively uninteresting precisely because of their predictability; they are usually intuitively obvious. It is the area between the extremes which is in need of study.

Another way of making this point, but from a different angle, is to introduce a 'scale of utilisation' of the formal linguistic features in English. At one end of the scale there are uses of English where the total range of conceivable linguistic forms might occur (as in literature); at the other end, there are uses where only a very small number of forms ever occur, some linguistic systems available in the rest of the language being completely unused – for example, in the language of knitting patterns, parade-ground commands, heraldic language, and certain kinds of weather-forecasting. For uses of this latter type, the label 'restricted language' has sometimes been used; but it is probably more useful to see these uses as being simply at the 'most restricted' end of a scale of increasing restrictedness, rather than to posit any difference in kind.

DIMENSIONS OF SITUATIONAL CONSTRAINT

For the analyses carried out in this book, the linguistic features of any utterance – apart from their fundamental role of producing intelligible language – were discussed in terms of their correlatability to different kinds of situational function. The linguist, having intuitively noted a particular feature as being stylistically significant in some way, attempts to rationalise the basis of his intuitive response by examining the extra-linguistic context in order to establish any situational factors which might account for restrictions on its use. To take a clear example, the use of 'thou/thee/thy/thine' in Standard English is restricted to those extra-linguistic contexts in which certain religious factors are dominant and obligatory, other factors being relatively random, and usually optional. It is by no means extravagant to conclude that an aspect or aspects of the context exercises some kind of conditioning influence on the feature in question, and the notion of *situation* has been set up to describe the kinds of conditioning influence. Similarly, any other feature which can be shown to display restricted occurrence in a sub-set of extra-linguistic contexts within the English speech community is by definition of importance for stylistic analysis. The stylistician begins by studying what the most significant deviations from random occurrence are, and why.

The entire range of linguistic features in a text functioning in the above way is plotted, and the notion of *situation* is broken down into *dimensions of situational constraint* (which we have so far been referring to rather loosely as 'situational variables'); and the role every feature plays is described in terms of one or more of these dimensions. For example, feature A may be seen to correlate with the geographical area the speaker came from, and is referred to as a *feature of* the dimension of regional variation, or *regional dialect*; feature B is seen to be a result of the kind of social relationship existing between the participants in a conversation, and is referred to as a *feature of* a different dimension (in this case the dimension we shall refer to below as *status*); and so on. Those features which have no situational correlates at all, apart from the stylistically trivial one of *occurring in an English-*

speaking situation, are noted for separate discussion (under the heading *common-core* features, *cf* below). We would again stress the hypothetical nature of these dimensions. There may be further kinds of constraint which we have overlooked; and further sub-classification of the dimensions will certainly be necessary as more material is analysed. We must remember that no one has yet described the full range of linguistic correlates of any one of these dimensions; nor has there been much experimentation – such as by systematically varying the extralinguistic factors and examining the accompanying linguistic variation. But it only takes a little analysis to clarify the nature of certain central constraints, and the following is based on the work done here.

Before describing these constraints in detail, we must consider the stylistically neutral, or 'common-core' features which an utterance displays – those linguistic features which the utterance shares in some degree with all other utterances in the speech community, which occur regardless of the situational dimensions outlined below. This is a different kind of descriptive dimension from the others, in that its variability is random in respect of situational constraints. The features of this dimension, taken one at a time, do not discriminate situations of the kind the stylistician is interested in, though he has to be aware of them in order to be able to discount them. Thus most of the segmental phonology of English, and most of the grammatical and lexical patterns are imposed on the language-user as being laws common to the whole community in all situations. For example, the existence of concord between subject and verb is not stylistically significant, nor is the fact that the article comes before the noun, that *man* has the irregular plural *men*, or that *pleasant* is the opposite of *unpleasant*. There is no variety which has no fricative consonants or falling tones, and none which finds it impossible to use colour terms. From the point of view of their form – *not* considering their distribution – such features of English are stylistically neutral, and are, moreover, in the vast majority. Uniquely occurring linguistic features are very much the exception: as we have already mentioned, all varieties of English have much more in common than differentiates them. This is not of course to say that such features as the above cannot be made use of for stylistic purposes at all: as soon as considerations of *frequency* of occurrence and overall distribution are taken into account, then most of the common-core features work in a different way – for example, a text consisting wholly of tone-units with a falling nucleus would certainly be stylistically distinctive. Most of the stylistic statements which we make in this book are in fact of this frequential or distributional type. But the study of constellations of these features is logically dependent on the prior establishment of an inventory, and for this a separate dimension of description is necessary.

All other features of utterance are, by definition, situationally restricted in some way. We shall distinguish eight dimensions in all, grouping these into the three broad types that may be seen in the following list. The reasons for this grouping will be explained below.

A

INDIVIDUALITY

DIALECT

TIME

B

DISCOURSE

(a) [SIMPLE/COMPLEX] MEDIUM (Speech, Writing)

(b) [SIMPLE/COMPLEX] PARTICIPATION (Monologue,

Dialogue)

C

PROVINCE

STATUS

MODALITY

SINGULARITY

INDIVIDUALITY

In unselfconscious utterance, certain features occur – relatively permanent features of the speech or writing habits – which identify someone as a specific person, distinguish him from other users of the same language, or the same variety of the language. Such idiosyncratic features, not normally altering over quite long periods of time in adults, would be such effects as those constituting a person's voice quality or handwriting, which provide the basis of his recognisability. Also under this heading we might include 'pet' words or phrases with a very high frequency of occurrence. We are of course using 'individuality' in a wide sense, to cover both physical and psychological personal traits which could give rise to phonetic and graphetic distinctiveness of any kind. It is also important to note the qualification 'unselfconscious' used above. Obviously, we would not want to deny a speaker the possibility of adopting an alien voice quality or style of handwriting for some purpose (for example, the mimicking of a famous person to make a humorous point), but such usage would have to be described in terms of a very different set of presuppositions. The kind of idiosyncrasy described in this section is also different from the relatively temporary, and usually conscious activity associated with individuality in a literary or other context, which we shall discuss under the heading of singularity below (*p 76 ff*).

DIALECT

Other features in a person's usage will give an indication of his place of geographical origin (*regional* dialect) or his location on a non-linguistically based social scale (*class* dialect) – what we might refer to as the linguistic correlates of the sociologist's 'primary group'. These too are relatively constant features of language, only altering in humorous situations, or in cases of intense social pressure which cause someone to conform to dialect patterns other than his own. Both types of feature are presumably too familiar to need exemplification; they have been centres of linguistic attention for some years. But it should be noted that social dialect features of a wholly predictable type are rare in English: certain tendencies emerge (for example, in choice of vocabulary,[2] or in the use of certain vowels), but there is little which is very systematic.

TIME

Another familiar dimension of description covers those features of an utterance which indicate exclusively diachronic information – the temporal provenance of a piece of language. Such information would be of primary importance in any historical study of English, both in the general sense of the language as a whole, and in the particular sense of the development of the language habits of a single human being (linguistic *ontogeny*). Temporal features are the third kind of fairly stable feature in the utterances of an individual.

The relatively permanent features of language which we have just discussed can largely be taken for granted by the stylistician. They are very much background features, which the general or descriptive linguist will be interested in for their own sake, but which are stylistically less interesting because of their insusceptibility to variation in most situations. These features are rarely able to be manipulated by language-users in the way that the remaining groups of features are. One should also note the corollary, that with the dimensions of description so far described there is a powerful mutual predictability between language and situation: if the relevant extra-linguistic factors are known, then certain linguistic features will be readily predictable, and *vice versa*. Of course these extra-linguistic factors are not the same for all the dimensions: compare, for example, the sense in which the vocal characteristics of a child, as opposed to an adult, can be said to be predictable (on physiological grounds) with the sense in which dialect features are predictable (if one knows the dialect in advance). The point is that within some set of predetermined criteria, there is predictability. And what stylistics is trying to do, in a sense, is to place the other dimensions of situational constraint on a comparably clearly definable footing by trying to specify the relevant extra-linguistic factors precisely. (When one considers the amount of detailed study which traditional dialectology has entered into as a matter of course, it is plain that stylistics, in our sense, has got a lot of work to do before it can ever be as explicit.)

DISCOURSE

We subsume under this heading two kinds of variability in language: the difference between speech and writing, usually referred to under the heading of *medium*, and that between monologue and dialogue, which results from the nature of the *participation* in the language event. This too is not a dimension in precisely the same sense as those shortly to be described, since most of the variability attributable to it could be taken care of by reference to other dimensions, particularly *modality* below. The distinctions that we are seeking to make here are best seen as referring to given, fundamental features of language in use, features which are worth attention not for the descriptive information they are likely to yield but for their value as explanatory clues – by referring to the linguistic differences associated with these distinctions we may be able to explain more adequately the characteristics of certain varieties. This happens, for example, when a specimen of written language shows a number of features that would usually be associated only with informal speech, or when a specimen of spoken language is found to contain constructions typical of writing, or when someone introduces features of dialogue into a monologue; in all cases, the features may be more satisfactorily described by making appropriate reference to distinctions in discourse.

Spoken and written language may be defined by reference to two distinct but overlapping sets of linguistic and non-linguistic characteristics, conveniently summarised by the labels *speech* and *writing*. The distinction is important to maintain for methodological reasons, in addition to the relevance that it has for stylistics. Essentially the distinction is non-linguistic, concerning the primary choice of method or substance with which to communicate – air, or marks on a surface. (We do not discuss here other communicative methods, such as the pictorial, musical, and so on.) But the dichotomy is important for the stylistician, just as it is for the general linguist: speech needs to be handled initially at the phonetic/phonological level, and writing at the graphetic/graphological level. In each case, a different descriptive framework is involved. From the situational point of view, not only are there central functional differences between the two (speech being relatively transient, writing relatively permanent; speech implying personal contact of some kind, writing not – apart from its illustrative function, as on a blackboard in a classroom), there is also the absence of complete formal parallelism between spoken and written varieties of English. No spoken varieties can be written in traditional orthography so as to reflect all contrasts present in speech (consider the range of non-segmental information omitted, for example, or the pressures against writing certain obscene words), and there are many cases of written language which it is impossible to speak without destroying the original graphetic coherence of the text (for example, the punctuationless nature of much written legal language, which has to be broken down into units if it is to be spoken aloud, though these units do not exist in the graphic form). Substantial differences of this kind make the central distinction between speech and writing a very relevant one in linguistics, with clear implications for stylistics.

Under the heading of *participation* in discourse, we distinguish between *monologue* (utterance with no expectation of a response) and *dialogue* (utterance with alternating participants, usually, though not necessarily, two in number). We note this distinction, along with medium, under the same general heading, discourse, for a number of reasons. First, like medium, it operates at a more general level of abstraction than do any of the other situational dimensions put forward in this book. Second, as far as intuitive identification of varieties is concerned, there are clear and central co-occurrences between the categories of medium and those of participation, irrespective of the other dimensions: spoken and written monologue and spoken dialogue are common, as is – perhaps less obviously – written dialogue (used, for example, in filling in and returning forms, in some exchanges of letters, or in some kinds of party game). Third, there seem to be important functional similarities between medium and participation. In both, there is rarely a real choice as to which category is used in any given extra-linguistic context: one cannot speak to someone out of earshot; one does not use monologue when other people are present, unless for a temporary effect (*cf p* 88); one does not usually use writing to communicate with someone in the same room; and so on. Again, there are no further possibilities of linguistic contrast within either dimension.

The categories of medium and participation may also function in a 'removed', or 'explanatory' way. This point may be clarified if we consider the case of a category of medium which is being used as a means to an end, instead of as an end in itself; that is, the category is serving as a stopgap in a situation, a temporary device intended to facilitate a transfer to the alternative category at some later stage. We shall refer to this phenomenon as *complex medium*. Thus language which stays within the one category (*ie* spoken to be heard, written to be read) will be formally distinct in certain respects from language which involves a switch (*eg* language which is spoken to be written, as in dictation, or language written to be spoken, as in news broadcasting), and this possibility of systematic difference has to be built in to our theoretical framework. The introduction of phonological criteria into a discussion of written literature (describing the effect of alliteration, assonance, and so on) is a technique which would be covered partly by this dimension. Further sub-classification of complex medium is theoretically possible ('language written to be read aloud as if written', and so on),[3] but it would seem wise not to introduce further complications until the initial distinction has been tested as fully as possible.

The 'explanatory' function of the monologue/dialogue opposition may be seen when it is necessary to account for the presence of dialogue features in an utterance produced by only one person (a common literary device), or for the tendency for monologue to be introduced into a conversation, as when someone tells a joke. Both the joke and the short story may include spoken monologue to be uttered as if dialogue, different accents sometimes being adopted to indicate the change of speaker, and so on; and in drama the relationship between an author and his characters can perhaps be thought of as a function of written monologue which is to be spoken as dialogue (along with all the associated conventions). In these cases, then, we are trying to explain certain features of a variety which would fall as a general rule within one kind of discourse by reference to features which would normally be expected to occur only in another. We shall refer to this as *complex participation*.

The remaining dimensions of constraint all refer to relatively localised or temporary variations in language, and provide the central area of stylistic study.

PROVINCE

In this dimension we describe the features of language which identify an utterance with those variables in an extra-linguistic context which are defined with reference to the kind of occupational or professional activity being engaged in. Province features provide no information about the people involved in any situation – about their social status or relationship to each other, for example; they are features which would be found to recur regardless of who the participants were, and ·which relate to the nature of the task they are engaged in. The occupational role of the language-user, in other words, imposes certain restraints on what may be spoken or written (or, to put it positively, suggests a particular set of linguistic forms which a speaker is at liberty to use). It is these, along with other restraints (of *status* and *modality* in particular) which we shall shortly discuss, which form the stylistic basis of any variety. Clear examples of provinces would be the 'language of ' (shorthand for 'distinctive set of linguistic features used in') public worship, advertising, science or law – contexts in which the sociologist would consider 'secondary groups' to be operating. Each of these contexts, it should be noted, has an intuitive coherence and identity which may be defined in non-linguistic terms – though this is not of course to imply that all provinces have comparably clear, readily definable extra-linguistic correlatives.

The situational variables in the contexts referred to may be defined at different levels of generality, depending on the nature of the linguistic features which are being considered. It would be possible, for instance, to speak of 'advertising', as opposed to 'television advertising', as opposed to 'television advertising of washing powders', and so on. Two questions immediately arise: what is the most general level at which a province may be identified, and what is the most specific level? As an example of the kind of problem posed by the first question, we may take the following. Having noticed certain linguistic features of different categories of advertisement, such as public announcements of forthcoming events, newspaper advertisements, magazine advertisements, television advertisements (*cf pp* 218–226), does one then refer to these as different provinces, or does one go to a more general level and refer to them all as aspects ('sub-provinces') of the one province of advertising, or, at a still more general level, the province of propaganda? Clearly, if this process were continued, all varieties would ultimately fall under the heading of one major province, which might be labelled 'communication', or something of the kind, and the point of the exercise would have been lost.

At the other end of the scale, to examine the second question raised above, it is futile to continue sub-classifying situations when there are insufficient linguistic formal differences to warrant further analysis. 'Washing-powder advertising on television making use of a blue-eyed demonstrator on a Sunday', to continue the example, would not be differentiated, one would hope, because it would not be very difficult to show that there was no significant language difference between this and the language used by other demonstrators of different ocular persuasions on other days of the week. Exactly how much sub-analysis can be justified is something yet to be decided: there is certainly no obvious cut-off point. It is thus essential to view all labels used to refer to different provinces with the greatest suspicion, until further descriptive work has been done – and this applies as much to the labels used throughout this book as elsewhere in literature on stylistics. The concept of province, and the other concepts which we discuss below, must be taken as being simply a basis for investigation, nothing more. The first question to be asked on being given a label such as 'the language of X' is always: What formal features make this use of language unique and correlatable only with this situation? Is the label too broad? Or is it too narrow? How far is there an unclear boundary-area between this and other 'language-of' situations? We shall be looking at a number of these commonly used labels in this way in the course of this book, and finding that many of them are inadequate from a linguistic point of view.

Meanwhile, we should note three further general points about the concept of province. First, province features should not be identified with the subject matter of an utterance, as has sometimes been suggested in connection with the notion of 'register'. Subject matter, in so far as this is a question of the use of distinctive vocabulary, is but one factor among many which contribute to a province's definition, and in any case has predictive power only in a minority of extremely specialist situations. Knowing the subject matter of an utterance is no guarantee that it is possible to define its situational origin, as consideration of the following chapters shows. In those cases where it is the subject matter (as opposed to the situation) which totally dictates the form, then of course this is not a stylistic matter at all.[4]

Second, we shall be applying the term 'province' to the notion of conversation, but one must remember that conversation is different from all other provinces in that it is the only case where conventional occupational boundaries are irrelevant: whatever conversation is linguistically, it may occur within and between any of the restricted uses of language which one would want to classify as provinces. It is however this very generally which makes it as clear a notion as any of the other provinces, comparable to them in situational distinctiveness; and in view of the fact that conversation may be defined, albeit negatively, with reference to other provinces, it would seem to fall within the terms of the definition given at the beginning of this section.

Lastly, it should be noted that, apart from the distinctions in discourse outlined above, which are fairly fundamental for linguistics as a whole, there is no theoretical ordering between the dimensions, no established priorities, to demand, for example, that province features should always precede status features in description. There is no theoretical hierarchy here. In fact, it is usually easier to begin by looking for province features in any analysis, presumably because province is a more readily established stylistic concept, the relevant variables being easier to specify and label. But one should note that this is a procedural convenience, and not in any sense a theoretical requirement: it does not lead us to develop a 'theory of province', in the same way that some scholars have done with a 'theory of register' (thus to all intents and purposes equating 'register' with 'stylistics'!).

STATUS

In this dimension we describe the systematic linguistic variations which correspond with variations in the relative social standing of the participants in any act of communication, regardless of their exact locality. The audience may be an individual or a group. It is postulated that status variations occur independently of province variations, although there are some restrictions on co-occurrence (see p 89). The semantic field which may be subsumed under the label 'status' is of course complex: it involves a whole range of factors related to contacts between people from different positions on a social scale – factors intuitively associated with such notions as formality, informality, respect, politeness, deference, intimacy, kinship relations, business relations, and hierarchic relations in general. A number of areas may be clearly distinguished within the dimension of status in any language, various kinds of formal and informal language being perhaps the most noticeable (though one must be careful to distinguish between formality in a stylistic sense, and the grammatical category of formality which occurs in, say, Japanese, where social status is reflected paradigmatically through many of the forms of the language). Exactly how many categories of status there are awaits elucidation. Joos has postulated five degrees of formality in this connection (namely 'frozen', 'formal', 'consultative', 'casual', and 'intimate'),[5] but we feel this to be premature. It is likely that a scale of formality exists, but the number of linguistic terms along the scale, and the nature of the polarities, are still matters for speculation. Utterances may be found which seem to fit neatly into the above five slots; but these are far outnumbered by utterances which do not. As with province, therefore, we shall not claim too much for the categories of status which we make use of in our analysis.

MODALITY

This dimension has not usually been systematically distinguished in stylistic discussion. In it we describe those linguistic features correlatable with the specific purpose of an utterance which has led the user to adopt one feature or set of features rather than another, and ultimately to produce an overall, conventionalised spoken or written format for his language, which may be given a descriptive label. Modality can be described independently of province and status, in that on the whole a choice of some kind exists regardless of a language-user's specific occupational role or relationship to other participants. For example, there would be linguistic differences of modality if, within the province of conversation, in its written form (what might be called 'correspondence', for the sake of convenience), one chose to communicate a message in the shape of a letter, a post-card, a note, a telegram, or a memo; or, within the province of scientific English, if one chose to write up a topic in the form of a lecture, report, essay, monograph, or textbook. In each case there would be linguistic as well as extra-linguistic differences, and it is the overall pattern produced by the former which would be the basis of any decision assigning a text to a particular category of modality. The familiar distinction between 'genres' (traditionally well-recognised divisions in (usually literary) language) could also be seen in terms of modality, though we must remember here that the term 'genre' has never been given a precise, generally agreed definition, and is regularly used to refer simultaneously to varieties operating at different degrees of theoretical abstraction – for example, 'poetry' *v* 'prose', as well as 'essay' *v* 'short story', which are sub-categories of prose. Most kinds of joke would be describable in terms of modality, and here we can see very clearly the linguistic basis of the format – opening formulae (such as 'Have you heard the one about . . .'), the 'punch line', the various prosodic and paralinguistic accompaniments, and so on. Other examples of modality distinction would be those between types of spoken or written monologue such as anecdote, proclamation, poster, and testimonial.

Modality is clearly partly a question of the suitability of form to subject matter, but it cannot wholly be discussed in these terms, as very often the conventional linguistic format is a result, at least in part, of a tradition whose synchronic relevance has long been lost, as in the form of lettering in many legal documents. We should also like to emphasise the independence of modality as a dimension of stylistic description, particularly in view of the failure to differentiate modality from province hitherto. To think of what is conveniently labelled 'sports commentary' as a province, for example, is to overlook the fact that there are two theoretical variables involved, which should be kept distinct. There *is* a basis for a province here, namely, the business of reporting sports; but commentary is a function of modality (which should be clear when one considers the other linguistic formats a sports reporter could use – newspaper article, retrospective radio report, and so on). Modality differences may both cut across provinces – it is possible to have a commentary about sport or cooking or even a scientific experiment, for example – and also occur within them, some provinces having a very restricted variability (the liturgical English discussed in Chapter 6, for example), others having a great deal of flexibility (such as the wide range of modalities which exist in legal or literary English).

SINGULARITY

Once the linguistic features of a text have been described in terms of the above dimensions, features may still be left which cannot be related to anything systematic amongst the community as a whole, or some group of it, but only to the preferences of the individual user. A user may display in his utterance occasional idiosyncratic linguistic features which give a specific effect within the framework of some conventional variety, *eg* when an author introduces a linguistic originality into a poem. Along with idiosyncratic deviations from a person's normal linguistic behaviour of any kind in any situation, they may be studied *en bloc* as yet a further possibility of variation, and, if they appear regularly in a person's usage, can be regarded as evidence of authorship. We use *singularity* as a cover-term for these personal, occasional features.

This is thus the only dimension which takes account of linguistic idiosyncrasy: other dimensions are either non-linguistic or non-idiosyncratic. Singularity features are different from the vocal or written reflexes of personality traits mentioned under the heading of individuality above, in that the former are typically short, temporary, and manipulable, usually being deliberately introduced into a situation to make a specific linguistic contrast, whereas the latter are relatively continuous, permanent, and not able to be manipulated in this way – in short, non-linguistic. It can be difficult to decide which dimension a feature belongs to, especially with an unfamiliar speaker; for example, there is the case of the joker who begins by impressing his audience with linguistic ingenuity, such as punning, but who ends up by being a crushing bore, through continual introduction of such devices into his speech. There comes a time when what has been taken as a singularity feature, in our sense, turns out in fact to be an individuality feature: this point is not always easy to detect, however.

We ought also to indicate a procedural difficulty in determining whether a linguistic contrast in a text is a marker of singularity or not, namely, that an intuition of authorship will depend on familiarity – the more one reads of or listens to a person, the more recognisable will be his idiosyncrasies. In the initial study of a text which is largely unfamiliar, there is no way of deciding whether a contrast belongs to province, status, or modality on the one hand, or to singularity on the other. This is only a temporary difficulty, of course, as further analysis of other texts by the same and different authors will in all probability provide sufficient data to suggest the likelier solution; but it is as well to be aware that the difficulty does exist.

We have decided to use the term 'singularity' to avoid the over-general implications of the word 'style' (*cf* p 9 *f*), but it should be emphasised that what we are referring to is in no sense new. To talk of studying the 'style' of an author does not usually imply a study of *everything* in the language he has used, but only an attempt to isolate, define, and discuss those linguistic features which are felt to be peculiarly his, which help to distinguish him from other authors – a common use in literary criticism and questions of authorship identification, for example. As far as the student of the language of literature is concerned, styles may well be the most interesting things to study; but we must point out that before he can study these systematically and comprehensively, he must first be able to identify, and thus eliminate, all the variables which are non-idiosyncratic in the language situation – *ie* variables belonging to the other dimensions outlined here – otherwise he will attribute a feature to the style of an author which is in fact a common feature of usage in the language as a whole. This does not happen so much in the study of modern literature, but it is a common mistake to take too much for granted in the study of older literature, where there is no intuitive awareness of the everyday norms of the spoken or written language.

OTHER DIMENSIONS

It would be strange if the complexity of language variety could be explained by reference to the above four variables alone, and so we were not surprised to find that, while they accounted for the majority of our data, there remained a number of cases of language use which could not be explained in their terms. For example, there is the kind of language used in talking to babies, which can hardly be called a province in the same sense as above, nor even a sub-province (of conversation); and none of the other dimensions seems relevant. Then there is the case of what is sometimes called the 'fire and brimstone' sermon. In a sermon, a preacher usually conforms to a certain phonological minimum which allows us to identify the variety; but he may introduce a further range of phonological effect into the sermon, such as extra rhythmicality, loudness or pitch width, all of which would be permissible within the province, and which would provide the basis, along with certain grammatical and lexical features, of the 'fire and brimstone' category of sermon. It is important to realise that this is a linguistically conventional type: any preacher wanting to give a sermon which would be recognised as belonging to this category would be forced to use a particular sub-set of linguistic features, and these would not occur in the same way in other contexts. But it is not easy to define the situational variable involved here. It is not province, as the same extra-linguistic factors may underlie the more usual kind of sermon, too; nor is it accountable for by reference to any of the other dimensions.

A stylistic theory should provide further dimensions of description capable of accounting for all such features, but with very little analysis having been done the nature and definitions of the required dimensions are by no means obvious at present. We feel that one potentially relevant dimension might take account of features in terms of whether they reflect a conventional orientation, a generally accepted way of treating some aspect of the communication situation – the subject matter of an utterance, the audience, some feature of expression or of the speaker's situation – within a stylistically restricted context. Such a dimension (which might be called *point of view* or *attitude*, as long as it was not confused with the more general, stylistically unrestricted senses of these terms) might well be able to handle many, though not all, of the above examples. We have not studied a sufficient number of cases, however, to justify setting this up as a separate dimension, consequently we have not given it any theoretical status in the present introductory investigation.

Perhaps causing the most difficult stylistic problem of all are those uses of language which cannot clearly be specified in terms of the above set of dimensions, because the phenomena referred to cut across all these dimensions and require specification with reference to qualitative, non-linguistic criteria. 'Literature' and 'humour' are the two central cases which need to be given separate theoretical status in this way. They are essentially different from other varieties, being fundamentally unspecifiable linguistically, and thus stylistically: it is impossible to list a set of features and predict that the configuration will be called literary or funny. There is a crucial qualitative distinction, which does not occur elsewhere at such a fundamental level, which the linguist, *qua* linguist, is not competent to assess. It is perhaps worth stressing, in view of the tension which has existed in the past between literary critics and linguists, that any decision as to what is of literary value and what is not is not the linguist's to make. His role in relation to literature is to ensure that all relevant linguistic variables prerequisite for understanding are in fact understood before this qualitative assessment is made.

We do not therefore wish to sidetrack ourselves into any discussion of the meaning of 'literature', and related issues. But we do wish to emphasise that there *are* certain factors, which could be considered stylistically distinctive in our sense, in most language normally put under the heading of literature (as defined by a consensus of opinion among those who consider themselves to be literary critics, and who would be considered by others as being so). Such central factors would be the relatively high proportion of singularity features, in the sense described above, the variability of modality (the question of 'genres' again), the high frequency of overt indications of attitude (*cf* p 78), and, most important of all, the possibility of introducing any kind of linguistic convention without its being necessarily inappropriate – features from any other variety can be made use of in a literary context (or a humorous one) for a particular effect. Literature can be mimetic of the whole range of human experience – and this includes linguistic as well as non-linguistic experience. In a poem or novel, one may find pieces of religious or legal English, or any other, which have to be understood in their own right before one can go on to assess their function in terms of the literary work as a whole. Most literary works weld together contrasts which derive from different varieties of language – Eliot's *The Waste Land* and Joyce's *Ulysses* are particularly well-constructed cases in point.

One should also note that literature and humour, more than any other varieties, introduce a large number of descriptive problems which our theory in its present form cannot handle. For example, the above dimensions cannot satisfactorily explain the stylistic differences which exist between such widely varying aspects of literature as oral-formulaic verse, drama involving artificial but conventional vocalisations (such as expression of grief), the use of a chorus, the effect of stereotyped forms such as the limerick or nursery rhyme, and the whole question of introducing such literary effects as bathos. Or, in the case of humour, it is difficult to know how to account for the 'standard' kind of joke, where the familiarity of the linguistic pattern in the narrative is the main source of the effect (such as in the 'shaggy dog', or 'Englishman, Irishman, Scotsman' types, or in the more transient crazes for particular jokes involving outrageous puns or illogicalities). Again, the question is, how does one account for the standardness which is an intrinsic part of the variety and responses to it?

While on the subject of literature, we would point out that our approach in many ways parallels that adopted by textual critics in general. Indeed, some critics (for example, those associated with the methods of *explication de texte*) have markedly similar aims and techniques. The linguist's aim is to ensure that the total range of linguistic features bearing on the interpretation of a text can be made explicit. The normal critical apparatus of editor's notes, biographical allusions, and so on, where of linguistic relevance, is thus subsumed by our approach. This is especially desirable in the case of historical stylistics, where of course one has no direct intuition of the state of the language concerned.

We have not attempted to apply our approach to any literary texts in this book, partly for pedagogical reasons, partly for reasons of space limitation. But in view of the way in which books, articles and theses on stylistics these days tend to concentrate on literature to the exclusion of all else, some further explanation is perhaps necessary. Our omission is not, of course, due to any lack of interest on our part in literary language; indeed, we feel that the application of stylistic techniques to the study of literature is perhaps the most important reason for carrying on this business at all, and ultimately might well provide the most illuminating information. But no introduction to stylistic analysis should begin with literature, as this is potentially the most difficult kind of language to analyse – not only because it allows a greater range and more extreme kinds of deviation from the linguistic norms present in the rest of the language,[6] but also because it presupposes an understanding of the varieties which constitute normal, non-literary language, as we mentioned earlier. One has to be aware of the normal function of the linguistic features constituting these varieties in non-literary English before one can see what use the author is making of them. Which is why the application of stylistic techniques to literature should be the last part of a stylistician's training, not the first. Moreover, in view of the vast range covered by the many different kinds of language which have been gathered together under the heading 'literature' – everything from the most conversation-like of drama to the most esoteric poetry – we feel it would be distorting to select but one or two short extracts for analysis in this book. Clearly, a separate study is needed to cover literary English adequately, and we hope it is not long before such a study is attempted.

Such work, however, will become possible only when stylisticians have appreciated sufficiently the complexities of 'ordinary' language, and have mastered the tools of analysis to the extent of being able to talk reasonably precisely, systematically, and objectively about the phenomena they are observing. So far, there is little evidence that anyone has reached this stage: most stylistic analyses carried out by linguists so far have been severely censured by literary critics for being unhelpful; and few books written by literary critics which purport to discuss an author's language have achieved anything like the degree of precision required to make their observations meaningful to the linguist – or to anyone who concedes the importance of objective, verifiable descriptive information as a critical tool.[7] But it would be premature to condemn the linguistic approach to style before it has had a chance to prove itself: appreciation of the aims of stylistics will only come once an appreciation of the aims of linguistics as a whole has been attained. Meanwhile, we trust that, by restricting our attention to more mundane matters in this book, we can contribute a little towards the clarification of stylistics as a discipline.

We may summarise this discussion by saying that, in any text, the stylistically significant characteristics can be classified into types which correspond to the set of questions outlined below. Putting it crudely, the general question to be asking is, 'Apart from the message being communicated, what other kind of information does the utterance give us?' There are at least thirteen sub-questions here:

Does it tell us which specific person used it? (*Individuality*)

Does it tell us where in the country he is from? (*Regional dialect*)

Does it tell us which social class he belongs to? (*Class dialect*)

Does it tell us during which period of English he spoke or wrote it, or how old he was? (*Time*)

Does it tell us whether he was speaking or writing? (*Discourse medium*)

Does it tell us whether he was speaking or writing as an end in itself (see p 70), or as a means to a further end? (*Simple v complex discourse medium*)

Does it tell us whether there was only one participant in the utterance, or whether there was more than one? (*Discourse participation*)

Does it tell us whether the monologue and dialogue are independent, or are to be considered as part of a wider type of discourse? (*Simple v complex discourse participation*)

Does it tell us which specific occupational activity the user is engaged in? (*Province*)

Does it tell us about the social relationship existing between the user and his interlocutors? (*Status*)

Does it tell us about the purpose he had in mind when conveying the message? (*Modality*)

Does it tell us that the user was being deliberately idiosyncratic? (*Singularity*)

Does it tell us none of these things? (*Common-core*)

Any one text will provide us simultaneously with information about each of these questions. Occasionally it is not possible (as was mentioned earlier) to allocate a linguistic feature or set of features to one dimension rather than another, but this is to be expected in the present stage of study. Ambiguous features in a text can be classified as such for the time being, and given further study at a later stage.

Once the stylistician has become aware of the kind of theoretical variability involved in work of this kind, he has two main tasks to carry out: to specify the number of (formally and functionally) distinct categories within each dimension, and plot the extent to which categories from different dimensions may co-occur. A *variety* will then be seen as a unique configuration of linguistic features, each feature being referable to one or more of the above dimensions of description; the variety displays a stable formal-functional correspondence, which is the basis of the intuitive impression of coherence and predictability that may then be labelled. (One will usually have given it an impressionistic label already, of course, to facilitate discussion. In an ideal world, linguistically based and impressionistically based varieties would coincide: how far they do in fact remains to be seen.) Within each dimension, one may distinguish a number (to be defined) of situational *categories*, such as 'formal', 'informal', 'religious', 'legal'. Different dimensions will have different numbers of categories. A switch in the categories at any one dimension (*eg* legal English becoming religious English, formal English becoming informal English) thus by definition produces a different variety. Some categories are naturally going to be closer together (share more linguistic correlates) than others, such as 'informal' and 'colloquial'; and therefore some varieties will be much closer together than others. But we have not tried to group varieties into more general types here; this is a task which remains to be done.

The categories in turn are defined with reference to sets of linguistic features which correlate with the distinctiveness of a situation, and which operate at some or all of the levels of description specified in Chapter 2. These situationally bound linguistic distinctive features we refer to simply as *stylistic features* (or, if one wishes to get away from the term 'stylistic', *variety-markers*). The diagram on *p* 84 may help to interrelate these concepts more clearly.

ORGANISATION OF
STYLISTIC FEATURES IN ANALYSIS

Let us now examine in detail the process whereby we build up our picture of the stylistic structure of a text. For each intuitive selection of a linguistic feature, we make two simultaneous decisions: one decision is to allocate the feature to a particular level of analysis; the second is to allocate the feature to one or other of the stylistic dimensions. Thus we are continually thinking in terms of a two-fold description for every feature, *eg* a *phonological* feature of *province*, a *grammatical* feature of *status*, and so on. We regularly work with two sheets of paper in front of us, one listing the levels as we have described them, with sub-categories outlined (see below); the other listing the various dimensions of description, with any sub-categorisation which we have discovered being indicated. The first sheet of paper, listing the linguistic features occurring at each level, is in effect a kind of informal matrix. By definition, it covers all contrasts available in the language, and thus all which are potentially relevant for the characterisation of any variety. It therefore provides a common yardstick for all texts in a language; all features can be referred to the same basic framework (see *p* 85), and thus more readily compared.

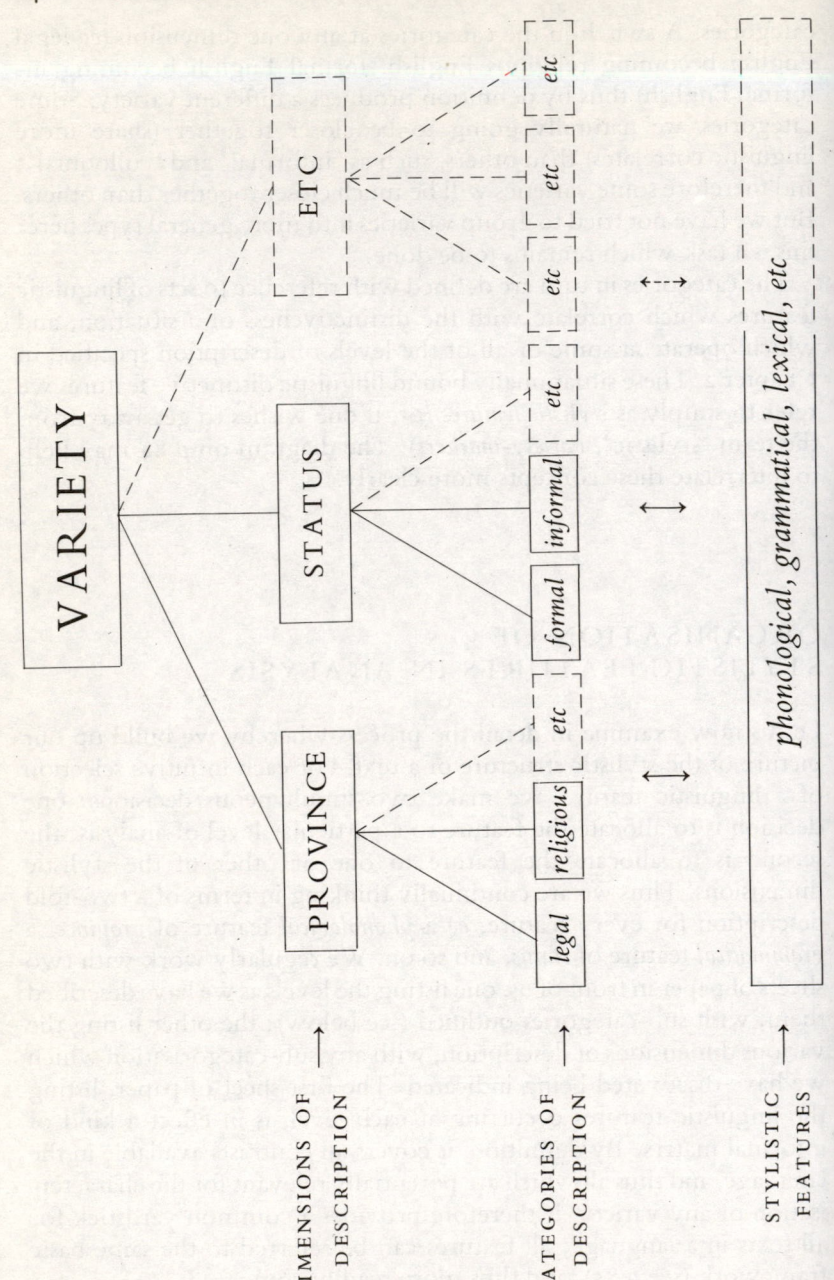

ANALYTICAL FRAMEWORK		TEXT
Specification	Phonetics	Statement
of range of	Graphics	of the
linguistic	Phonology	stylistic
features	Graphology	features
so far	Grammar	noted in the
noted in	Vocabulary	text being
English	Semantics	studied

The phonological component of this matrix might take the following form:

phonology
segmental { vowel, consonant contrasts classified and listed
non-segmental { pitch, loudness, *etc* contrasts classified and listed

Thus a given text might display a proportion of repeated initial consonants which distinctively characterises it, or a specific range of pitch contours not found elsewhere, and these would be noted in the matrix as distinctive features of this text, without which its identity and relationship to a given situation would be reduced or lost.[8] Features which do not seem to be significant would be passed over in silence. The point is that with such a framework in mind, it is highly unlikely that anything of significance would be omitted: the analyst, if he works systematically through the matrix, is forced to consider a very wide range of contrasts, which ultimately should comprise all the contrasts available in the language.

This matrix allows maximum systematisation and quantification of a text's stylistic features, all levels being treated in the same way: grammatical features would be listed in terms of some model (see above), as would features of phonetics, graphology, vocabulary, and semantics. Cross-referencing between levels would be dealt with as discussed above (*pp* 15, 20–1). This is the aim. Naturally, in view of the unfinished state of linguistic description of English at the moment, we can only go part of the way towards filling in the matrix completely, and only use that information which has already been accumulated about English structure – but in principle the matrix would provide comprehensive specification of the entire range of features relevant for stylistic analysis.

We now turn to the second sheet of paper which we have before us in carrying out our analysis, which contains headings of the different dimensions of stylistic description. On the first sheet we are organising our information linguistically. But it must be remembered that our motivation for choosing one item from the text and not another is a stylistic one; that is, we feel that there is some situational variable involved. On the second sheet, then, we note this variable under the appropriate heading. For example, if we see a text spattered with contracted verbal forms (*he'll*, *etc*), this would have been noted on the first sheet, under the heading *grammar*, as a feature of the verbal groups of the text; on the second sheet, we enter it under the general heading of *status*, with the specific indication *informal*, this being our intuitive feeling about its stylistic function. All decisions on this second sheet are hypotheses, as of course are the categories (such as *informality*) which we set up. We are trying to build up a coherent and consistent picture of a text as a whole. We make the assumption that the text is homogeneous, and we therefore expect the stylistic features to show a consistent function. But we cannot be sure of this before we begin; consequently, any conclusion about the function of a feature must be in the form of a hypothesis, which will become progressively more likely as more and more features get examined and are shown to fit in with it. For example, we may note at the beginning of a text a feature which strongly suggests that the text should be placed in a category for which the label *informal* seems appropriate; further down, we find other examples of the same feature which reinforce this decision, and different features which also suggest that this category is viable. If at the end we find that all these features fit into the informality category, and none into any other dimension, then we are justified in calling our text 'informal'. Of course we have to be careful that we do not allow our initial decision about a feature to colour our decisions further down. This is a danger which is always present in any work of this kind: to minimise its influence an attempt has to be made to take each feature in its own terms, to see, independently of what has previously been decided, exactly what its stylistic function is. To obtain greater objectivity here, it is helpful to refer specific problems to the intuition of a colleague who is not familiar with the text being worked on: a second opinion provides a useful corrective to any theory which may be forming too prematurely.

If, when a text is being examined in this way, no wholly consistent pattern emerges, and a feature occurs which contradicts the initial hypothesis about the text, then we must stop and look for reasons which will explain the presence of the contradictory feature. If, for example, in a text under analysis in which feature after feature has indicated informality, there is suddenly found a feature which indicates, without any doubt, formality, then its presence must be explained, since such an occurrence will be an important factor in any final assessment of the variety as a whole. A text cannot be labelled 'informal' if it can be shown to contain one or two features of formality. Further examination is sure to reveal that the change in formality has been produced by some kind of situational change, for instance of speaker, audience, or author's attitude, and so on.

It must also be remembered that the categories of description on this second sheet are no more firmly established than the linguistic categories on the first. We cannot say with certainty how many categories of status there are, or how far a province may be legitimately sub-classified – though of course the existence of certain categories will become clearer to the analyst as his experience increases. Consequently, decisions frequently have to be made as to exactly where and how to place a stylistic feature on this sheet. Three categories of formality may be needed to account for all the variations in the text, or perhaps four, or more. Once a theory has been agreed which allows for the existence of, say, six categories (or possibly 'degrees') of formality in English, then this scale can be used for all variations; but until some such scale has been established, work has to go on in an *ad hoc* manner. The title of this book is an attempt to recognise that we ourselves are compelled to work in exactly this way.

The process of stylistic analysis we are recommending is therefore one in which ordered selection and comment are carried out within parallel frameworks, one stylistic, the other linguistic. The stylistic framework contains the dimensions of description and their sub-classification; the linguistic framework contains the levels of analysis and their sub-classification. There are two distinct places where stylistic decisions enter into the analysis: at the beginning, when they may be used intuitively, as the motivation for selecting a text and a set of linguistic features to talk about; and at the end, when the aim is to formalise intuitions by establishing the entire range of linguistic correlates, and by pointing to the pattern which is felt to be there. The process should enable statements to be made about the range of varieties which exist within a language, and thus provide a basis for comparing languages from a stylistic point of view. It should also make possible comparative statements of a different kind – that variety X is primarily marked by phonological features, variety Y by lexical, and so on. This is the kind of statement which is particularly appropriate to literary contexts, where the concern is not so much with varieties in this general sense, as with individuals, and exactly what it is that differentiates one author from another. If it can be shown that author A tends to use his language in one kind of way, author B in another, then this would seem to be a justification for the method, and a prelude for the more important interpretative statements which must follow.

SOME FURTHER OBSERVATIONS

We will conclude this chapter with a few comments about various features of the theoretical framework just outlined, seen as a whole. Firstly, the stylistic dimensions are synchronic concepts; that is, the linguistic variables are correlated with the situational variables in the contemporaneous extra-linguistic context, and no recourse is had to feature of a context's history in order to explain a linguistic form. For example, the use of specifically religious language is related to the religious environment in which it is being used, and not to the cultural situation which generated it in the past. Occasionally, there is no synchronic explanation for a feature, as in the case of particular kinds of lettering being entirely a product of tradition, and these must be regarded as exceptional. But in all cases where there would be a choice, such as explaining a literary verse-form either synchronically or diachronically, we adopt the former method, as being more consistent with our general linguistic position.

Secondly, the view that a variety is a complex of features describable by reference to every dimension should not lead us to conclude that each dimension provides precisely the same amount of stylistic information. Not every situation requires the same degree of functional participation from each dimension. Thus in some provinces, it might be impossible to have any variation in modality at all (some of the maximally restricted kinds of English referred to on *p* 63), whereas such variation might be common elsewhere (as in conversation, where a switch from dialogue to temporary monologue to produce an anecdotal format – to take but one example – is common). This has implications for the use of terms, also; for example, to say that a sermon is 'formal' is not the same thing as saying that a lecture is 'formal', for the latter has a greater possibility of becoming informal than the former.

Within a given dimension, thirdly, the categories are set up without reference to the categories of other dimensions; but when viewed in combinations constituting a variety, they are not always independently varying. There are strong tendencies for certain categories from different dimensions to co-occur. At least four types of inter-relationship exist:

Mutual dependence (*ie* redundancy), as between 'legal' and 'formal' language, 'conversational' and 'dialogue' language.

Probable co-occurrence, as between 'conversational' and 'informal' language.

Possible co-occurrence, as between 'religious' and 'informal' language.

Highly improbable co-occurrence, as between 'legal' and 'colloquial' language.

Various existing combinations might then be taken for more detailed study, such as 'spoken informal dialogue conversation' (less redundantly, 'informal conversation', or simply 'conversation'); 'spoken formal religious monologue sermon' (or, more economically, 'sermon'); or 'written informal scientific textbook monologue' (which might have the mnemonic label 'popular science').

While co-occurrence of categories from different dimensions is restricted in this way, co-occurrence of categories from the *same* dimension is of course impossible: the labels, by *linguistic* definition, are mutually exclusive. For example, in this sense it is impossible to have, within the dimension of medium, spoken written English, or, within status, informal formal English, or, within province, scientific journalese, because the linguistic features entering into the definition of the respective labels are contradictory, at least in part. This does *not* mean, however, that some sense cannot be given to the idea of 'scientific journalese', let us say; it is merely that this idea would not be the same as ours, in that it would not be based primarily on an examination of linguistic features, but would rather be the product of a notional approach of a completely different order. It follows from this, we might add, that any descriptive labels found to co-occur in this book must therefore belong to different dimensions.

Finally, it is important to ensure that different degrees of abstraction from the data are kept apart terminologically in any theoretical discussion, and that the same descriptive label is not used inconsistently. It is undesirable, as we have seen, to use a label like 'genre' to refer simultaneously to the kind of difference existing between poetry and prose on the one hand, and essays and letters, both in prose, on the other. Similarly, province should not be used to refer to the differences between scientific and religious language as well as to the differences between the language of physics and that of chemistry. But a full terminology for stylistics, taking into account such different degrees of abstraction, has yet to be worked out and agreed upon.

It should be clear from this chapter, and the one which precedes it, that we view the business of stylistics as being the description of the linguistic characteristics of all situationally-restricted uses of language. Stylistics thus subsumes the first two senses of 'style' referred to on *pp* 9–10 above, and excludes the third and fourth. It is not concerned solely with literary language, although its techniques are most widely used in this context; nor is it concerned directly with evaluation, with personal opinion about the way language is being used from the viewpoint of enjoyment, and so forth. While it is important that people should be able to cultivate a personal and sensitive response to matters of language, stylistics hopes to provide a more objective basis for understanding, appreciating, and sharpening this response. Why *should* some language have a powerful effect on us, while other language leaves us relatively unmoved? Can we make more explicit the ways in which language has been manipulated to produce its final impression? What do we hope to gain by making distinctive uses of language, and correlating these with different social situations? Few people have such a naturally developed sense of style as to be able to answer these questions to their own satisfaction, and even fewer have the skill to be able to explain the answers to others. One normally needs assistance to catch all the linguistic nuances in a text that is at all unfamiliar and specialised, and a critical apparatus and terminology to discuss these nuances with others. Stylistic analysis, when done properly, has as its end the clarification of the full meaning and potential of language in use. The purpose of this book is to consider one possible technique whereby the mass of linguistic patterning can be reduced to a more comprehensible shape for the attainment of this end.

Notes

1 M. A. K. HALLIDAY, A. MACINTOSH, P. D. STREVENS, *The Linguistic Sciences and Language Teaching*, Longmans, 1964, *pp* 88–9.

2 *Cf* the (oversimplified) distinctions noted in A. S. C. ROSS, 'Linguistic Class-indicators in Present-day English', *Neuphilologische Mitteilungen*, 55, 1954, *pp* 20–56.

3 M. GREGORY, 'Aspects of Varieties Differentiation', *Journal of Linguistics*, 3, 1967, *pp* 177–98.

4 We are thinking here of cases such as the distinction between laws and definitions (as may be found, for example, in scientific language), where certain linguistic features are obligatory, as they refer to various logical operations which form the basis of the distinction. This, just as much as vocabulary, seems to be a part of subject matter. There are very few cases like this, however. Another possible example would be the use of various traditional literary forms (such as pastoral and lyrical poetry) at different periods of history, so that a particular form was said to be most appropriate for a particular subject matter, and *vice versa*.

5 M. JOOS, *The Five Clocks*. Publication 22 of the Indiana University Research Center in Anthropology, Folklore and Linguistics, 1962.

6 This point has been well discussed already, for example by R. QUIRK, *The Use of English*, Longmans, 1962, Chapter 13; or by J. P. THORNE, 'Stylistics and Generative Grammars', *Journal of Linguistics*, 1, 1965, *pp* 49–59.

7 But *cf*, for example, the clarity of W. NOWOTTNY, *The Language Poets Use*, Athlone Press, 1962.

8 This decision, as already mentioned, is essentially an intuitive one: the more experienced the analyst at variety analysis, the more likely he will be to spot the distinctive features of a text rapidly. For someone who has not carried out any such analysis before, it may well prove more convenient to begin by choosing some variety as a norm, describing this in detail, and then relating other texts to it. Such a norm is essentially a means to an end, its value getting less as comparative information about different varieties accumulates, and experience of analysis develops. The norm should not be taken as an obligatory category of stylistic theory, only as an optional procedural device (*cf p* 42).

Other aids for identifying stylistically significant features include: (*a*) replacing one linguistic item by another, in order to see if there is a consequent change in stylistic effect; and (*b*) inserting a supposed feature in a range of alternative contexts so as to discover whether an impression of incongruity, humour or an intuitive recognition of the original context is produced.

Part Two Practical Analysis –
specimen texts
with commentary

As a preliminary to the following chapters, we must explain certain points connected with the selection of the extracts and the conventions of presentation used. To avoid the possibility of our analytic results unconsciously influencing decisions about selection and transcription, all our texts were isolated and transcribed well over a year before the stylistic analysis was made. The provenance of each text is outlined in the relevant chapter. We have tried to select texts which are representative of ranges of usage that we intuitively recognise, and which would generally be considered to be typical and successful examples of their kind. Our descriptive statements are primarily concerned to elucidate the structure of these texts. However, in the process of selection, we found ourselves examining many other samples of the same varieties, and from time to time we have introduced into our discussion information which goes beyond that found in the illustrative text. Whenever we generalise on the basis of our impressions, without having any specific data in mind, we say so. Unless otherwise stated, all texts are examples of standard British English; all the accents used are types of Received Pronunciation, as normally defined.[1]

The conventions which need to be explained are as follows.

Whenever we have omitted sections of a text, the omission is indicated using the convention ... ...
To facilitate reference, the lines of each text are numbered in fives. Where there is more than one text in a chapter, each is given a Roman numeral, and the line numbering continues consecutively. In Chapter 9, however, which provides practice material, the lines are left unnumbered.

[1] For example, by D. ABERCROMBIE, *Problems and Principles in Language Study*, Longmans, 1963, Chapter 4.

Chapter 4

The Language of Conversation

There are a number of good reasons for choosing relatively informal conversation between educated people as the opening variety for linguistic analysis. Conversation, in the sense described in this chapter, is without doubt the most commonly used kind of English, and consequently a variety which will be more familiar to the vast majority of English-speaking people than any other. We can confidently claim that everyone makes use of this kind of English every day, whereas this claim could not be made of any other variety of English we might want to describe in a book such as this. Also, from the pedagogical viewpoint, the sort of English used in conversational situations, with the extreme kinds of non–fluency mentioned below removed, would seem to be the most useful and least artificial kind to teach foreign students of English as a means of everyday communication. Such practical reasons are quite important.

But we would also point to theoretical and procedural reasons for taking this variety first. It is the least 'marked' kind of situationally-influenced English. By this we mean that, whereas the other varieties in this book are clearly restricted to a particular situation (always to a certain degree specialised) and would be intuitively associated with that situation, conversational English has no comparable situational specificity. It is, situationally speaking, the most neutral kind of English one can find. For this reason, as well as in view of its frequency, it seems the obvious variety to choose for an introductory illustration of our analytic procedure, and as a basic measuring-rod for the language of other situations as and when necessary. We have already discussed the need for comparative statement in stylistic work, and the way in which the existence of a yardstick of some kind may facilitate this (*cf* *note* 8, *p* 91): the present variety would seem to be the most suitable for this purpose, and we shall consequently have cause to refer to it often.[1]

A relevant procedural reason for choosing this variety first is that conversation is a very convenient kind of English, in that it provides us with a great deal to discuss at all levels of analysis. Very often in stylistics, much of the interest in a text is concentrated at one level – a variety may be primarily distinguished through its phonology, or vocabulary, for example. Here, however, all levels of analysis provide important information about the character of the variety. There seems also to be a much greater flexibility of usage in this variety than in any other: there are fewer restrictions on the kind of structures that may be used, consequently one is liable to find in any extract of conversation that a wider range of contrasts operates at any level than could be expected elsewhere. A further procedural point for a pedagogically orientated book is that as this is the most familiar variety in English, it will be easier for readers to check the linguistic facts presented in our description with their intuitions, and thus make their own assessment of the extent to which our extracts are a representative and helpful sample, than if some less familiar variety had been chosen.

In view of these factors, and the general agreement in linguistics on the primacy of speech in language study, it might seem odd that so little linguistic research has been carried out into this variety of English. There have been occasional informative articles, such as those by Abercrombie and Quirk,[2] but these are sporadic in their comments; their main value is to focus attention on certain dominant and yet neglected features of this kind of English. There is little else, and no detailed survey. Far more is known in fact about such varieties of spoken English as advertising or preaching. There is however one very good reason for this lack of information, namely, the procedural difficulty of obtaining reliable data to investigate. It is well-known that most people will behave differently if they are aware of being tape-recorded, and as a result the language they use simply cannot be taken as a reliable sample of spontaneous informal conversation. Even if it seems that they have 'forgotten' about the microphone, the data cannot be trusted. In our experience, there seems to be a cyclic pattern of forgetting and remembering about the microphone, with consequent alterations in the manner of speaking. The only safe way of obtaining data is through the technique of 'surreptitious' recording, and this requires a degree of technical preparation which precludes its frequent use. This was the method used for obtaining the material in this chapter: the participants in the conversations, apart from speaker B in extract **IV** below, were not aware that a recording was being made.[3]

The relationship of the speakers to each other in the extracts **I**, **II**, and **III** which follow is that both are housewives with a general professional background (A in teaching, B in business); they are in the same age-group (mid-thirties) and have known each other for some time. The occasion is that B was invited to A's house for an evening chat over coffee. In extract **IV** (see *p* 116), which is a conversation over the telephone, speaker A is female, speaker B male; they are close friends who shared the same university educational background as mature students; A is a housewife, B a lecturer, and both are in their mid-thirties.

The first text consists of three extracts, labelled **I**, **II**, and **III**, taken from the beginning, middle and end of an evening's conversation respectively. They display some obvious differences – the anecdotal character of **II**, for example. Consequently, to call the language used throughout the text, along with the extract of telephone conversation, **IV**, a single variety may be a little premature, though we feel there is sufficient evidence to justify our doing so (see *p* 116). A clear central area of distinctiveness can be defined, but there are a number of very uncertain marginal issues, which reflect the way in which what is intuitively labelled 'conversation' can blend imperceptibly into other varieties that are labelled differently, such as 'discussion', 'talking shop', *etc.* We shall be looking at this problem again with special reference to extract **IV**.

I

'alleg'	A 'you got a |$_h$CÓLD|' –
'lax'	B |"NÒ| · 'just a |bit' ↑$_n$SNÌFFY| cos I'm –
'dimin'	I |"ÀM CÓLD| and I'll '|be all 'right 'once
'alleg piano'	I've 'warmed ÙP| – 'do I |LÒOK as
	'though I've 'got a ↑CÓLD|' 5
	A no I |$_n$thought you SÒUNDed as 'if you
	were
'pianiss'	B '|M̀|' – –
'piano'	A '|pull your CHÀIR up 'close if you WÁNT|'
	|is 'it – *(obscured speech)* 10
'piano'	B *'|YÈS|' · |I'll be all 'right in a
	$_n$MÍNUTE|* it's |just that I'm ·

'allegriss   A ('|ₙwhat have you GÒT|')

piano wide'   B ↑STÙpid| I |had ə about ↑↑five 'thousand

'low'   BÒOKS| – 'to |take 'back to 'senate   15

HÒUSE ₙYÉsterday|' – and I got |all

the 'way 'through the ₙCǑLLege| tō̄

'accel' |where the CÀR was| 'at the |parking

meter at the ↑ÒTHer end| and |realised

I'd 'left my' · ↑ç̧ÒAT| in my   20

'alleg' |ₙLÒCKer| 'and I *|just couldn't'*

'piano'   A *'|ₙM̀|'*

'accel'   B F̱ĂCE| 'going |all the way ↑BÀCK

again| with |this great' · 'you

know my |"ÀRMS were 'aching| 25

'piano'   A '|ₙM̀|' –

'piano'   B 'and I thought |ₙWÈLL| I'll |get

it on ↑↑TÙEsday| – it's a bit

|SĬLLy| cos I |NÈED it|' ·

'piano narrow'   A '|M̀| · it's gone |very CǑLD| 30

|HÀSn't it|'

'piano'   B '|M̂| – – – it's |FRÊEZing|' ·

'piano'   A '|ₙM̀| – *I'm |(2 syllables)|'*

'piano'   B *'you're |KNÌTTing|' · (laughs

'spread'   quietly for –) '|what are you   35

KNÌTTing| |that's 'not a 'tiny

ₙGÁRment|'

'low'   A '|NÒ|'

B (laughs for --) –

A |no 'it's for MÈ| but 'it's |very   40

PLÀIN|

'piano'   B 'it's a |lovely ↑CǑLour|' – –

'high piano'   A 'it |is NÍCE|'

'piano'   B '|ₙYÈAH|' – I |never 'di I could |never

TÀKE to ₙKNÍTTing| ex|cept on these   45
+double o 'needles with +S̱TRÌNG|
'you |KNÓW| |that's ₙMỲ sort of
'knitting|

  A *|ₙYÈAH|*

'giggle' B 'it |ₙGRÒWS' 'quickly| 50

  A |ₙYÈAH| · |I get 'very fed ÙP|

  B |(3 or 4 syllables) the ↑PRÒCess
though| 'do 'you |SĚW| · I |used

'narrow' to SÈW a 'lot| *'(when)*

  A *|N̄Ò [I |DÒN'T]|*   55

  B in the |days when I was a 'human
+BÈing|'.
. . .   .
.

II

'dimin' B 'and |conver"sàtion"| · |went like
"narrow" +THÌS| · |THÌS sort of conver'sation|
'affects posh accent' əmː' – – [ɹ] – ' "|"have you ᵥNÒticed"   60
"high forte" ₙPRÍNcipal| · that əm – – the
"descend" "|boiled ÈGGS| at |sunday *BRÈAKfast|" '* –

  A (laughs for –)

'high forte wide' B ' "|always HÀRD|" ' – – 'and |principal
"posh accent" SĀID| · "|ÂH [|WÊLL]|" ' · the |simple   65
'piano'
"breathy" +TRÙTH [|ÌS]| that · |ÎF you're 'going
to 'boil 'eggs| · |CŎMMunally| – they
|"ₙMÙST be 'hard| · (A and B laugh

'forte' "high" loudly for – –) 'and |"every"body

"alleg" +WÀITed| "and she |said you ↑SĒE|" '   70

'high' – – 'you |have to 'crack the +HEÀD'
of an 'egg| · when you |take it 'out

'alleg' "high" of the +PÀN| · '|"otherwise" it 'goes

                   on' �470CÒOKing| · (*A and B laugh for*

'alleg'   – – –) 'and |so we ↑↑DÌD the 'eggs| 75

"high" "narrow" |"every"body 'made their contri"BÚtion"|'

'allegriss'   'from |all 'over the 'senior CÒMMon

               · room| about |their 'point of 'view about

               ↓ÈGGS|' |they were |some would 'rather

               'have them ↑MŪCH too 'soft| than |much   80

               too ₙHÁRD| and |some people would

'alleg'   '↑rather not 'have an 'egg at ↑ₙĂLL|'

'allegriss'   and – |SÒME 'people| ɔːm · 'thought (well)

               the 'thing (to do was) just |"put them in

               the 'water and take them ↑ÒUT again| 85

               and |"THÈN let them go on 'cooking|

'alleg'   with|out' 'cracking their HÈADS| –* you

'laugh' |KNÓW| you got' '|every possible' ↑point

               of VÌEW|*

              A *(*laughs*)*   90

'high'   B a|bout 'boiled ÈGGS| '|THÉN| · you |went

               on to the ↑NÈXT 'topic| it was |like ·

               as |though there was an 'un'written'

               a↑GÈNda|

'piano'   A '|ₙYĔAH|' –   95

'alleg'   B 'and |everybody 'made their 'contriBÚtion|

               |then –you went on to the' · ↑NÈXT 'point

               on the a'genda| – and then |mary

               ↑johnson ↑SĀID| – |ₙÌ 'have a THÉOry| ·

               that · ɔːm · |one should ĒAT| – – |altĔRnately| 100

               |liquid and solid MÈALS| – |SŌ| · |I

               eat · ↑liquid at BRÈAKfast| – I have

               |liquid BRÈAKfast| · |solid LÙNCH||liquid

               TÈA| · and |solid DÌNNer| *(laughs for – –)*

               |SÒMEbody*   105

	A	*(laughs)*	
'alleg'	B	I told THÍS to| 'said she |probably' ·	
		knocks back a ↑bottle of GǏN| for	
		|BRÈAKfast|	
	A & B	(laugh for – –)	110

. . . .

III

<table>
<tr><td>'narrow'</td><td>B</td><td>'wə \|one of \|one of thi · ↑GÒRgons\| at ·</td><td></td></tr>
<tr><td>"accel"</td><td></td><td>saint \|PÀUL'S\| "was \|talking a↓bout</td><td></td></tr>
<tr><td></td><td></td><td>this par'ticular SCHÓOL\|" and saying</td><td></td></tr>
<tr><td>"allegriss monot"</td><td></td><td>you're "\|"lucky to 'get them in cos</td><td></td></tr>
<tr><td></td><td></td><td>it's a very 'difficult 'school to</td><td>115</td></tr>
<tr><td></td><td></td><td>get" ÎNto\|' ·</td><td></td></tr>
<tr><td>'pianiss'</td><td>A</td><td>'\|ₙM̀\|'</td><td></td></tr>
<tr><td>'narrow' 'forte'</td><td>B</td><td>'and a \|very ↑GÒOD 'school\|' · 'it's</td><td></td></tr>
<tr><td></td><td></td><td>a \|"BEAÙtiful 'school\|' · *\|very NÌCE\|*</td><td></td></tr>
<tr><td></td><td>A</td><td>*\|ₙMÍXED\|* ·</td><td>120</td></tr>
<tr><td></td><td>B</td><td>\|ₙNÕ\| ·</td><td></td></tr>
<tr><td>'pianiss'</td><td>A</td><td>'\|ₙM̀\|' · *"this \|single* ↑sex BŪsiness\|'</td><td></td></tr>
<tr><td>'piano'</td><td>B</td><td>*(\|single) –* \|ₙYÈAH\| · \|ₙYÈAH\| – – –</td><td></td></tr>
<tr><td></td><td></td><td>\|this s s 'you \|ₙKNÓW\| it's a · sort</td><td></td></tr>
<tr><td>'forte'</td><td></td><td>of – – '\|"out'dated ↑PÒLicy\|' 'which</td><td>125</td></tr>
<tr><td>'alleg narrow'</td><td></td><td>↘\|just 'goes 'on and ÒN\|' – it \|"still</td><td></td></tr>
<tr><td></td><td></td><td>'tends to be ₙTRÙE\| that \|most of the</td><td></td></tr>
<tr><td>'dimin'</td><td></td><td>'↑"BÈST 'grammar 'schools\| are \|single</td><td></td></tr>
<tr><td></td><td></td><td>SÈX\|'</td><td></td></tr>
<tr><td>'piano'</td><td>A</td><td>'\|ₙM̀\|' – –</td><td>130</td></tr>
<tr><td>'alleg'</td><td>B</td><td>'as \|far as I can ↑GĂther\|' · \|best</td><td></td></tr>
<tr><td>'narrow'</td><td></td><td>in 'terms of – – '↑you *\|KNÓW\|'*</td><td></td></tr>
<tr><td>'piano'</td><td>A</td><td>*\|records* ↑to SHÒW\|'</td><td></td></tr>
<tr><td>'piano'</td><td>B</td><td>'\|ₙYÈS\|'</td><td></td></tr>
</table>

'piano'	A	'|m̌|'	135
'piano'	B	'|ₙYÈAH|' – –	
'piano narrow'	A	'of course the |l c ⌃c seem to be	
		'goin͞g| – |ᵢback to this 'single ⌃sex	
		ₙBÚsiness| |DÒN'T they|' – – –	
'pianiss'		*'(obscured speech)'*	140
'high'	B	*'|this* 'is 'the TÈNDency|' |ĭsn't it| –	
'alleg' "monot"		'(I mean) I was "|talking to	
		'somebody on the 'phone this" ⌃èvEning	
		a'bout 'this| and we were |ₙSĂYing|' ·	
		you |know that in ⌃RÙssia| |after	145
'rhythmic'		the revo⌃LÙtion| '(a) |national	
'piano'		'policy of 'co educÀtion|' 'and |then ·	
		it swung ⌃right BÁCK|'	
'piano'	A	'|m̌|' – – I |can't see WHỲ| be|cause ·	
'lento'		I'm con⌃vinced that · '⌃mixed 'schools	150
		– – 'are the |"SÒUNDest|' – – I |mean	
		⌃over⌃ÀLL – [the |ₙSÒUNDest]| –	
	B	well it |ₙFÈELS 'healthier|	
		|DÒEsn't it|	
	A	*|ₙYÈS|* ·	155
	B	and |SÈEMS 'healthier|	
'piano'	A	'|ₙYÈS|'	
	B	the |"THÈOry ís| that · they	
'high'		dis|'TRÀCT' each 'other| – – but	
		that's |LÌFE| |ĭsn't it|	160

It does not require a very close examination to see that these extracts display certain linguistic characteristics of considerable importance, transcending whatever differences exist between them. Three factors seem to us to be central. First, there is the inexplicitness of the language, which is to a large extent due to the participants' extreme reliance for much of their information on the extra-linguistic context in which the conversation is taking place. This manifests itself through the frequent use of apparent ambiguities, 'apparent' in that these are only ambiguous when isolated from their context, as on a tape. For example, there is the use of many anaphoric features of language (such as the substitute-word 'one', or the demonstratives), which produces sentences like 'That's a big one', which are unintelligible on tape without further explanation. (Tape recordings of other varieties are on the whole very explicit, and do not produce many ambiguities of this kind.) Also, there is the frequent 'incompleteness' of many utterances, this again being but superficial, as the context makes perfectly plain to the speakers what was being intended, thus making redundant its vocal expression. There is in addition a large amount of phonologically obscure utterance on the tape, which is not due to the quality of the recording, but to the participants lowering their voices to an inaudible mumble, or to their simply tailing off into silence. This is also tolerated, along with other obscurities in the course of utterance, because of the permanent possibility of recapitulation upon request by the listener, a possibility present only in certain types of dialogue, and rarely present in writing. The other aspect of conversation's inexplicitness derives from the extent to which the participants have a common personal background – in the present case, the fact that the participants knew each other well meant that they were often able to take a great deal of what they were trying to say for granted. The more one knows somebody, the more one can rely on abbreviated forms, in-slang, subtle references, family jokes, and so on. All these features of inexplicitness, which are diagnostic of conversation in the sense being discussed here, are evident throughout the extracts.

Secondly, conversation is characterised by randomness of subject-matter, and a general lack of planning. The three extracts, on the same conversational occasion, are very different: compare the relatively brief and domestic exchanges of **I**, the monologue on a particular theme of **II**, and the greater discursiveness of **III**. It is not possible to predict at the beginning of a conversation how it will end, or how it will develop within any period. Conversation, as opposed to such concepts as discussion or debate, regularly lacks an overall theme. This unpredictability is of course optional. It is always possible to guide the course of a conversation towards a given theme. The point is that at any place in a conversation one may, if desired, 'change the subject' without this being felt to be linguistically inappropriate. It is this *potential* for change which is the important feature of the variety. The informality of the conversation situation is also reflected in the fact that any kind of language can occur, without its being necessarily linguistically inappropriate, including such extreme examples as complete switches in accent or dialect for humorous effect (*cf* the professional use of this technique by comedians), or the introduction of recognisable (albeit artificial) dialect forms to indicate familiarity or intimacy. It is significant that in an informal language situation, very formal language may be used from time to time, as in argument or humour, without its being out of place, whereas the reverse is not true. It is this juxtaposition of usually separated linguistic features which is a major characteristic of conversation. The only other variety where a comparable flexibility may be found is literature.

The third general feature of this kind of English has been regularly noted by scholars, and probably over-rated, namely, the phenomenon which has been called 'normal non-fluency'. Informal, spontaneous conversation is characterised by a very high proportion of 'errors', compared with other spoken varieties, involving hesitation features of all kinds,[4] slips of the tongue (though these are by no means restricted to this variety), and a substantial amount of overlapping or simultaneous speech. There are two points to bear in mind about these features, having noted their existence. First, it is not their occurrence as such which is significant, but their distribution: as has been suggested,[5] hesitancy is strongly influenced by periods of creative thinking – the more one is thinking what to say, the more likely hesitation features are to appear – and this tends to produce a cyclic pattern. Secondly, and more fundamentally, even the distribution of errors has to be seen within a wider perspective. As recent discussion of the distinction between competence and performance has suggested,[6] the actual occurrence of given features in a text is only one sub-set of the possible occurrences of the features in the language as a whole, and one should not pay too much attention to individual occurrences without bearing this in mind. The really significant fact about informal conversation is the toleration of these features when they occur, and indeed the expectation that they will occur. Perfect fluency in this variety tends to produce the wrong effect, for psychological and other reasons – one gets labelled a 'smooth' talker, for instance – which rather suggests that hesitation phenomena are of primary significance in determining the acceptability or otherwise of conversation. What must be avoided at all costs is prejudging this issue by inculcating a pejorative attitude towards hesitation features in conversation: to refer to conversation as if it were 'disjointed', or to talk about these features as if they were 'errors', without further qualification (which is why we put our use of the word 'error' in inverted commas above) is in fact to judge conversation against some other (usually written) standard, such as is manifested by the regular omission of these features in written forms of conversation, novels or dramatic dialogue. Considered in its own situation (that is, with gestures, facial expressions, and so on all included), conversation does not seem 'disjointed' at all.

These general points are perhaps fairly obvious. Taken along with the less obvious and more detailed features of linguistic behaviour which occur in the above texts, there would seem to be very clear evidence that there is a valid linguistic basis for regarding this kind of language as a variety, in the sense in which this term was discussed in Chapter 3.

There is relatively little of significance to be noted about conversation at the phonetic level of analysis. A basic point which must be made is that as there are no restrictions on who may participate in a conversation, and as there is no formal training required, the range of voice qualities one finds being used is entirely random and without pattern – as opposed to the more predictable qualities of certain other varieties (*eg* television advertising, sermons, spoken legal language). Otherwise, the only features which regularly occur (though they are not much in evidence in the texts used here) are the use of a wider range of sounds from different air-stream mechanisms and other configurations of the vocal tract than one finds in other varieties of English (vocalisations such as 'tut tut', various whistles (*eg* of amazement), artificial clearing of the throat or coughing for purposes of irony, and other snorts and sniffs, to communicate disgust and other attitudes), and the greater use of and permissiveness for onomatopoeic words and sounds, such as 'whoosh', 'boing', 'brrr'.

The segmental phonology is also restricted in the amount of stylistic distinctiveness it contains. All speakers in these extracts used their normal varieties of Received Pronunciation, apart from during the single anecdotal excursus in **II**. The possibility of switching accents, already mentioned, is in evidence here, as indicated rather crudely in the margin to line 60. Frequent use is made of lexical items with an abnormal syllabic structure for English, such as 'sshhh', 'mhm'. Another feature, not indicated in our transcription, is the regular use of the assimilations and elisions which have been noted as characteristic of informal English,[7] and which are largely absent from many other varieties of speech, where they tend to be avoided, either for clarity of enunciation (as with the public-address system on railway stations, or in certain kinds of radio broadcast) or because of a misguided fear of being criticised as careless in articulation.

The phonological distinctiveness of conversation lies mainly in the use of non-segmental features of language. First, conversation, unlike all other spoken varieties apart from spoken literature and humour, will allow the occurrence of the entire range of prosodic and para-linguistic effects. Contrasts such as *sob* and *cry* occur relatively frequently, compared with elsewhere. There would seem to be no social restrictions on the range and depth of emotions which might be displayed in a conversational situation, the controlling factors being rather a question of personal relationship between the participants; consequently the linguistic expression of emotion, primarily a function of non-segmental features, is similarly unrestricted. In principle, then, anything may occur. In practice, within any given stretch of utterance, very little occurs; which leads us to a second main characteristic of conversation, namely, the tendency to make frequent use of a small number of basic prosodic configurations. This may be seen in a number of ways throughout the above texts. The relatively standardised, narrowed pitch contours for many of the monosyllabic response utterances provide a specific instance (22, 26, 30, 33, 44, 49, 51, *etc*), as does the very high proportion of simple falling tones. Another example of the tendency would be the frequency of a 'stepping down' kind of head within tone-units, that is, a sequence of gradually descending syllables from the onset to the nucleus, and the almost complete absence of a 'stepping up' type of head (where the syllables gradually rise), or heads involving wide pitch jumps between the syllables, which are common in most other spoken varieties of English. Again, while tone-units may be any length in conversation, within normal physiological limits, extending in our data from one to twenty and more words – another variation on the 'anything goes' theme – there is a strong tendency to keep them short, to break up potentially lengthy tone-units wherever possible. The average length of the units in this text is considerably shorter than that of any other variety, the vast majority falling within the range of one to five words. Moreover, a relatively high proportion of tone-units are incomplete, largely due to the nature of the interchange, often accompanied by reduced loudness (a 'tailing off' of the voice, *eg* 6, 12). Related to this is the frequent absence of end-of-utterance pauses, due to the rapid taking up of cues. (Similar effects to these last are often introduced into radio drama dialogue which tries to simulate fluency and informality of this kind.)

These are only tendencies towards uniformity, of course; any danger of a mechanical repetitiveness arising within the speech of an individual is avoided through the introduction of a large number of other prosodic contrasts at various points within the tone-unit. (There is little chance of uniformity between speakers, in view of the substantial phonetic differences between voice qualities.) Contrastive (non-final) tonicity is extremely frequent in this variety (3, 4, 6, 9, 16, 19, 23, 25, *etc*), and to a certain extent correlates with the high frequency of compound tones, especially the fall-plus-rise (which is particularly common in extract **I**). There is also the occasional completely unexpected placement of nuclear tone (54), which is only likely to happen in informal kinds of speech. The tendency noted above towards the use of simple falling tones is also varied somewhat, particularly through the use of low rising-type tones on statements (especially in **I**, where the normal emotional value of these tones, informal friendliness or politeness, would be most appropriate), the occasional use of very emphatic tones such as the rise–fall (32, 65, 66, *etc*) and fall–rise (30, 42, *etc*), and the high proportion of narrowed tones throughout. A further means of variation is the common use of high unstressed syllables, especially in the prehead of the tone-unit (24, 40, 47, 53, *etc*).

As already mentioned, a familiar point about informal conversation is the frequency of silence for purposes of contrastive pause, as opposed to its being required simply for breath-taking. Voiceless hesitation is always much more frequent than voiced in any variety of English, but in this variety its frequency is significantly high (especially of the brief pause within tone-units) and it tends to occur relatively randomly, not just at places of major grammatical junction, which is more the pattern in examples of written English read aloud.[8] Voiced hesitation is not frequent in most speakers, but what is important is the wide range of exponence one may find for this phenomenon. In the present extracts, apart from the occasional *əm*, there are hesitant drawls (17, 20, 46), and unfinished tone-units; and in everyday conversation one frequently hears phonetic oddities of every description occurring as hesitation, such as clicks, trills, and intakes of breath. One should also note the stylistic implications of introducing hesitation phenomena of any kind into more specialised discussion (*eg* 125 *ff*): the effect of 'word-searching' helps to avoid the impression of being too knowledgeable about a topic, and builds up an alternative impression of informality. Some varieties make regular use of rhetorical tricks of this kind – for example, the cultivation of apparent spontaneity in lecturing, or in television news reporting. In the latter, the principle is often taken to extremes, pauses occurring regularly in places that normal informal conversation would rarely make use of, such as after the definite article; for example, note the pause in the second nominal group in the following:

   . . . gave it to the ÀRCHitect| – the · |ĂRCHitect . . .

As a result of the permissible hesitation frequency in conversation, the tempo is characteristically uneven within and between utterances, though inter-pausal stretches (especially those with relatively few un-stressed syllables, reflecting the absence of technical polysyllabic words) have a marked tendency towards subjective rhythmic iso-chrony (see *p* 36). Absolutely speaking, the speed of conversation is quite fast, but this is not the linguistically relevant point which has to be made, which is that there is no conventional pressure for con-versational speed to be regular; tempo is as flexible as one wishes it to be. Linguistic contrasts in tempo do occur, of course: *allegro* is very frequent in **II**, for example. As far as other non-segmental features are concerned, one should note important variations in loudness to suggest the relative importance of what a speaker is saying. Consider the normally *piano* expression of phatic information (see *p* 121), the *high forte* used as anecdotal utterance initiators (see 60 *ff*) or at the climax of jokes. The overall prosodic build-up for a dramatic climax is in fact well illustrated by the second extract. Finally, paralinguistic features of significance in this variety are – as one might expect – the use of *laugh* (50, 88), *spread* (35), and *breathy* (65).

The evidence of these extracts suggests that in conversation there is a marked tendency for non-segmental features to form a basic set of recurrent patterns, which is occasionally disturbed by the intro-duction of specific prosodic and paralinguistic effects. The precise nature of these patterns varies to a certain extent depending on such factors as the fluency of an individual or the modality he is using. If we compare extracts **I**, **II**, and **III** from the latter point of view, certain formal differences immediately emerge: the anecdotal character of **II**, for instance, exercises a strong influence on average tone-unit length. Also, level tones are frequent in **II** (six occasions), but are completely absent from **I**.

One of the interesting things which in a way helps to distinguish this use of language from all others is the kind of descriptive problem it poses, particularly as regards the grammatical delimitation of the utterance and the sentence. In most other varieties, utterances are usually clearly definable, and sentences much more so than here. The problem is readily illustrated from extract **I**. The notion of utterance subsumes any stretch of speech preceded and followed by a change of speaker (*cf p* 45). This suggests taking lines 23–9 as two utterances on B's part, though there are extremely cogent grammatical and semantic reasons for taking them as one. Interpolations of the kind used by A in line 26 are very significant in this variety. They are usually interjectional in character; their function is primarily to indicate that attention is being maintained. We need only try taking part in a conversation and withholding all such 'noises off' to prove their integral role – the conversation rapidly breaks down, as soon as our interlocutor begins to wonder whether we are really listening. However, in view of the fact that they are grammatically optional (as opposed to the *m* used in reply to a question, *eg* 32), that their distribution is governed mainly by semantic criteria, and that they could have occurred simultaneously with the interlocutor's speech, it is proposed to treat 'broken' utterances of this type (*eg* 23–9 and similar cases) as single utterances. We are accordingly in a position to make the descriptive generalisation that the length of utterances in this variety is much more variable than in any other variety of English. There are of course certain tendencies to adopt a given length depending on whereabouts in a conversation an utterance occurs; in the data we have examined, utterances are relatively short at the beginning, longer as topics are introduced, longer still as argument develops or an anecdote begins, and short again as the end approaches. Changes in modality and status also condition variations in utterance length. No other variety has such short utterances, telephone conversation providing an even clearer illustration of this point (see p 120).

A similar problem arises over the sentence. Before we can make any statements about relative length of sentences and relative complexity of sentence structure, we must first be clear as to our criteria for delimiting sentences from each other. This problem has already been mentioned in Chapter 2 (see *p* 45), and it exists in its most marked form here. Informal conversation is characterised by a large number of loosely coordinated clauses, the coordination being structurally ambiguous: it is an open question whether one takes these as sequences of sentences or as single compound sentences. The situation is complicated by phonetic and phonological ambiguity other than that caused by the intonation: the generally rapid speed of speech and the absence of inter-clausal pause, in particular, *eg*

I |"ÀM CÓLD| and I'll |be all 'right . . . (*p* 97, *l* 3)

(*Cf* the more normal kind of problem, involving pause, illustrated by line 16, and the completely unambiguous coordination of line 64.)

The choice of solution has implications for the stylistic analysis. Thus if we take all such sequences as separate sentences, then we can make a statement such as 'sentence length is relatively short, and in structure displays predominantly the simple type'. On the other hand, if we take such sequences as units, then our analysis must point to a significantly high proportion of longer, more complex, and more varied sentence-types. We have adopted the former solution here, on the grounds that it produces a simpler description. To take such sequences as single sentences would force us to make a highly complicated sub-analysis of compound, complex, and mixed sentence-types (79–87 would be one type, for example), which would be of little relevance for the description of most other varieties.

Having said this, we may now qualify the point made above by noting that if utterances do reach any substantial length, it is because of this phenomenon of loose coordination. It might be better, indeed, to refer to such a feature without using the term 'sentence' at all, talking instead of 'clause-complexes'. Such a procedure would certainly clarify a very important point about the way in which conversation progresses, more in a series of loosely coordinated sentence-like structures than in a series of sharply defined sentences; but it would be a bad procedure from a stylistic point of view, as we should thereby be setting up a different grammatical theory simply to account for this variety, and this would complicate our comparative statements, producing an undesirable overlap between the notions of clause and sentence which we have carefully tried to avoid (see *pp* 46–7).

Other than these loosely coordinated types, sentences tend to be short. Often, a number of sentences, not separated by any kind of pause, are found within a single utterance (*eg* 11–12, 35–6, 46–7).

Minor sentences are extremely frequent, especially as response utterances (though 'response' must here be given a fairly wide definition, to include utterances which are not straight answers, such as the noises of agreement already mentioned). Non-response minor sentences are also frequent in these extracts, particularly through the use of summarising statements (as either introductions or afterthoughts), *eg* 59, 119, 122. Apart from this, sentences are all of the SP(CA) type, further complexity being introduced by increasing the number of adverbials, usually in sentence-final position, *eg* 76 *ff* SPCAA, 142 *ff* SPCAAA. One should also note the high proportion of parenthetic compound types of sentences (see *p* 48), in these extracts, particularly through the introduction of *you know* (24, 47, 87, 124, *etc*), though other interpolations could have been just as appropriately used (*eg I mean, you see*). It is probable that a modality difference conditions usage here, as such interpolations are rare in anecdote, and common in more serious types of conversation.

The use of minor sentences, along with the loose coordination discussed above, is almost certainly the basis of the impression of 'disjointedness' which many people feel is characteristic of this variety (*cf* our attitude to this, *p* 105). This is further reinforced by the absence of a stable pattern of rhythm or tempo at the phonological level. This naturally depends to a large extent on the fluency of a speaker, on his familiarity with the topic being talked about, on his experience of discussion, or joke-telling, and so on; but in view of the fact that the vast majority of conversations are not between 'conversationalists', in any 'professional' sense, it does not seem unrealistic to stress less fluent conversation as being the expected kind. Moreover it is very much to be doubted whether a more fluent norm for conversation would in fact strike people generally as being more desirable in view of the observable tendency, already noted, for too much fluency in an informal conversation to be stigmatised. The theoretical distinction between competence and performance (*cf p* 104) does not seem to take sufficient account of material of this kind: it is not at all clear to what extent all the non-fluencies in the above extracts can be 'dismissed' as performance, in view of their frequency, their undeniable distribution in terms of regular syntactic and phonological patterns, and their clear relation to a standard behavioural response on the part of the language-user.

The disjointedness referred to, moreover, is increased by the fact that many sentences and clauses (*eg* 6, ?10, 24, 44, 79) are incomplete.

This is sometimes due to a 'syntactic anacoluthon' on the part of a speaker, a re-starting of a sentence to conform more to what he wanted to say (as in 79); but it is also fairly common for A to complete B's sentence, or *vice versa* (*eg* 133), or for the two speakers to provide an ending for a sentence simultaneously – a situation frequently parodied by comedians. Once again, the linguistic point to be made is that, whether such things happen or not in any given piece of conversation, they *could* have taken place without being felt to be inappropriate. We should also note in this connection the way in which the characteristic 'give and take' of a successful conversation is maintained (see extract **III**, in particular, where things have really 'warmed up'): the pace of the dialogue is kept up by the 'agreement' question–tags and the phatic interpolations. In a dialogue of this type it is sometimes difficult to find an obvious stopping-point for extracting a linguistic sample: in the present case, the cut-off in **III** is quite arbitrary, as the topic continued to be discussed for some minutes.

There are a few other points to be noted at the level of sentence and above. Overt, inter-sentence linkage is very marked: the extracts provide illustrations of all the types referred to on *p* 44 (personal pronoun reference, cross-reference using the articles and determiners, ellipsis, *etc*). Interrogative sentence types are particularly frequent. Imperatives are few, and when they do occur, their force is 'softened' through some device (*eg* the additional clause in 9), as better befits the informality of the situation. Finally at this level, one should note the frequency with which speakers make use of different grammatical modes of reference, such as reported speech, directly quoted utterance (both of these especially in **II**), and undefinable mixtures, such as the structure in line 27.

There is little to say about clause structure. Vocatives are common, especially in initial position, though this is not well represented in the above extracts, presumably because the identifying or attention-getting function of the vocative is not likely to be frequently used in conversations involving only two people. Nominal groups tend to be infrequent as subject; the personal pronoun is more in evidence – especially the first person, which is an expected, but nonetheless a distinctive feature of conversation. One might also note in this connection the use of the informal *you* (71), in its impersonal function as against the more formal *one* or in place of the third person pronoun (91).

Group structure, both nominal and verbal, is relatively uncomplicated. The former tends to be of the simple type *Determiner* (*Adjective*)

Noun, with little postmodification or adjective sequence. There is a tendency for nominal group structure to increase in complexity as the level of seriousness of the conversation increases (*cf* **I** and **III** from this point of view). Within the nominal group, one should note the frequent use of a very limited range of adverbial intensifiers such as *very*, *a bit* (contrast lecturing, with its use of *highly*, *notably*, *etc*); relative clauses usually omit an optional relative pronoun (*eg* 105); it is normal to put the preposition in a relative clause at the end (*eg* 107). .

Verbal groups are also simple in structure, usually one auxiliary with a lexical verb, though the whole range of auxiliary combinations is possible. A significant flexibility is that conversation allows the occurrence of the whole range of tense-forms and aspects. Also highly distinctive is the occurrence of contracted verbal forms (*he's*, *I'll*, *etc*); the frequency of informal 'filler' verbs, such as *got* (5, 16, 88, *etc*); the tendency to use phrasal verbs (probably below conversational average in the above extracts); the infrequency of passives; and the use of colloquial ellipses (*eg* 1, 62–4).

Finally, at the grammatical level, informal conversation provides the best example of a variety wherein points of disputed usage tend to be passed over unnoticed. It is perfectly possible to hear two people continually using alternative constructions in the same conversation, neither noticing the difference introduced by the other, and often a person will be markedly inconsistent himself, without this being noticed. They only become sensitive to points of usage in a relatively self-conscious or formal situation, when pressures to use a particular form and reject another on some obscure ground of 'correctness' regularly come to the fore. As a result, one is liable to find in conversation instances of both a favoured and a condemned form (by the standards of traditional grammar books). For example, in 76 one finds *everybody made their contribution*. The linguistic point which has to be made immediately is not that *their* is wrong and *his* right, or *vice versa*, but that *in this variety* either is permissible, and will be used depending on one's linguistic background. In normal conversation, no comment would be made on the choice of usage: only the pedant, whom one trusts to be exceptional, tries to introduce 'linguistic disharmony' into this variety. Similarly, repetitious structures, looseness of syntax, 'weak' words like *got* and *nice*, and so on – all of which would be condemned, and with good reason, in children's school essays and elsewhere – are a standard and indeed a valuable part of informal conversation. Formal written English and informal spoken

English are two very different varieties, and the criteria of acceptable usage must not be confused.

Probably the most noticeable aspect of informal conversation is its vocabulary. Words tend to be very simple in structure: even when discussion is well under way (as in **III**), there is an avoidance of specialised terms and formal phraseology, and whenever they are used, their force is usually played down by the speaker, through the use of hesitation, or the use of *you know, sort of*, and so on (*eg* 124). The lack of precision in such matters of word-selection does not seem to matter; inexplicit references are accepted (*eg* 112); and it is even possible to replace a lexical item by a completely non-specific prop word, as in the use of *thingummy, what-do-you-call-it, you-know-what-I-mean, etc*, which may all function as nouns. On the whole, the vocabulary reflects the relative domesticity of the subject matter – knitting, education, table, the weather – with the addition of a great deal of phatic ('atmosphere-setting') vocabulary, and the vocalisations (such as *m*) which keep the conversation going.

The informality of this text is evident throughout, particularly because of its readiness to use certain items which are highly frequent in conversational English, *eg yeah* (44, 49, 51, *etc*), *cos* (2, 29, 114), *got* (1, 5, 13, 16, *etc*), *all right* (3, 11), *just* (2, 12, 21, *etc*), *a bit* (2, 28), *fed up* (51), *sort of* (124), *sniffy* (2), *I mean* (142), *knocks back* (108), *warmed up* (4), *take to* (45), *a lot* (54), and *phone* (143). One finds in the extracts a representative number of colloquial idioms, such as *in a minute* (11), *just couldn't face* (21), *the simple truth is* (65), *the thing to do* (84), *as far as I can gather* (131); and also the occasional cliché, such as *that's life* (160) – though again this does not have the undesirable connotations that clichés have in certain other varieties. Informal conversation is also characterised by a great deal of lexical hyperbole, usually with phonological support, *eg stupid* (14), *five thousand* (14), *freezing* (32), *every possible* (88), *on and on* (126), *all over* (77). 'In-group' slang is also frequent – for example, the use of abbreviations familiar to both participants, such as *St Paul's* (112), *LCC* (137). One should also note the tendency, illustrated in the piece of telephone conversation below, to use such phrases as *ie, eg, a, b, c*, in a speaker who has been educated to a reasonably high degree. Familiar euphemisms can also be expected to occur – *tiny garment* (36) is in fact a humorous query as to the possibility of A having become pregnant. Finally, one should note the deliberate introduction of incongruous or humorous items of vocabulary into an informal conversation, the nature of the wit of course largely depending on the common background of the speakers. In the present case, we have *human being* (56), *gorgons* (111), and possibly *eat liquid* (102) and *string* (46). Related to this is the introduction of vocabulary normally part of another province or idiolect for dramatic or humorous effect, as with *communally* (67), *principal* (61), and *did* (75).

Semantically, the most important feature of this variety is the randomness of the subject matter, the lack of an overall contrived pattern, the absence of any conscious planning as conversation proceeds. Conversation does not take place in a series of coordinated blocks, but – especially as someone searches for the beginning of a topic – in a series of jumps (as in extract **I**). There is a general absence of linguistic or cultural pressures to make the conversation go in a particular direction,[9] and there is a corresponding admission of all kinds of spontaneous effect, especially switches in modality. Many features are indicative of this: the simultaneous start given to an utterance (*eg* 33–4), A supplying B's image (133), the occurrence of afterthoughts (118 *ff*, 153 *ff*), the loose stringing together of ideas (90 *ff*, 141 *ff*), the rough synonymy (118 *ff*), the repetitive nature of certain parts of the discourse (such as the multiple agreement in 134–6), and the redundancy which allows omissions (24). Other important semantic points have already been mentioned: the freedom to introduce material of almost any kind (the limits depending on the sex, class, and intimacy of the participants), such as jokes, bathos (*eg* 61 *ff*), irony (64 – *cf And Sir said* . . .), and accent- or dialect-switching (as in 60 *ff*);[10] the importance of intimacy-signals, silence-fillers, 'rapport-makers', or whatever one calls them; and the importance of the context in which the utterance took place, so that omissions go unnoticed (24), speech which is obscure to the analyst is understood by the participants (10), and so on.

To call the language used in the above situation a 'variety' is perhaps a little premature. The term 'informal' is readily correlatable with certain linguistic variables, operating at all levels, and reflecting the parity of social status of the participants and the spontaneity of their expression. The term 'conversation' is not so clearly distinguishable from other terms which come to mind, in particular the notion of 'discussion'. It may well be that a useful linguistic distinction can be drawn between 'conversation' and 'discussion', in terms of the degree of seriousness of the subject matter, or the formality of the occasion, and it is not difficult to think up probable linguistic correlates – for example, at the semantic level, the relatively monothematic nature of discussion would condition a markedly different semantic structure for the discourse from that which exists in conversation. But it is unlikely that there is a clear boundary between conversation and discussion: there are many intuitively clear stylistic categories within which elements of both conversation and discussion combine – the concept of 'talking shop', for example. As a consequence, we do not wish to suggest that any clear lines of stylistic demarcation have been drawn in the present instance. We have tried to point at the centre of a peripherally unclear stylistic issue; we feel that there is sufficient evidence to make the postulation of a variety warrantable; but there is much which remains to be investigated.

We shall conclude this chapter by examining one outstandingly neglected area in greater detail, namely, the question of how far other kinds of informal conversation occurring in a more restricted situation may best be analysed: whether they should be described as instances (more precisely, sub-provinces) of the same province, or as separate provinces. The answer will of course depend on the extent to which these more restricted varieties of conversation share the properties of the variety which we have described so far. If there is a very close linguistic similarity, the former solution will be preferable; if there is little in common, then the latter, and a label other than 'conversation' will have to be found.[11] We have chosen an extract of telephone conversation to illustrate this problem.

IV

A |highview double three four FÍVE|

B good |MÒRNing|

A *(hel|LÒ| |ÁRthur|)*

B *|"VĂLerie|*

A |YÈS| †good |MÒRNing|†   5

B †thi this† is |ÀRthur SPÉAKing|

A hel|LÒ|

B ə |SÔRRy I've 'been so 'long in
   'getting in TÓUCH 'with you| I

|rang a ↑cÔuple of times YÉsterday| 10
and you |weren't ÌN|
A |ₙNÒ| I was in |cÒLLege 'yesterday|
B you |WÈRE|
A |YÈS| *and I*
B *|aHÁ|*   15
A |thought that might ₙHÁPpen|

'high'   'but |not to WÓRRy| · |what 'I
            wanted' to say to you ↑RĔALLy| was
'alleg'   əm – 'I |didn't know 'whether you
           were 'going to say' · that you ↑could   20
'alleg'   come or you ↑CÒULDn't| 'but I was
"monot"   "|going to say 'could you 'make it" '
'rall'   'the ↑FÒLLowing 'saturday|' ·
'alleg'   B əːm '|ₙYÉS| |well' – ÓNE| |I was ↑going
           to 'say that I · that we ↑"WÈRE CÓMing| 25
           A |YĔS| · *|SPLÈNdid|*
'alleg'   B *|and ₙTWÓ|* · wē '|CÀN make it the
           'following 'saturday|'
           A |ₙCÁN you| |only əm it's it's a ↑MÌNor
           complicÁtion| but əm   30
'alleg high B '|sǑRRy| |didn't GÉT 'that|'
  narrow'   A the |point is that my ↑CHĬLdren| –
           are |going away for the ↑weekÉND| –
           B |YÉS|
'alleg'   A 'and it was |going to be ↑ₙTHÌS   35
           weekend| and |now it's going to be
           ↑NÈXT| *and*
'creak'   B *'|oh'*
           A it's |really more con↑VÈnient for me| if they're |not
           HÈRE| be|cause ↑otherwise I ↑have to   40
           keep ↑flapping arÓUND|' and

B m| H́M|

A |DÈALing with them| *'you* |KNÓW| –

'low creak' B *'|YÈP|'*

A |sō̄ əm · we'll 'make it the ↑FÒLLowing   45
ₙSÁTurday *then|*

'low' B *'that's* |FÌNE| |YÈS|' |same TÍME|

A |same TÌME| |YÈS|

B |GÒOD|

'alleg' "high" A əm ' "|do 'you think" – |I don't even   50
know �ꜛwhich · I |can't even re'member
what the chap's ↑NÀME is|' the |other
chap in your dePÀRTment| · |BÈRnard
ís it|

B |bernard blū əm: · |GRÈEN'field| ·   55

A yeah |not BLÒOMfield| (laughs)

B |ₙYÈAH| ·

'accel' A 'so |could you 'mention it to HÌM|
cos |I've in'vited him as WÈLL|'

'low creak' B '|YÈS|' – – *'|oꜛK|'*   60
'high'

'alleg' A *|oǨ|* · '|FÌNE| |everything 'all RÍGHT|'

'high' B |ÓH| |FÍNE| '|was 'there 'anything'
ÉLSE| əm:

A |NÒ| I |just ə I've |left some ↑RÈCords|

'accel' in |smart's RÒOM last 'night| 'which   65
I was all |PÀNic 'stricken a'bout| cos
they're |not MÌNE|' ·

B |Ḿ| ·

A but I |told NÈIL| and I |hope hē̄ əm ·
got the PÒINT| so I *|just wanted to*   70

B *ə I |don't* · I'm |not sure whether he
'quite 'got – the MÈSSage| |would you

'tell me a↓GĀIN 'please|

A |YÈS| |there's ǝːm · ǝ ↑RÈCords| in |smart's RÒOM| it's |measure for 75 MÈAsure| · |in |in an ÀLbum| – –

B |YÉS| ·

A and ǝm I |left them last NÌGHT| by mis|TÀKE|

B |Ḿhm| 80

'alleg' A and they're |not MÌNE| so '|that means I've 'got to take 'special ↑ₙCÀRE of them| and I |want to col'lect them to↓MÒRROW|' ·

B |ₙYÉS| do you |want me to 'get HÒLD 85 of them ₙFÓR *you|*

'alleg' A *'|could* you just 'put them͞' somewhere CÀREfully †FÓR me|†

B †|put them† SÀFE| ·

A *|ₙYÈAH|* 90

B *|YÉS|* · I'll |DÒ that|

'alleg' A '|thanks very MÙCH 'arthur|'

The telephone situation is quite unique, being the only frequently occurring case of a conversation in which the participants (and of course the contexts in which they speak) are not visible to each other. As a result, certain differences between this kind of conversation and that already described become immediately apparent. A different range of situational pressures is exerted upon the participants, and consequently the range of linguistic contrasts which they are permitted to choose differs somewhat. They cannot rely on the extralinguistic context to resolve ambiguities in speech (such as in the use of ambiguous demonstratives, pronouns, *etc*); visual feedback being absent, auditory cues become all-important, and in view of the diminished quality of the voice over the telephone, there develops a greater uncertainty and confusion in maintaining the 'give and take' of the dialogue (which was rarely impeded in extracts **I**, **II**, and **III**);

there is a strong pressure for greater explicitness, arising out of the quality of the medium of transmission, for example having to spell out words because of the distortion of certain sounds; and there is a tendency to avoid long utterances without introducing pauses which allow one's listener to confirm his continued interest, and his continued auditory 'presence'.

This last point is worth developing. The phonological system of pause that we make use of in English varies to a certain extent from variety to variety, and telephone conversation represents one extreme. Here the total number of contrasts available to most varieties is much reduced. We cannot make use of the longer pausal contrasts, because anything approaching a silence on the part of one of the speakers is either interpreted as a breakdown of communication (*Hello? Are you there?*) or as an opportunity for interruption which may not have been desired. This is particularly the case when such a conversation has not progressed onto a set theme: there is either a complete absence of pause, especially between sentences (*eg* 9, 12, 21, 24, 29), or a brief pause (*eg* 17). Longer pauses are usually restricted to grammatical contexts which are clearly incomplete (and which are therefore liable to be uninterrupted), and frequently reinforced by voiced hesitation (*eg* 19, 27). There is a tendency not to be silent before answering a question or introducing a new topic: if a delay is required, then voiced hesitation is usually introduced to 'fill the gap' (*eg* 24, 45, 50). As a result, voiced hesitation of different kinds (*eg* drawls, random vocalisations, repetitions of words) is proportionately more frequent here than elsewhere. The silent pause system, also, is reduced to a basic three terms, zero, brief (·) and unit (–), with double (– –) occasionally being used (*cf p* 35). There is nothing longer. We may contrast this with the opposite extreme, where maximum use is made of pausal contrasts, namely in the language of public speaking, where, in addition to the above, treble, and even longer pauses are possible. When there is no one to interrupt, a speaker can manipulate silence freely. (Interestingly, some of the best ripostes during a political speech come at a point when the speaker is trying to gain maximum effect through a rhetorical silence: it is easy for an inexperienced speaker to be thrown completely off balance by a punctured silence.)

There are a few other differences between telephone and other informal conversation. In view of the purpose of a telephone call, questions, responses, and imperatives are all likely to be frequent. Again, the purpose of a telephone call in the majority of cases implies a specific theme, or set of themes, which have to be raised, and this has implications for the semantic structure of the discourse. And there are undoubtedly some minor points which a full description would have to cover, for example, the different kind of formulaicness at the opening and close, or the different senses of *hello* (meaning 'I am here' or 'Are you there?' rather than simply 'Greetings'). But apart from this, it is difficult to suggest any linguistic features that could not equally well have turned up in the earlier passages of conversation. There is the same listing of dominant features at sentence, clause, and group levels, for example; the same descriptive problems emerge (*cf* the loose coordination of 78 *ff*, for example); in vocabulary there is the same use of colloquialism, idiom, and vocalisation, apart from the minor differences noted above. In other words, it can be argued that while the *range* of variety markers is considerably diminished in telephone conversation (as compared with **I**, **II**, and **III**), the *kind* of marker which occurs (with the one exception of the distinctive pausal system) is essentially the same. The conclusion which suggests itself, therefore, is that telephone conversation and other conversation are different only in degree, and that the former can most realistically be seen as a sub-province of the more general notion.

Exercises

1 Examine the markers of informality in the extracts and decide which have the most important stylistic function.

2 The extracts provide a clear example of the introductory, ice-breaking use of language known as 'phatic communion' (for a further discussion of which, see R. Quirk, *The Use of English*, Longmans, 1962, Chapter 4). But there is more to phatic communion in English than talk about the weather. To what extent does the kind of phatic communion vary depending on differences in (*a*) province, (*b*) status, and (*c*) dialect?

3 What other kinds of modality difference regularly occur in conversation?

4 In what ways does radio drama dialogue differ from the dialogue described in this chapter?

5 The following is an extract from *Everything in the Garden* by Giles Cooper. In what ways does this conversation differ from the kind illustrated in this chapter? What spoken information is left out of the written version?

Jenny: When do you want to eat?

Bernard: When I'm fed.

Jenny: No you won't, you say that but you never do and then it all gets cold while you finish something.

Bernard: What is it?

Jenny: What would you like?

Bernard: What is there?

Jenny: Nothing much.

Bernard: Then I'll have it cold with pickles.

Jenny: There isn't time, if I cooked it now it would take two hours and it wouldn't be cold till midnight.

Bernard: It was only a joke.

Jenny: I thought you meant the joint.

Bernard: No, you said nothing much, and I said I'd have it cold with pickles.

Jenny: I'm not there.

Bernard: Because you said what would I have and I said what was there, and you said . . .

Jenny (breaking in): All right, eggs?

6 How does the novelist try to reflect conversation? Discuss the linguistic features of the following extract, paying special attention to the way in which the author provides us with clues as to how the speech of the characters should be interpreted.

'Why don't you have a bicycle, and go out on it?' Arthur was saying.

'But I can't ride,' said Alvina.

'You'd learn in a couple of lessons. There's nothing in riding a bicycle.'

'I don't believe I ever should,' laughed Alvina.

'You don't mean to say you're nervous?' said Arthur rudely and sneeringly.

'I *am*,' she persisted.

'You needn't be nervous with me,' smiled Albert broadly, with his odd, genuine gallantry. 'I'll hold you on.'

'But I haven't got a bicycle,' said Alvina, feeling she was slowly colouring to a deep, uneasy blush.

'You can have mine to learn on,' said Lottie. 'Albert will look after it.'

'There's your chance,' said Arthur rudely. 'Take it while you've got it.'
(D. H. Lawrence, The Lost Girl*)

* Copyright 1921 by Thomas B. Seltzer, 1949 by Frieda Lawrence. Reprinted by permission of the author's agents, the Estate of the late Mrs Frieda Lawrence, and The Viking Press, Inc.

Notes

1 One might well find that for more restricted studies of English varieties a different yardstick would be more useful; for example, someone making a comparative study of written varieties might find it more valuable to choose a written variety as a basis for investigation; or a study of types of public speaking might be more usefully undertaken if a more formal variety of spoken English were chosen to begin with.

2 D. ABERCROMBIE, 'Conversation and Spoken Prose', *English Language Teaching*, 18, 1963, pp 10–16; A. H. SMITH and R. QUIRK, 'Some Problems of Verbal Communication', *Transactions of the Yorkshire Dialect Society*, 9, 1955, pp 10–20.

3 Naturally, permission was asked to make use of the recording, and all participants agreed. Further, to ensure complete anonymity, all names were altered to rhythmically identical equivalents, a procedure which we also use, for obvious reasons, in the extract of spoken legal language in Chapter 9.

4 These include phonological, grammatical, and lexical types, *eg* a higher proportion of anacolutha and word partials alongside the familiar 'ers' and 'ums'. *Cf* J. BLANKENSHIP and C. KAY, 'Hesitation Phenomena in English Speech: a Study in Distribution', *Word*, 20, 1964, pp 360–72.

5 For example, by F. GOLDMAN-EISLER, 'Sequential Patterns and Cognitive Processes in Speech', *Language and Speech*, 10, pp 122–32.

6 See N. CHOMSKY, *Aspects of the Theory of Syntax*, M.I.T. Press, 1965, p 3 f.

7 For example, by A. C. GIMSON, *Introduction to the Pronunciation of English*, Arnold, 1962, pp 263 ff.

8 It would be interesting to see how far silence in conversation was being supplemented at any given point by an overt reliance on context (*eg* by some bodily gesture, as when one finishes a sentence with a shrug of the shoulders instead of a word), but only surreptitiously filmed material will do this adequately, and expense makes research difficult.

9 Those cases where X comes to talk about a particular subject with Y would not be included by this statement; but these would tend not to be informal in character and would in any case involve a certain amount of random 'beating about the bush' before the participants got down to business. The only genuine exception which we can think of is the 'angry scene' conversation, which usually mixes informality with formality, where X wishes to get something straight with Y without further ado.

10 Here, one should note that it is necessary only to *begin* well, in imitating someone's speech informally, and to give an occasional reminder that one is still imitating. Absolute consistency is unnecessary (except in professional circumstances, of course, and even there few narrators are perfect): in the present

text B slips out of the Principal's accent quite quickly, and introduces the occasional grammatical change, *eg* the use of *have to* (71), where the Principal would probably have used *must*.

11 If one wished, the 'similarity' between the two texts could be quantified statistically (*cf p* 22 above). There is a finite number of linguistic parameters recognised in the description, and these are ordered in a given way; consequently it would not be difficult to arrive at an overall statistic which would characterise a text. One could plot degrees of similarity using standard techniques. The only problem would come when a text could be shown to fall perfectly in between two such extremes as conversation and discussion. In such a case (which we have not yet come across), one would have to postulate a new stylistic category, rather than force the text into either extreme.

Chapter 5

The Language of Unscripted Commentary

Most commentaries have something to do with description, explanation, or opinion. But the three are not always present in equal proportions. Some forms of written commentary, for instance, by providing the supplementary information which will enable a text to be more fully understood, set out purely to explain. In spoken commentary, on the other hand, the need for vivid description is often so strong as to reduce explanation to a minimum. And commentaries are to be found – notably of the political kind, both spoken and written – in which there is a great deal of opinion but precious little that is either described or explained. If it is remembered that the descriptions, explanations and opinions may, on different occasions, relate to an almost unlimited range of subject matter, it becomes obvious that the term 'commentary' has to serve for many kinds of linguistic activity, all of which would need to be represented in any adequate descriptive treatment, and would presumably require separate labels such as 'exegesis', 'political comment', and so on.

The aim of this chapter, however, is not to compile an exhaustive list of all the imaginable types, but to discuss one or two examples of what is meant by 'commentary' when the word is used in its commonest current sense. There is little doubt that for most people nowadays a commentary is a spoken account of events which are actually taking place, given for the benefit of listeners who cannot see them. There are of course many occasions when both commentator and listener are looking at the same event – notably on television – but here the activity is usually self-evident and most commentators are mercifully aware of the absurdity, or even impertinence, of reporting that the ball is in the net, the stumps are spreadeagled or the parade commander has fallen from his horse. In other words, the television commentator's most useful function is to provide background information or explain any bits of activity that do not explain themselves. In contexts where the audience cannot see the event the commentator must do more than this: he must recreate for his hearers a chain of activity as it is developing. Such contexts are almost exclusive to sound broadcasting, and so far as commentary is thought of as a variety at all there can be little doubt that it is popularly associated with the efforts of radio commentators. Consequently, we turned to radio as the most likely source of representative specimens on which to base this chapter. One of our choices is from a commentary on a very common event – a cricket match; the other is from an account of a state funeral, which is something that happens very rarely. We hoped by making such different selections both to give an idea of what we consider typical of commentary and to indicate the range of subject matter that this variety may include.

I

'piano'	and the '|score goes ↓up to · ↑thirty
	↑FÒUR [for |TWÒ]| · |ₙÉDrich| · |twenty
"accel"	↓TWÒ| · "and |CÓWdrey| |ÒUT this
"rhythmic"	MŎRNing|" "|caught 'burge ↑bowled
'cresc'	'hawke" – ↓TÈN|' – – ānd '|england ↑NÒW 5
'narrow'	[of |CÒURSE]|' – s meta '|PHÒRically
'rhythmic'	[|SPÈAKing]|' – '|on the 'back ↓FÒOT|' – – –
'low piano husky' 'alleg'	'the |batsmen' ↑still to ↑CŎME| "which
"low monot"	"|many of you' · no 'doubt will be"
'piano' "trem" "giggle"	↑counting ↑ŬP| – ' "and" – "|some" 10
"monot"	"↑englishmen may be" ↑ₙGLÀD 'that|' –
	|NŌW| that |jack ↑flavell ₙWÀS left
'dimin'	out| 'in |favour of a ↓BÀTSMAN|' –
'alleg' 'alleg'	|parfitt ↓NÈXT| – '|THÉN ↓SHÀRPE|' – '|THÉN
	↓PÀRKES|' – |THÉN ↓ₙTÌTmus| – |TRŪEman| – 15
'low'	|ₙGÌFFord| – |CÒLDwell| – – – 'now a'
	|little – – ↑FŬSSing| a|bout ↑someone ·
	be↓side the ↓sight SCRÉEN| – be|fore
	mc↓kenzie BÓWLS| to – – – |BÁRRington| –

'accel cresc'	'|barrington 'giving a ↑look round the	20
'high forte accel	↑FÍELD|' a '|slightly · "↑CLÒser" 'field	
narrow'"tense" 'dimin'	for ↓HÍM|' '|"THRÈE 'slips [|GÙLLy]|' ānd	
'alleg'	'|not ˑa LÉG 'slip| bμt a' · |"ḇack'ward	
	'short LÈG| |only 'just 'backward of	
'accel' "stac"	↓SQÙARE| · ' "|six ↓men ↓CLÒSE| –	25
"cresc" 'lento'	"mc|kenzie comes ₙÍN| |BÒWLS|" ' · ̄ānd – –	
"laugh"	"|BĂRRington| |makes a ↑most ↑unˑ"G̱RĂCEful|	
	|little ↑J̱ÀB ₙTHÉRE|' to a |BĀLL| that	
'cresc' 'high'	'|goes 'through to ↑GRÒUT|' · '|ĀND| – it	
"narrow"	|is I 'think sig "↓NÌFicant"| · |that · the	30
'alleg monot'	↑ball' ₙNÓW| '|seems to be' CŌMing| –	
'tense' 'monot'	'|"ŪP|' · '|on its 'way to the' ₙWÌCket	
'alleg'	'keeper| · in|stead of · 'almost' ↑"C̱LÌNGing	
	to the ₙGRÓUND| as it |did on ↓SÀTurday| –	
	mc|KÈNzie · |scrubs it ↑FÙRiously on	35
	his FLÁNnels| and |starts ↓ÒFF| – on	
	|that ↑rather ↑"ḇÙOYant| · |"BÒUNCing	
	'run of his| |ₙBÓWLS| · and |barrington	
'breathy'	'PLĂYS|' · |very pre'cisely ↓FÒRward THÍS	
	'time| – – his |foot is ↑"r̄īght 'down	40
'piano' "low husky"	'the ↓ₙLÍNE| · · "and he |pushes ↓back	
	↑down to the BÒWLer|" – |goes ÓUT| and' –	
	|sweeps a↓WĀY a| – |little · ↑loose	
'alleg'	↓ₙGRÁSS| or 'per|haps ↑sweeps away 'nothing	
'low piano husky'	'at ↓ÀLL|' · '|while he TRÌES to|' ·	45
'low piano husky'	|"ₙSÈTTle| · '|those ↑ever 'present	
'alleg'	↑BŬTTer'flies|' · '|settles to his' ↓STĀNCE|	
	|right 'shoulder ₙRÓUND a 'little| ·	
	mc|kenzie ↓moves ↓ÍN| · |BŌWLS| |ₙÁND| ·	
	|BĀRRington| |PÚLLing his ₙBÀT away| ·	50
	|takes that ↑high on the ↓ₙTHÍGH| ·	

	and it |pops ŏUT| · to |short LĔG| ·	
'alleg'	'and it |must've 'come ↑"BÀCK at him [a	
'allegriss'	|"ₕBĪT||' · 'in |ₙÓTHer words|' mc|KÈNzie's| –	
'alleg'	|ₗoff ↑"CŬTTer| |or 'the ↓one that he	55
'low piano'	'moves' ↑in off 'the ↓SÉAM| · '|ānd · it's	
'dimin'	↑picked ↓ₙÙP|' · by '|veivers 'coming 'in	
	from ↑short ↓LÈG|' – |three ↑SLĪPS| ·	
'narrow'	and a |GÙLLy 'THÉRE [|THÓUGH]|' · for	
	the |ball that 'goes 'the ÒTHer 'way| – – –	60
'low piano'	'|up 'aGÀIN| – |comes mc↑KÈNzie|' |ₕBÓWLS| ·	
'forte cresc'	and |barrington · '↑edges ↑ₙTHÁT|' "and	
"forte high cresc	it's |through the ↑SLĪPS|" · '|and he's	
wide"		
'forte high'	↑going to 'get ↓four 'runs ↓and a LĪFE|'	
	(applause)	

II

'descend' "high"	' "and |NŎW| · a|GÀIN| – the |TĬNkle|" ·	65
	of the |CĂvalry| · as the |second	
	divĭsion| · of the |HŎUSE'hold| ·	
	|CĂvalry|' · the |second con↑TÌNgent|	
	of the |ÈScort| – |these are ↓found	
'low'	by the ↑BLŬES| · '|on their ↑dark	70
	↓CHÁRgers|' · |come · ↑SLŎwly| · and	
	ma|JĔstically| · |into the ᵥSQUÀRE| –	
'alleg'	'we have |seen · MÁny HÒRses| this	
'high' "breathy"	|MÓRNing|' · ' "|ÉARLier|" · the po|LÍCE|' ·	75
	the |MÓUNTed poLÌCE| 'were |HĔRE| ·	75
	|quietly con'trolling 'the ↓CRÒWDS| ·	
	|QUÌETly| · |ₙSMÒOTHly| · di|recting	
'alleg low'	af↓FÀIRS| 'as they |always ↑DÒ| on	
	these |great 'oc'casions in LÒNdon|' ·	
'high'	'and to |them inDĒED| · has |fallen	80

the "ʷPRÌVilege|'ˌ' · of |ʷHÈADing| ·

'alleg' 'lento low' ''this |great' caval↓CÁDE| · ''which

|NŌW| · |wiñds awÁY| · ˈto|wards ˈthe

'high' ↓CÌTY|' − but |NÓW| · 'a|GÁIN| · a

|band APPRÒACHes| − a|GÀIN| · the   85

|PLÙMES| · |of the ↑CĂvalry|' − ˈbut

|on ↓FÒOT| − − − (band plays)

|THÁT| · was the |BĀND| of the |royal

ar↑TÌLLery| · and |they are ↓FÒLLowed| ·

by ˈthe |BĀND| of the |metro'politan   90

po↓LÌCE| · and |nō̄w ↑sÒMbre| · in

their |dark ùni'forms| − ˈthe

'wide' ''po|LÌCEmen|'ˌ· a |large con↑TÌNgent

ÓF them| in|cluding po↑lice ca↓DÈTS| − −

|these MĒN| who have |seeñ ↑so MÙCH| ·   95

'low' ' of |london's ˈaf↓FĀIRS| − |march ·

↑slowly ↓BÝ|' · ˈto|wards ˈthe TÀIL

'end| of the ˈpro|CÉSSion| · but ·

|ₕstill beHÌND 'them| · the |ci↑VÌLian| ·

'low' '|SÉRvice 'men|' · the |MĒN| · of the   100

|FÌRE bri'gade| · and the |civil de↓FÈNCE|

. . . .

|MŌving| · |FÒRward| · |ₕpast the ↓CRÒWDS

[|THÈRE]| · with a |BĂCKground| · of the

|modern BŬILDings| of the |ₕnew LÓNdon| ·

'high' which has |RÌsen| · '|"PHÒEnix' 'like| |in   105

this ↑"b̠attered ʷCÒRner| − |coming NŌW|

|into thi¹ · ↑pool of ʷSHĂdow| · |under

the ↑station RÒOF| · our |ĒYES| · |turn

to the LÈFT| · to the |station ʷÈNtrance| ·

¹ We adopt the phonetic representation *thi* whenever a speaker uses the 'strong'
form of the definite article (pronouncing it *thee*) before a word beginning with a
consonant. The strong form of the indefinite article is represented by *ei* (*cf p* 246, *l* 5).

'ascend'   'to |sēe| · the |fīrst| · |flash̄' of   110
                'bright wórk| · |on the ↓cár| ·
                re|flecting · the ↓lìghts| · which
                have |brought · ↑warmth · and ↑ᵂcòlour| ·
'low'   ˙to 'this '|gréy| |drab ᵂscène|' – |nów| ·
                the |motor héarse| · |enters the   115
                stàtion| – |passes the 'waiting pèople| ·
                |ₕcomes 'under the ᵂclòck| · which
                |shòws| · |twenty ↑twò 'minutes| ·
'low wide'   '|past òne|' – – – |six ↓cárs| – |come
                ín| – – ma|jèstically| · but |in ·   120
'low'   ↑such · "màrked [|còntrast]| – 'to the
                |ceremònial| ˙we |sāw| · |earlier
                in the ↓dày|' – – – the po|līcemen| –
                |stand to attĕntion| – – and a |sīlence| ·
'low'   '|falls 'over the ᵂ↓stàtion|'   125

The description of activity and the provision of background
information have been singled out as centrally important parts of a
radio commentator's function. But he is faced with two further
requirements which are perhaps even more fundamental and inescapable: the need to keep up an unbroken flow of speech and to
sound interesting while doing so. In most of the other situations that
call for non-stop language the speaker is either reading from a script,
reciting from memory, prompting himself with notes or talking
about a well-known topic that has been given careful consideration.
While a commentator may get some support from any of these aids
during the lengthier gaps in proceedings, only spontaneously produced speech is capable of following the fluctuations that are likely
to occur in even the most predictable of events. As a result of these
pressures, successful commentary is marked by a fluency far in excess
of that found in most other forms of unscripted speech.

Impressionistic judgments about fluency are quite easy to make
when listening to a commentator. To give a linguistic definition of
the notion is more difficult, and to point out the 'fluent' features of a
phonological transcription more difficult still; but the complete

absence of voiced hesitation in both specimens of commentary is one respect in which they may be said to be more fluent than, for instance, the conversation in Chapter 4. Another feature that may contribute to the impression of fluency is the habit of using intonation to connect separate items of information into quite lengthy, coherent sequences terminated by a contour – often an extra-low or extra-wide falling tone – that gives a clear indication of finality. There is a good example of this in 65–72, where a remarkable series of seven fall–rises is interrupted for a moment by two falls – not sufficiently wide or low to be interpreted as final – and then continues in very much the same way until the wide fall on *square* signals that the end of the sequence has been reached. The same process may be seen at work in **I**, where, as in lines 26–34, a whole series of different intonation patterns develops before the low fall on *Saturday*.

If convincing evidence of fluency is hard to find in a commentary that has been reduced to writing, there are many features that may be put forward as signs of the commentator's efforts to sound interesting. No doubt interest in the last resort is to be related to subject matter and choice of vocabulary, but it can be stimulated to a considerable extent by the use of varied phonological effects. Certainly, some commentators can be a delight to listen to while providing very little in the way of information. Since the two specimens of commentary are on such different events it is not surprising that they show phonological variety in different ways. In the case of **II**, the extreme solemnity of the occasion and the impressive slowness with which events took place render many effects either inappropriate or impossible. The commentator uses increased speed in only three instances (73–4, 78–9, 82) and slows down only once (82–4): elsewhere his language is as regular in speed as the procession he is describing, with only one or two local fluctuations in the form of drawled syllables. Variety is introduced largely by means of pitch-range, where the adoption of a relatively narrow norm for individual tone-units enables them to be linked in long sequences marked off by a high start and an extremely low end point, in which the frequent wide nuclei provide centres of contrast.

Extract **I** gives a good impression of the wide range of phonological features that an equally expert commentator may use when confronted with an activity that fluctuates rapidly and dramatically. A glance at the margins shows that there is a good deal of prosodic contrast in addition to a number of paralinguistic features. The systems of pitch, loudness, and speed are especially well represented, and both complex and simple parameters are needed in description. Even in the first fifteen lines or so, where very little is happening on the field, loudness varies 'from *piano*, through *crescendo* to the unmarked norm, which is then punctuated by a couple of short *piano* spells before tailing off in a *diminuendo*. Within the same stretch there is an *accelerando* (3–4) and an *allegro* (8–9) to vary the tempo; and pitch-range variations include *low monotone* (9) and a stretch of *monotone* followed by a narrow nucleus and a level nucleus (11–12), which adds up in effect to a passage of narrowed pitch-range that is in sharp contrast with the wide contours that precede and follow it. Add to these features the two *rhythmic* sections (4–5, 7), *husky* (8), *tremulous* (10), and *giggle* (10), and the picture of a type of discourse with a considerable amount of fluctuation and variety in its sound is established.

So far we have considered features which typically cover sizeable stretches of speech, usually extending across several tone-units; but if we examine shorter sections – the tone-unit and within – there is further evidence of variety. Many of the tone-units show highly varied patterns of pitch movement, not only during moments of excitement, but throughout the excerpt. In lines 53–4, for instance, where the comment is on an action that has just been completed, the falling nucleus on *back* starts at a high pitch and is followed by a most unusual nuclear 'tail' in the form of a high level subordinate nucleus on *bit*. And in lines 42–5, where the activity being reported is hardly of compelling significance, the mildly amusing information comes in a series of four tone-units, of increasing length in terms of stressed syllables, with progressively wider patterns of pitch movement in the head and greater drops before the nucleus, producing what amounts to an effect of inverse climax with considerable ironic effect. It would perhaps be surprising to find such varied contours in a correspondingly quiet passage of conversation, and it is worth keeping these differences in mind when considering the numerous similarities that the varieties show. Some of the extended rising contours that occur with statements, as in lines 9–10, 20–1, 27, and 37, would also be rare in conversation, where this kind of pitch pattern is reserved mainly for such structures as insistently repeated questions and emphatic denials.

The subject matter of extract **II** and the more even pace that it demands make it unlikely that there will be many of the highly varied tone-unit patterns that occur so freely in **I**; but this is compensated for by the very wide overall pitch range that we have already mentioned, and the contrast between the sequences of relatively narrow tone-units and the low pitch drops and wide nuclei by which they are terminated. The element of restraint is also noticeable in the tone-unit lengths of **II**, which, in both passages, even though these were separated by quite a long time gap, vary only between one and six words. By contrast, the commentator in **I** used tone-units of up to ten words in extent, with a larger proportion of single word tone-units. In this respect **II** is reminiscent of English that is being read aloud from a written version of some kind, whereas **I** represents a shift towards conversation, where it is by no means uncommon to find tone-units that range from one to twenty or more words in length. It seems reasonable to suppose that varied tone-unit length is one of the devices an expert commentator might make use of in seeking to avoid monotony and introduce, to events for which it would be appropriate, an impression of conversational casualness.

The two extracts show a comparable distinction as regards position and length of pauses: in **II** they are of remarkably consistent duration and occur, with few exceptions, at the ends of tone-units; in **I** pauses differ more in length and are found often within as well as at the end of the tone-unit. This again is characteristic of conversation; but whereas in conversation pauses may be divided into two main categories – those which result from the physical necessity of breathing and those provoked by hesitation – the pauses here seem also to fulfil a number of other functions. They may be used to gain added emphasis, as in – – *fussing* (17), *slightly · closer* (21), and *and* – – *Barrington* (26–7); or they may enable the commentator to cope with the changing tempo of events: *to* – – – *Barrington* (19), *other way* – – – *up again* – *comes McKenzie* (60–1). No doubt this ability to control pause and distribute it so as to suit the requirements of a situation is an important component of the 'timing' that is so necessary for all forms of public performance where speech is involved.

Pauses, as opposed to just plain silence, presuppose words; and in normal utterance so of course do the tone-units and the other prosodic features that we have been talking about. But words themselves can be articulated in many different ways, with many other prosodic and paralinguistic contrasts, which provide the speaker with further opportunities for introducing variety and for sounding interesting.

Both commentators have in fact made use of such opportunities, as may be seen from a glance at some of the features that affect individual words, syllables or segments of sound; but again, as might be expected, **II** is more restrained both in range of features and frequency of occurrence. Each of the commentators provides local speed variations in the form of *drawled* segments; but the counterpart of *drawled – clipped –* is found only in **I**. In the system of loudness contrasts, both make use of extra stress, which is one of the commonest ways of adding emphasis to words. The cricket commentator appears to supplement this device by means of the numerous *held* segments, such as those in *ungraceful* (27), *jab* (28), and *buoyant* (37), which help him to drive home colourful bits of information; and, in a similar way, he also uses the tension system to pick out important single words like *closer* (21) and *up* (32). Apart from extra stress and one instance of *held – in battered* (106) – the commentator in **II** is content to provide variety as far as individual words are concerned by using the pitch-range system to produce the very low drops and wide nuclear tones that were mentioned earlier. Frequent wide pitch jumps on stressed syllables are also a feature of extract **I**, and these again have been referred to in the discussion of tone-unit patterns. The variety of pitch patterns, however, is related to unstressed as well as to stressed syllables, and both extracts are notable for the number of unstressed syllables that are at a higher pitch than would normally be expected. Examples may be seen in lines 41, 45, and 56 in **I**, and in **II** in lines 96–8, where the effect is to produce contours of a kind that would be rarely met in conversation and that are in fact more reminiscent of some styles of oral reading in which high-pitched unstressed syllables provide one of the devices by which 'expressiveness' is achieved.

Fluency and variety are perhaps to be expected of all successful commentary, but since commentators are forced inescapably to follow the course of an event as it is actually developing, there arises in some instances an even more obvious phonological characteristic: an unusually high degree of differentiation between the language used to describe important parts of the action and that used for filling in the background. This prosodic marking of transitions is usual in sports commentary because of the rapid fluctuations inherent in most sporting activities; but the degree and nature of the marking will vary between sports such as horse-racing, which may produce a lengthy build-up to one major climax; soccer, in which the activity is continuous but interspersed with many local climaxes; and tennis or cricket, where the structure of the game ensures that bursts of activity will alternate with quiet spells.

In **I** there are several points at which the commentator's personal response to exciting activity, coupled with a desire to recreate the excitement for listeners, has produced passages which stand out because of thickly clustered prosodic features. A relatively mild example is seen in lines 25–9, where the words describing the bowler's run-up and delivery are marked off, appropriately enough, by an *accelerando* passage reinforced by *staccato* and *crescendo*. This is terminated by a sudden switch to a stretch of *lento*, punctuated with *drawled* and *held* syllables, which, along with a significant chuckle on *Barrington*, effectively puts over the commentator's amused concern for the safety of a batsman who has just indulged in a rather risky shot. The best example, however, is found in the closing lines, 62–4, where there is a transition from *low piano* to a complex of *forte*, *crescendo*, *wide*, and *high* which culminates in a long and varied final contour and is admirably suited to the corresponding fuss on the field.

It is worth noting that even in such passages as the one we have just mentioned the commentator is bound by the constraints, common to all broadcasters, which demand a high level of clarity and intelligibility: he must be capable, after all, of restraining his enthusiasm ·before it overloads the microphone. The absence of both *pianissimo* and *fortissimo* is probably attributable to pressures of this kind; and although *allegrissimo* and *lax* – features which are sometimes associated with obscurity – do occur, they do not reach the extremes that are frequently found in such features in conversation.

Prosodic marking of changes in activity no doubt varies in keeping with the sharpness of the changes themselves: if, as in extract **II**, the activity shows only very slight fluctuations, then sudden prosodic switches are inappropriate. In view of the possibility of commentaries that proceed on a very even phonological keel, it may be best to think in terms of commentary as a generalised kind of variety, reducible to various combinations of modality features and province features, the selection of the former being determined by the situation which underlies the latter. Thus, a radio sports commentator will use the sub-set of commentary features most appropriate to the action in progress; for non-sporting public occasions a different, but overlapping, sub-set will probably be necessary; and so the process will go on for each occasion that is to be reported. The two extracts in this chapter seem to give clear evidence of this, at least at the phonological level.

When we were talking about fluency earlier on we mentioned intonation as one of the means by which items may be linked into coherent sequences. Many of these sequences, when looked at from a grammatical point of view, will of course turn out to be sentences. This is so in lines 29–34 of extract **I**, part of an example that was used to illustrate fluent discourse. Here it is worth noting the way in which contours with a connective function, such as the narrow falls on *significant* (30) and *wicket-keeper* (32), the level tones on *coming* (31) and *up* (32), and the narrow rises on *now* (31) and *ground* (34), are used to tie the parts of the sentence together before the low fall on *Saturday* signals the end of the sequence. This linking function, however, is not restricted to grammatical units below sentence level: it is an important means of linking one sentence to another – a means, in other words, of building up coherent sequences in which the units themselves are sentences. The connection between the sentence we have just been discussing and that which precedes it is partly brought about by a prosodic link: the function of *and* in line 29 is reinforced by the fall–rise nucleus on *Grout* which is a signal to the hearer that the sequence has not yet come to an end. Another good example of the way in which a series of sentences may be given additional coherence by prosodic means is provided by lines 16–25, where lexical and semantic links are supplemented by a succession of nuclei, all of which, including the falls in 22 and 24, are non-final in relation to the low pitch reached on *square* (25).

The occurrence of such sequences in commentary is one of the features that help to distinguish it as a variety from conversation, where, although intonation plays an important part in sentence linkage, the participants are seldom subjected to the kind of pressures that make it desirable for commentators to present their information in an orderly way. Commentators, however, like conversationalists, have to do most of their talking spontaneously, so that it is perhaps not surprising that they frequently make use of the loose grammatical linkage of sentences – especially with *and* – that is so common in conversational usage. Quite often, this kind of linkage occurs along with prosodic indicators of coherence, as may be seen from the three last sentences in extract **I**. At other times the *and* may come immediately after a contour which clearly suggests the end of the preceding sentence, as, for instance, with *two* (3), *ten* (5), *London* (79), and *police* (91). It is perhaps worth noting that the commentator in **I** has a habit of marking *and*, in its sentence-linking function, with a drawl on the vowel (5, 26, *etc*); in two places (29, 49), he even goes so far as to give it separate tone-unit status. This is probably idiosyncratic, but it seems a regular idiosyncrasy, and may be evidence of a tendency to distinguish by prosodic means a frequently used element of discourse connection.

Another consequence of spontaneity is that there is always the likelihood of the occasional grammatical discontinuities which are found in conversation, but which would not be tolerable in most forms of written English. One of these is to be found in the early part of the cricket commentary, when the sentence *the batsmen still to come which many of you no doubt will be counting up* (8–10) – itself containing a grammatical anacoluthon in its use of *which* – is broken off to allow the insertion of a remark about one of the players. Although this aside is clearly marked off, especially by the lowered loudness at beginning and end, the sequence of sense is such that when the list of batsmen (14–16), which it is the purpose of the interrupted sentence to introduce, does eventually come along, no feelings of discomfort arise from the fact that it is grammatically quite separate, and that the clause commencing with *the batsmen still to come* is never in fact finished. It is questionable whether any of the listeners who heard the original commentary were aware of the break; and of the people who have listened to the tape from which the transcription was made none has called attention to it. The ability to accommodate all manner of grammatical discontinuities within a smooth flow of speech is no doubt another characteristic of the skilled commentator.

The list of batsmen we have just mentioned is a reminder of the fact that commentators may often find it convenient to present some of their information in the form of lists. This is especially so with sports commentary, where there are teams to name and scores to be reported; but it can be true also of other forms of commentary. In fact, much of the commentary from which extract **II** was taken consisted of elaborate listing of parts of the funeral procession, which provided the main centres of interest, the activity itself being so regular and predictable as to warrant only occasional comment. The lists, of course, may take numerous grammatical forms, and may involve the linking not only of individual words or nominal groups, but also of complete sentences. Items within a list tend to have common grammatical as well as semantic features, and it is the repetition of similar structures in a series that is particularly effective in distinguishing from a more normal conversational type of usage any variety in which the process occurs at all frequently. The list in lines 14–16 of the cricket commentary, with its close phonological linking of a succession of minor sentences, provides an interesting example of this type of verbal behaviour.

Most of the sentences used in commentary will of course be statements; but questions do turn up occasionally. Where several commentators are covering an event or where there is a commentator plus someone else whose function is to advise or summarise, the normal process of communication is bound to lead to questions: *Is this a record for an opening stand by two left-handed batsmen on a Thursday, Arthur Wrigley?*; *Now what did you think of that round, Barrington Dalby?* In such instances it may be fair to say that the variety has temporarily ceased to be commentary; but there are times, especially at moments of great tension, when it seems a characteristic habit of commentators to insert into a break in the action some such question as: *Now, can he hole this putt for the championship?*; or *Will his clutch hold out for the three remaining laps?* These questions are not addressed to anyone; but they cannot be called rhetorical in the usual sense. Rather, they convey the commentator's anticipation and identify him, in his inability to give the answer, with the audience. As such, they appear to be an important, if relatively infrequent, variety-marker.

As regards sentence structure there is, as we have noted, the possibility that incomplete sentences will be used occasionally. The business of presenting information accurately and concisely may be facilitated by a reasonably early appearance of the main verb, with any extra weight coming towards the end of the sentence; and any long and elaborate structures of subordination are unlikely. The taste for fairly uncomplicated sentences is evident in extract **I**, where there is a strong preponderance of simple sentences; and it is also to be seen in **II**, but to a lesser extent. This is not to say that commentary is devoid of complexities as far as sentence structure is concerned. In both extracts there are plenty of dependent clauses, non-finite as well as finite, functioning adjectivally, adverbially, and as object of a verb; compound sentences are to be found, as in 35–8 and 88–91; and both commentators make use of a number of complex sentences. In **I**, the best example of a complex sentence, at least by traditional standards, which were often based on the written language, is that in lines 29–34. It is interesting to note that this sentence occurs at the only point at which the commentator turns to the significance of something that has just happened, instead of restricting himself largely to description and information. A complex sentence that is fairly typical for the second commentator is to be found in 74–9, and there is also a compound-complex, or mixed sentence, in lines 114–19.

There is in fact a good mixture of sentence types – and even of sentence lengths – in the two extracts; and the impression of varied sentence structure that this gives is supported when account is taken of what is probably the most important characteristic of commentary when considered at sentence level: the high incidence of minor sentences. Many of these occur when the commentator presents an essential item of information in the form of a nominal group, often with an attendant adverbial element, and omits as redundant a transitive verb and subject – or the intransitive verb – that would be necessary for a major sentence. For instance, in 85–7, the sense of *again the plumes of the cavalry but on foot* is quite clear, and it would have added very little for the commentator to say something like *... we see the plumes of the cavalry ...*, or *... the plumes of the cavalry appear ...*; nor, in *six men close* (25), is it necessary to be told that *there are six men close* or that *six men are standing close*. Other examples of this type of minor sentences are to be found in 91–4, and 98–101, and there are many instances in **I**, such as the sequence of names in lines 14–16, and the cluster of sentences describing the placing of the fielders in 21–5, the concluding one of which we have already quoted.

The cricket commentator also makes use of a number of minor sentences which consist basically of a verb, with or without an adverbial element, from which one may imagine that a subject has been omitted. An example is: *settles to his stance right shoulder round a little* (47–8); and, again, the addition of some such subject as *Barrington, he,* or *the batsman* could provide nothing that is not already obvious from the verbal context. A sentence of this type turns up several times, closely linked by intonation to a preceding major sentence, in the kind of characteristic sequence that is seen in: *McKenzie comes in bowls,* in line 26, and again in lines 35–8, 49, and 61.

All the minor sentences quoted so far are simple sentences; but there are numerous instances in the two extracts of complex minor sentences, as in 16–19, where the clause *before McKenzie bowls to Barrington* is dependent on the minor clause *now a little fussing about someone beside the sight screen*; and in lines 65–72 the dependent clause *as the second division of the Household Cavalry the second contingent of the escort . . . come slowly and majestically into the square*, which is itself interrupted by an embedded sentence, is dependent upon the minor construction – in this case a nominal group – *the tinkle of the cavalry*. There is even one example of a mixed minor sentence in extract **I**, in lines 42–7. Other varieties of English, such as those used in conversation and advertising, also make considerable use of minor constructions in independent function, but these usually occur without any dependent clauses and function as simple minor sentences. It is difficult to think of a variety other than commentary that provides the same opportunities for complex minor sentences, and the frequency of their occurrence may well be one of its most important defining characteristics.

It seems a reasonable inference that commentators will try to reduce as far as possible the element of repetition which is likely to enter into the description of events – particularly events which involve recurrent sequences of activity such as those that occur in most sports; and it is possible that the omission of elements of sentence structure which have low information value – in other words, the process which gives rise to minor sentences – is evidence of a sensitive commentator's anti-repetitiveness. At the same time, when describing repetitious activity, a certain amount of repetitious language is inescapable. We have already referred to the characteristic sequences that recur in 26, 35–8, 49, and 61, and in lines 1–5 there is an example of a sequence giving details of the score which is of a type that turned up quite frequently in the rest of the commentary from which the extract was taken. Regular recurrences of this kind are rare in other varieties of spontaneous spoken English, where they are felt to be generally either unnecessary or undesirable, and this is probably worth bearing in mind as another possible distinctive feature of commentary.

The elements of clause structure in our two extracts usually occur in the expected order for statements, with the Subject preceding the Predicator. The cricket commentator, however, makes use on one occasion of the inversion of Subject and Predicator that is possible with verbs of motion after a place adverbial: *up again comes McKenzie* (61), where the order of elements is AAPS. If it were used in conversation this construction would sound archaic, whimsical or reminiscent of nursery-rhymes. And in extract **II** the much greater formality of the situation allows the commentator to make use of a similar construction: *and to them indeed has fallen the privilege . . .* (80–1). But perhaps the most notable feature of clause structure in this variety is the high frequency of adverbial elements, especially those which relate to motion, place or direction, and present time.

In both extracts there is a mixture of nominal group types – simple, premodified, postmodified, and mixed. There are no very large nominal clusters of the kind associated with some varieties of written English; but on the other hand the picture is certainly more complex than is usually the case with conversation. The commentator in **II** occasionally goes in for quite lengthy strings of postmodification which have a distinctly literary flavour, as may be seen from the examples in lines 81–4, or 103–6; and a similar tendency, although less marked, is not entirely missing from **I**: see, for instance, lines 8–10 and 23–5.

Premodifying adjectival elements are an obvious and economical device for making nominal groups more precise in their specification and for adding descriptive detail. The commentator in **II** is usually content with single adjectives as in *dark chargers* (70), *great cavalcade* (82), *new London* (104), and so on; but he does use the sequence *grey drab* in line 114. In **I**, the premodifying structures have a tendency to greater complexity, and include a number in which the adjectives themselves are modified by adverbial intensifiers: *slightly closer field* (21), *most ungraceful little jab* (27–8), *rather buoyant bouncing run* (37–8), and *ever present butterflies* (46–7), for instance. A further way of gaining specificity and descriptive detail is to place in apposition to a nominal group another which adds to or expands the information contained in the first. This device, with its opportunities for balance and parallelism, seems to be especially suited to the dignified progress of **II**, and is seen in lines 66–9, 74–5, and 99–101; and a related, though not exactly similar kind of structure occurs in lines 92–4. The commentator in **I** also makes use of apposition, as in 20–1, and the coordinated nominal groups in lines 54–6 have roughly the same kind of function.

Since our two samples of commentary deal with such completely different topics, it is hardly to be expected that they will resemble each other very much in vocabulary, a great deal of which is determined by subject matter. It is also necessary to remember that one of them – the cricket commentary – was addressed to an audience that could reasonably be expected to contain a good proportion of listeners with some specialist interest in the subject who would accordingly be prepared for, and would understand, a fair sprinkling of technical words; while the other was aimed at a general audience.

There are, however, similarities. Both make use of what might be called a basically 'domestic' vocabulary in which many of the nouns really can be said to name things and the verbs to denote actions. There are no learned words, unless we include under this heading technical terms like *off cutter*; and it is difficult to imagine any commentator making use of *volition, perspicacious,* or *ratiocinate,* unless perhaps for humorous purposes. Both extracts contain numerous fixed collocations, some of which, like *now again* (65 and 84), *the score goes up to* . . . (1), . . . *moves in bowls* (49), and so on, were used many times in the course of the respective commentaries. In some varieties efforts are often made to suppress or vary fixed patterns of this kind, but in most commentary they seem to be an acceptable or perhaps even an expected part of the linguistic framework. At the same time there are in English a number of high frequency phrases – *you know, I mean, you see* and so on – which most commentators, like those in both of our extracts, will be at pains to avoid.

Although commentary thus provides opportunities for the use of much that is normal in the way of vocabulary, and also for regularised patterns of vocabulary within different areas of subject matter, commentators are constantly coerced by situational pressures that demand vivid and interesting descriptive language. An obvious way of meeting the demand is by making the kind of effective lexical selection that can be seen in *a most ungraceful little jab* (27–8), *furiously* (35), *buoyant bouncing* (37), or in *sombre* (91) and *phoenix like* (105). Another feature that may be common to most commentaries, and of which both extracts contain a hint, is a more than usually high proportion of proper nouns – especially names of people and places.

But otherwise, the two extracts are very different as regards vocabulary. The considerable number of technical terms in **I** is fairly typical of commentaries intended for specialist audiences. It is perhaps worth noting that most of these terms consist of words and phrases taken from everyday life, but here given a restricted, and usually fairly precise, meaning, as in *field* (21, *etc*), *short leg* (24, *etc*), *down the line* (40–1), *the other way* (60), and *life* (64). But there are a few, such as *off cutter* (55), which could occur only in a cricketing context. In **II** there are no technical terms in this sense and in fact hardly any at all, unless we include words like *division* (67), *contingent* (68), *escort, found* (69) – in its rare sense of 'provided' – *work* (111), and perhaps *Blues* (70). The frequency of words with ceremonial associations or with a slightly archaic flavour – *cavalry* (66, *etc*), *chargers* (71), *majestically*

(72. *etc*), *cavalcade* (82), and so on – contributes to the much greater formality of **II** as compared with **I**, where, in addition to the more informal quality of the vocabulary generally, the commentator constantly used the kind of colloquial contractions, avoided by **II**, that were referred to when we were discussing the verbal group.

Commentary sets out primarily to provide information about events, and to this extent its language is likely to be factual and non-figurative; but the commentator has also to give an adequate visual impression of the events and of their setting, and this gives him the opportunity to be descriptive and impressionistic. It is therefore not surprising that, as our previous sections have perhaps at times suggested, commentary should reveal these twin situational pressures in language that is at one time reminiscent of a news broadcast and at others of descriptive journalism. The process is intensified by the fact that commentators are inescapably tied to the events in front of them: events usually fluctuate, and periods of intense activity will test the commentator's capacity for informative conciseness, while the slack spells will give him all the opportunity he needs – and perhaps more – for indulging in descriptive afflatus. All this ties in quite nicely with the need to communicate enthusiasm and demonstrate personal involvement – a need which is met on the one hand by passages in which terseness of grammar and vocabulary combine with appropriate phonological effects to convey excitement, and on the other by passages in which significant detail culled from the scene has been used to sketch a convincing background. The selection of surprisingly minute, even totally irrelevant, detail for comment, as in 42–5 and 118–19, tends to be characteristic of commentary and is as effective in convincing the listener of the reality of the scene as it is in helping the commentator to handle awkward time gaps.

Both the informative and descriptive passages must be recognised when considering how meaning is organised and presented in commentary; but so also must the occasions – marked, possibly, by a crucial switch of tense – on which the commentator stops commentating and, as it were, begins to comment – to discuss the significance of events rather than the events themselves, to refer to previous as well as to present happenings, and to venture opinions instead of reporting facts. The cricket commentary from which excerpt **I** was taken seemed to progress in a series of episodes, many of which had a characteristic structure. It may be helpful to attempt to summarise this (semantic) structure in some such table as the following:

EVENTS	LANGUAGE
1 No noticeable activity (cf 1–16)	Information about the state of the game. Description of background detail. Casual comment
2 Activity that is not centrally important to the game (cf 16–25)	Description of the activity as a means of filling time and creating atmosphere
3 Activity that is predictable within the framework of the game (cf 26)	Very brief information in standard form that tends to be used repeatedly
4 Response that 3 produces (from the other players). Probably less predictable (cf 27–9)	Information with or without emotional overtones, according to whether response is exciting or not
5 Comment (ie the commentator and his opinions temporarily become the most important feature of the situation (cf 29–34)	Information of a less factual kind. Perhaps significant changes of vocabulary, different selections from pronoun system, switch of tense

The order which this table may seem to imply changed a good deal, and sections 1, 2, and 5 were often omitted as optional; but, allowing for local variations, the pattern was repeated throughout. It is conceivable that many sports commentaries would show evidence of similar repetitive patterning; although the episodic structure could be expected to vary considerably according to the nature of the event. Even the state funeral commentary from which **II** is taken showed some evidence of a comparable periodic fluctuation, but on a completely different time scale.

Finally, it is important to remember, when considering the way in which a commentator parcels out the information he wishes to communicate, that he can usually assume that his audience will be familiar with the basic structure of the events he is describing. Thus, when a cricket commentator says *and now Jones to Smith*, he can rely upon its being interpreted as *Jones is bowling to Smith*, not as *Jones is speaking to Smith* or *Jones is walking up to Smith in order to shake hands with him*. Similarly, racing enthusiasts may be expected to handle without difficulty sentences like *round the bend through the dip and into the home straight Lucky Strike by a short head from High Life*. In other words, the commentator is able to work within a stable frame of reference known both to him and to his audience. Even in the relatively rare cases in which the commentary is about an unusual kind of event the commentator will probably take pains to establish such a frame of reference as quickly as possible. When he has done so, he can use it as the basis for precise items of information strung rapidly together with a minimum of connective irrelevance. Thus he is able to achieve the economies of grammatical structure we have mentioned, in this way reducing the element of repetitiveness that is so often forced upon him, and increasing the descriptive immediacy on which he relies so much for effect.

Exercises

1 In the discussion of the extracts above, a good deal of space has been given to listing the linguistic similarities. Attempt to make as full a list as possible of the numerous differences, paying special attention to contrasts in status. Having done so, do you agree with our conclusion that both extracts can be said to belong to the same variety?

2 List the phonological characteristics you would expect to find in commentaries on sports other than cricket. (It would be a good plan to test your ideas by listening to actual examples on the radio.) Is there any evidence that the type of sport compels the commentator to adopt a distinctive phonological norm (of speed, loudness, *etc*)? If there is, does this affect our decision to regard all sports commentary as implying a single variety?

3 The commentator in **II**, Raymond Baxter, is very well known for his sports commentaries. Listen to some examples of these, and compare what you hear with the kind of English he is using above.

4 What stylistic differences are there between a radio and a television commentary? (A good way of highlighting the idiosyncrasies of the former is to turn down the sound of a television commentary while listening to a radio commentary on the same event.)

5 Printed below are two extracts of written English which would often be referred to as 'commentary', though in a sense different from that used above (*cf p* 125). The first is part of a commentary on a literary text, and is described as a 'commentary' by the author; the second is a discussion of linguistic features in some examples of seventeenth-century prose. Does a consideration of these extracts reveal any grammatical features in common with the above samples of spoken commentary?

(i) [*Miss.* Lord! Mr *Neverout*, you are grown as pert as a Pear-monger this Morning.

'as pert as a Pearmonger': recorded first in 1564, it became, c. 1800, mainly rural. The variant (now dialectal) *peart* appears in the 17th–20th century, mainly Devonian, 'as peart as a sparrow'; the 19th–20th Lancashire–Yorkshire 'as peart as a robin'; and the Oxfordshire 'as peart as a maggot'. 'As pert as a pearmonger' has the semantic variant, 'as pert as a pear-monger's mare' (Ray, 1678). As a costardmonger (coster-monger) sells costard apples, so a pearmonger . . . Here, *pert=* lively.

(From *Swift's Polite Conversation*, annotated by E. Partridge)

(ii) Three features distinguish prose of this type. The vocabulary is quite ordinary; there is no straining after effects with unusual words or expressions. Secondly, no grammar yet written offers an adequate description of its syntactical structuring – indeed the idea of a 'sentence' or of 'sentence-structure' receives a severe shock when faced with L'Estrange's 'Now to his Business;' and one would be hard put to explain in traditional terms the syntax of Walton's 'not to exceed'. We are clearly face to face with the so far undescribed 'grammar' of spoken English, which is only now beginning to engage the attention of linguistic scholars. The third feature is astonishing, in the light of the first two: the three passages cited are extremely effective pieces of *written* prose. Not a word could be eliminated or displaced without affecting the meaning or the tone. Their clarity, and non-ambiguity, is absolute. In L'Estrange even the puctuation carries authority, a series of expression-marks indicating the stress, juncture, and intonation of live speech.

(From I. A. Gordon, *The Movement of English Prose*)

Chapter 6

The Language of Religion

The kind of language a speech community uses for the expression of its religious beliefs on public occasions is usually one of the most distinctive varieties it possesses. Very often, it is so removed from the language of everyday conversation as to be almost unintelligible, save to an initiated minority; and occasionally one finds a completely foreign tongue being used as the official liturgical language of a community, one well-known instance being the use of Latin by the Roman Catholic Church. As far as the study of contemporary English is concerned, the situation has been complicated by powerful movements, within the major religious dominations, for a revision of the kind of language traditionally used in the context of public worship. These movements have been largely successful, and at present any survey of liturgical and biblical language has to take account of new translations of the Bible alongside the old, and more modern versions of prayers which used to exist only in older forms of English. Such changes, of course, have not been able to take place without a great deal of discussion and controversy; moreover, the movements underlying them are not yet complete, new versions still being seen as experimental in character. By the time this book appears, **IV** and **V** below will have been superseded. Consequently our review of religious language has had to be selective, and we have focused our attention in this chapter on those varieties in current use which have achieved in their time some measure of general acceptance in a liturgical context.

We do not restrict ourselves entirely to the modern state of the English language in this chapter, however. We have found it necessary to add an illustration of the older kind of religious English (which is still used), partly as a perspective for assessing the more modern versions, but also because the older versions are of greater linguistic significance within the speech community as a whole, having had more time to become part of its 'linguistic consciousness', as it were.

One pointer to this is the number of traditional biblical phrases which have now passed into general usage, such as *the powers that be, the sweat of your brow, prodigal son*, and *mess of pottage*.[1] Another pointer lies in the way that the linguistic importance of liturgical and biblical language is not restricted to religious situations, though of course its primary function is there. Whether one believes in the content of the language or not, the fact still remains that its style has a cultural function and a linguistic impact which is generalisable beyond the original religious context in which it appears. This generalisability is also true, in different degrees, of other varieties of English – legal language, for instance. As a source of linguistic effect, religious language is very evident within literature, where a deliberate, evocative use may be made of its terminology and phraseology; or in humour, where one may readily cause laughter by discussing a non-religious topic, such as a cricket match, in the tone of voice, grammar, and vocabulary associated with the extracts below – a device frequently used by satirists on radio and television. This awareness of an incongruity testifies to a national consciousness of the form and function of religious language which is not limited to those who actually practise the religion. It is therefore of more general linguistic interest than is often realised.

But of course before we can hope to understand the way in which literary or humorous effects are made using religious language, we must first of all be fully aware of the primary purpose and meaning of such language within its own context, *ie* in a church or similar building, or in surroundings which are religious in character, such as a graveside. The extracts which follow are therefore mainly discussed in this light. They represent the liturgical language of contemporary Christianity, this being the dominant religion of the English-speaking world with which most readers of this book will be familiar. There are of course other kinds of religious language than the liturgical, but these are sufficiently different in form and function to be better considered elsewhere: the language of sermons, for example, has more in common, stylistically, with other varieties of public speaking, and has accordingly been grouped along with them in Chapter 9; and the language of theological discourse is also very different – this might be treated along with other examples of learned descriptive or discursive narrative (such as the language associated with the presentation of such non-scientific academic subjects as history or philosophy), though we do not have space to cover such a field in this book.

Again, the language of biblical translation is in many important respects different from that used in many public prayers: in this particular case, however, we have allowed it into this chapter, because formal reading from the Scriptures plays a main part in most liturgical services, and has been the primary influence on the forms of many non-biblical prayers. Of course there are overlaps between all of these areas: obviously they will share a great deal of vocabulary; biblical quotation will naturally occur in all religious contexts, either explicitly or implicitly; and sermons, for example, often deliberately echo liturgical language. But when one considers the whole range of linguistic features that characterise liturgical language, it becomes clear that the differences which exist between this and the other kinds of religious language are more striking than the similarities.

We must also bear in mind the particular cultural and linguistic background to liturgical language, which exerts a unique range of pressures on the choice of forms to be used. There seem to be three main influences. Firstly, there are the linguistic originals. In the case of the Bible, and with many of the common prayers, the requirement of conformity to the sacral character, as well as the sense, of the text in the original language is a restriction on one's choice of English which does not normally apply to other varieties. Similarly, there are traditional formulations of belief of doctrinal significance, which are difficult to alter without an accusation of inconsistency or heresy being levelled; clear traditions of devotional writing in English which have often established intuitive norms; and familiar words and phrases which have a widely revered ancestry, and which many people would prefer to see stay as they are (as with many idioms from the Authorised Version, for example). These are all important factors.

Secondly, there is a strong concern over speakability. Clearly, the choice of a liturgical language must pay careful attention to the fact that its main use is in corporate public worship, either by groups of people speaking together aloud, or by individuals speaking to a congregation. The need for clear cues as to how such language should be spoken (bearing in mind the complexity of some of the prayers), and the avoidance of unnecessary difficulties of pronunciation, should be obvious. Indeed, one can find indications of the importance attached to this point going back to the Middle Ages and beyond.[2]

Thirdly, there are strong pressures deriving from popular attitudes towards the appropriateness and intelligibility of the language to be used. When one is devising a new form of language for large numbers of individuals, particularly in a context such as that of religion, one must try to choose language which the majority of would-be users do not revolt at (what is normally referred to as the 'middle range' of churchgoers). On the one hand, one needs to avoid too intellectual, obscure or unintelligible language (and older versions of liturgical language have been criticised for involving too high a proportion of archaism, theological jargon and complex construction); on the other hand, a variety of English which was too colloquial and informal (such as that exemplified in Chapter 4) would equally be anathema. One needs a balance between intelligibility, pronounceability, relative dignity, and formality; a balance between the ordinary and the obscure; and this is not easy to achieve. Also, one needs euphony, one criterion of which, according to the Roman Catholic International Committee on English in the Liturgy, is that many texts must be suitable for both saying and singing; and this has important phonological implications. Of course, it is impossible to please everyone, as people's ideas of what is dignified, beautiful, and so on in language differ markedly. The important point is, that whatever decisions *are* made, the basis on which the choice was made should have been presented clearly, and the linguistic issues involved in the language being reformed understood in their own terms. In fact, the current tendency is to orientate liturgical language towards what is normally referred to as 'contemporary living usage': this amounts to a significant reduction in the number of archaisms used, a paraphrasing of theological technical terms (*eg consubstantial* becomes *one in substance*), and a tendency to avoid complicated sentences. As we shall see, the overall effect is still fairly formal, and distinctively religious. It is highly unlikely that any proposals for linguistic reform would be accepted which produced a kind of English totally identifiable with some other variety, as this would inevitably produce an equation or confusion of the overtones associated with this other variety, and the distinctive purposes of the religious language (*eg* the addressing of a deity) would become blurred with other – and, to the believer, more trivial – occupations (such as addressing anyone else).[3]

We may usefully begin with a brief excursus into biblical language, as it is this – and in particular the language of the Authorised Version (AV) – which has done most to inculcate a national consciousness of a religious language in the English-speaking countries. Almost everyone agrees that this translation, while retaining a certain grandeur and power of evocation lacking in other versions, is no longer relevant to modern needs, because the linguistic differences between the language of the late sixteenth and twentieth centuries are sufficiently marked to provide regular obscurity and often unintentional humour. It is not simply a question of certain words having changed their meanings; the changes have affected syntax and phonology too (see below). Extract **I** by no means covers the entire range of the AV's distinctive language, but it does illustrate clearly a number of influential linguistic forms which are still intuitively recognised as having religious connotations.

I

MATTHEW 13   [from *The English Bible in Five Volumes*, Vol. V, The New Testament, ed. W. A. Wright, Cambridge, 1909].
The same day went Iesus out of the house, and sate by the sea side.
2. And great multitudes were gathered together vnto him, so that hee went into a ship, and sate, and the whole multitude stood on the shore.   5
3. And hee spake many things vnto them in parables, saying, Behold, a sower went foorth to sow.
4. And when he sowed, some seedes fell by the wayes side, and the foules came, and deuoured them vp.
5. Some fell vpon stony places, where they had not much earth: 10 and foorthwith they sprung vp, because they had no deepenesse of earth.
6. And when the Sunne was vp, they were scorched: and because they had not root, they withered away.
7. And some fell among thorns: and the thornes sprung vp, and   15 choked them.
8. But other fell into good ground, and brought foorth fruit, some an hundred folde, some sixtie folde, some thirty folde.
9. Who hath eares to heare, let him heare.
10. And the disciples came, and sayd vnto him, Why speakest   20 thou vnto them in parables?
11. He answered, and said vnto them, Because it is giuen vnto you to know the mysteries of the kingdome of heauen, but to them it is not giuen.
12. For whosoeuer hath, to him shall be giuen, and he shall haue   25 more abundance: but whosoeuer hath not, from him shall be taken away, euen that hee hath.

13. Therefore speake I to them in parables: because they seeing, see not: and hearing, they heare not, neither doe they vnderstand. 14. And in them is fulfilled the prophecie of Esaias, which saith, 30 By hearing ye shall heare, and shall not vnderstand: and seeing yee shall see, and shall not perceiue.

First, the language of this text is distinguished at the phonological/ graphological level through a number of features: one should note in particular the carefully controlled rhythmical framework of the whole, involving balanced structures (*cf* especially the antitheses in verses 12 and 13) and a generally slow rate of progression (through the splitting up of the text into 'verses', and the frequent use of commas). There are numerous graphological features distinctive of an earlier stage of the language (though these are frequently modernised in present-day editions of the AV), some of which reflect old writing habits (*eg vp* for *up*, *Iesus* for *Jesus*), some of which reflect older pronunciations (*eg sate* for *sat*, *sunne* for *sun*). Also, the use of punctuation devices (*eg* the colon) is not the same as in modern usage.

. The main area of grammatical distinctiveness is the verbal group, where the use of the old third person singulars (*hath, saith*), old strong forms of verbs (*spake, sprung*), and the inflected second person singular (*speakest*) is common. Many of the verbs no longer enter into the same kind of grammatical relationships, *eg* the transitive use of *speak*, where these days we would use *tell* (6), or the phrasal verb *deuoured vp* (9), which nowadays lacks the particle. Closely connected with the verbal group is the use of the archaic pronominal forms *ye* and *thou*, which are readily associated with a religious province.

. Other grammatical points should also be noted, particularly the common inverted order for elements of clause structure, PS, where these days we would use SP (1, 28), and the dominant use of an initial coordinator (here mainly *and*). The sentence structure also displays this coordinating tendency, many verses being essentially loosely coordinated complexes of simple sentences. Unexpected ellipses – unexpected, that is, from a modern point of view – are regularly seen (25, 26, 27), as in the old 'absolute' participial construction (29, *etc*). Otherwise, the overall effect is obtained through an accumulation of isolated points, such as the indefinite article form *an* preceding *hundred* (18), the use of distinctive pronominal paradigms (*eg whosoeuer*, 25), and a different plural form from modern English (*eg other*, 17).

The vocabulary provides the third area of distinctiveness. We note the wide range of archaisms, some (such as *vnto, foorth, multitude*) being used very frequently throughout the AV: *behold, foorthwith, deepenesse, brought foorth*, (go) *foorth, folde, abundance, wayes side*. Then there are the relatively technical religious terms, such as *parables, disciples, prophecie*; the formal locutions such as *gathered together, perceiue, therefore* (cf also *had not* in the verb, 10, 14); and the words which have changed in meaning, such as *foules* (9), which no longer has the general sense of 'birds' but is restricted to a specific kind of bird.

It is such points as these which provide a basis for the tradition of religious language which has lasted until the present day. A second dominant formative influence on religious language also emerged at about the same time, however, and this too must be taken into account – the language of the Book of Common Prayer (BCP). If we examine two extracts from this text (**II**, **III**, below), we can see the existence of certain common forces at work, but it is also possible to point to significant additional factors not to be found in the AV. This is primarily due to the fact that the BCP was much more of an innovation in its use of language than the AV, being really the first systematic attempt to adapt English to the needs of a formalised liturgical language.[4] We have also recorded one of the prayers in its spoken form, to provide further relevant stylistic parameters. These, along with the remaining extracts in this chapter, are all examples of liturgical English in the sense discussed above, though they are at different ends of a historical scale. We shall discuss all four extracts simultaneously, however, as, despite the diachronic differences, they have so much in common. Extracts **II** and **III** are spoken by one person; **IV** and **V** are normally uttered in unison. The last two, representing an aspect of the movement to modernise liturgical language, are taken from an experimental version of the Roman Catholic translation of the Mass which was used throughout England in 1964. It has since been replaced by a more internationally used translation, but is a good example for our purposes. It has of course been criticised both for going too far and for not going far enough in its reforms. In **II**, the capitalisation of the written text has been retained.

II

COLLECT FOR THE SUNDAY AFTER ASCENSION DAY

'narrow'   'O |God the 'King of GLóry|' –
who hast ex|alted thine +only ₙSÓN|

|Jesus CHRÍST| with |great TRÌumph

unto thy 'kingdom in ‚HÉAven| — we

be|sēech thee| |leave us not còmfortless| ·   5

but |send to 'us thine ✦Holy 'Ghost

to ↓còmfort us| and ex|alt us 'unto

the ✦same PLĀCE| |whither our

↑Saviour 'Christ is ✦gone beFòRE| —

'descending'   'who |liveth and RēIGNeth| with   10

|thee and the 'Holy ‚GHÓST| |one

GŌD| |world without ēND| a|MÈN| '

III

PRAYER OF CONSECRATION AT THE COMMUNION

Almighty God, our heavenly Father, who of thy tender mercy
didst give thine only Son Jesus Christ to suffer death upon the
cross for our redemption; who made there (by his one oblation   15
of himself once offered) a full, perfect, and sufficient sacrifice,
oblation, and satisfaction, for the sins of the whole world; and
did institute, and in his holy Gospel command us to continue, a
perpetual memory of that his precious death, until his coming
again; Hear us, O merciful Father, we most humbly beseech thee;   20
and grant that we receiving these thy creatures of bread and
wine, according to thy Son our Saviour Jesus Christ's holy
institution, in remembrance of his death and passion, may be
partakers of his most blessed Body and Blood: . . .

In the following texts, we have added main stresses (') and pauses
(indicated by | and | for short and long respectively) to the normal
punctuation of the printed version.

IV

GLORIA [from *The Rite of Low Mass*, edition by Burns & Oates]

The celebrant begins:
'Glory be to 'God on 'high . . . *and the people continue with him:*   25
and on 'earth 'peace to 'men of 'good 'will.|
We 'praise thee.|

We 'bless thee.|
We a'dore thee.|
We 'glorify thee.| 30
We 'give thee 'thanks for 'thy great 'glory.|
'Lord 'God,| 'heavenly 'King,| 'God the 'Father al'mighty.|
'Lord 'Jesus 'Christ,| the 'only-be'gotten 'Son.|
'Lord 'God,| 'Lamb of 'God,| 'Son of the 'Father.|
'Thou who 'takest a'way the 'sins of the 'world,| 35
    have 'mercy on us.|
'Thou who 'takest a'way the 'sins of the 'world,|
    re'ceive our 'prayer.|
'Thou who 'sittest at the 'right 'hand of the 'Father,|
    have 'mercy on us.| 40
For 'Thou a'lone art 'holy.|
For 'Thou 'only art the 'Lord.|
'Thou a'lone art 'most 'high,| O 'Jesus 'Christ.|
With the 'Holy 'Ghost,| in the 'glory of
    'God the 'Father.| A'men.| 45

V

CREDO [from *The Rite of Low Mass*, edition by Burns & Oates]

The celebrant begins:
'I be'lieve in 'one 'God . . . *and the people continue with him:*
the 'Father al'mighty,| 'maker of 'heaven and 'earth,| and of
    'all 'things 'visible and 'invisible.|
And in 'one 'Lord 'Jesus 'Christ,| the 'only-be'gotten 'Son
    of 'God.| 'Born of the 'Father be'fore 'all 'ages.| 50
'God from 'God,| 'Light from 'Light,| 'true 'God from 'true 'God.|
Be'gotten not 'made,| 'consub'stantial with the 'Father:| through
    'whom all 'things were 'made.|
Who for 'us 'men| and for 'our sal'vation| came 'down from
    'heaven.| (*Here all kneel*) 55
And 'was in'carnate by the 'Holy 'Ghost of the 'Virgin 'Mary:|
    'AND 'WAS 'MADE 'MAN.|

As we shall see, the grammatical and lexical levels provide the
majority of evidence which would lead one to conclude that these
texts are instances of a single variety. The phonetic/phonological and
graphetic/graphological levels contribute towards this, but at the same

time display important modality and complex medium differences which reflect differences in the context in which a particular text is used. In this respect, a dividing line has to be drawn between **II/III** and **IV/V**. Both pairs are cases of written English read aloud, but in the former pair, the reading is usually carried out by one person – the officiating clergyman – in the latter, the whole congregation is speaking in unison. The repercussions of this functional difference are quite marked. First of all, from the graphological point of view, the person reading **II** and **III** will not normally require any help in order to read the texts, either because he will have read them many times before, or have had plentiful experience of reading aloud in public. They do not need to be printed in any special way. An inexperienced reader may well put some mark as a mnemonic at those places where extra emphasis might be laid, or a pause introduced, but this would be done in an *ad hoc* way, and would never be considered a requirement when printing the text itself. In **IV** and **V**, on the other hand, while the readers are usually fairly familiar with the texts, they are not used to reading aloud in unison; consequently the cardinal requirement is to give sufficient clues to enable them to determine as unambiguously as possible how the text is to be read. Not all editions of these texts do this equally well, of course, as financial considerations enter in – the more typographical variation one introduces, the more expensive to print – but *some* such unequivocal instructions to the reader must be introduced. Texts **IV** and **V** are taken from an edition which tried to introduce a large amount of explicitness of this kind.

The main graphological devices one can make use of are paragraphing, spacing, and capitalisation, alongside the normal range of other punctuation marks, some of which tend to be used idiosyncratically for this variety. The central feature is the combination of all these factors to split the text as a whole into clearly demarcated graphic units, which are sometimes sentences, sometimes not (*cf* p 160). The initial letter of each of these rhythm-cum-sense units is always a capital; they always end in a period; in all cases but one (50) they begin on a separate line; and when they contain more than one line, all lines except the first are set a little way in from the margin. The consequence of this clear demarcation of sense units is that the reader is guided through the text in a series of jumps, and not in a smooth, continuous flow; this facilitates his speaking in unison, and also reduces the likelihood of losing the place.

Another factor facilitating unison speech is that the punctuation on the whole is very simple, and is given a clear phonetic value. This emerges if one compares the phonetic marks in the above texts (based on a tape-recording of a service) with the graphological marks in the text which the clergyman or congregation was reading. There is an almost complete coincidence of periods with major pauses, and commas with brief pauses; and there is little variation in the length of pauses of both types throughout any given text. Perhaps the most interesting thing is the way in which the phonetic criterion dominates the grammar. Normally in English a period is used at the grammatical end of a major sentence; but here it is used depending on how long a pause is required – regardless of whether the preceding structure is grammatically a major sentence or not. Periods in liturgical English follow major and minor sentence types in about equal proportions. Other marks of punctuation are infrequent. The colon (52, 56) has little distinctive phonetic value, being sometimes equivalent to a comma, sometimes to a period: its purpose seems purely semantic, usually indicating that the structure which follows is a climax or summation of some kind. Semi-colons and other punctuation marks do not occur in this edition; nor are they frequent in other editions and elsewhere in liturgical language. However, it is impossible to generalise from the punctuation system of this edition to that of others: other editions sometimes split up the text in quite different ways (for example, one edition of text **V** replaces most of the periods by commas). All editions, though, agree on the use of capitalisation, which is a distinctive feature of this variety. Capitalisation is used for proper nouns, as is normal, but is also used for personal titles of the deity (*eg Lamb, Lord, Light*) and for certain pronouns referring to him (*eg Thou*), which is not found in other varieties, apart from occasional usage in such formal written contexts as invitations and legal language (*cf p* 199). The distinction between titles on the one hand and epithets describing the deity on the other in fact depends on this use of capitalisation. 'O' is conventionally always a capital (as 'I' in English as a whole). Finally, any utterance which needs to stand out from the rest of the text is given a distinct typographical identity, for example the printing of the procedures (either descriptions of what the priest is doing, or instructions to the congregation) in red, or in italics; or the highlighting of a phrase of central doctrinal importance, as in 57.

The clarity of the graphology is an important reason contributing to the reader's having very little difficulty with such texts. The stretches of utterance in between punctuation marks never pose any problem of speakability. The reader moves from punctuation mark to punctuation mark, knowing that at each point there will be a definable pause. Between pauses, the overall pace of articulation is slow and regular: all lexical words are given a degree of strong stress, and there is a marked tendency to keep the time-intervals between stresses isochronous. Moreover, there is frequent parallelism between interpausal units of this kind – largely due to the repetition of similar grammatical structures containing words not too different in syllabic structure (*eg* 27–30, 32 *ff*, 51 *ff*) – a rhetorical feature which reaches its extreme in the speaking of litanies – and consequently there develops a regular rhythmical balance between lines, or between the parts of a line, which also contributes towards mass fluency. Factors such as these combine to produce a standardising of effect, reducing the idiosyncratic extremes between people. Thus, a naturally rapid speaker will tend to slow down, and *vice versa*. Occasionally it is the case that a person has such a rapid rate of articulation that he cannot accommodate this to the conventional rhythm that the majority are using; but it is interesting that such a person always obeys the main pauses. He may finish a unit before everyone else, but he will always commence the next unit in unison.

From the point of view of non-segmental phonology, each punctuation group is a prosodic unit, but it is a prosodic unit of a rather different kind from the tone-unit which is found in all other varieties of spoken English, as it requires only two obligatory prosodic features – a most emphatic syllable, and stress conforming to the distribution of lexical words within the unit. Whether one introduces variation in nuclear tone type, or in pitch-range is optional. One may, if one wishes, articulate the words with as much feeling as possible, introducing a wide range of pitch patterns; but as far as the total, cumulative, auditory effect is concerned, such effort is unnecessary. A congregation – or any speakers in unison – has very much one voice. When a group speak an utterance together, differences in the phonetics and phonology of their articulation become blurred, and one is left with a 'single voice' impression, which, to the ear of the outsider listening in, consists solely of variations in emphasis. The relatively low monotone pitch level which tends to be used may at times vary: towards the end of a longer stretch of utterance than normal there may be a noticeable descending movement. This is absolutely predictable at the very end of a prayer, where the 'Amen' (and often the words immediately preceding it) is given a marked drop in pitch. But otherwise pitch contrasts are regularly reduced to zero, leaving monotone and rhythmicality as the defining characteristics of unison liturgical prayer. The similarities to chant should be obvious.

So far, we have been discussing the main phonological markers of unison speech. If we compare now the phonology of text II, which is the speaking aloud of a prayer by one person, certain similarities immediately emerge. In particular, we would point to the marked narrowness of pitch-range, including a high frequency of level tones, the gradual descent of pitch at the end, the tendency to keep units short and rhythm isochronous, and the absence of marked prosodic or paralinguistic features from any of the other systems available. There is also the related point that this is one of the few cases where one is allowed to speak with little or no significant kinesic accompaniment – one finds a minimum of facial expression and bodily gesture in this category of religious language, a marked contrast with sermons.

The linguistic features which uniquely identify texts as belonging to the single variety of religious English are concentrated in the vocabulary and in certain parts of the grammar. Beginning with grammar, we may start by noting that the sentence structure is quite remarkable. **II** and **III** are in fact single sentences, as is **V** – if one ignores the special punctuation introduced to facilitate readability (see below). Taking the two prayers of address to God first (**II** and **III**), despite the great difference in length and internal complexity, it is the case that the underlying sentence structure is quite simple. **II** is of the form:

Vocative – dependent structure – spc – p(imperative)c – conjunction p(imperative)ca – conjunction p(imperative)ca – dependent structure – Amen.

III has the structure:

Vocative – dependent structure – dependent structure – conjunction dependent structure – conjunction dependent structure – p(imperative) vocative – parenthetic spc – conjunction p(imperative) – dependent structure – dependent structure

From a comparison of these and other prayers, we can deduce the following obligatory minimal underlying structure for texts of this kind:

Vocative – dependent structure(s) – P(imperative)C – dependent structure(s) – Amen.

Further optional vocatives may be introduced at various points, as may idiomatic parentheses (some of which, such as *we beseech thee*, are very frequent); and an apparently indefinite amount of recursion is allowed, particularly of dependent clauses qualifying the initial vocative, and of imperative structures. The length and complexity of these sentences is quite abnormal for imperatives, which are always short and relatively simple in other varieties of English.

V is different in one central respect, namely, that being an affirmation of belief, it is cast in the form of a number of grammatical statements. The first half of the *Credo*, which constitutes extract **V** above, is, if one ignores the punctuation, a single statement. Whether one chooses to ignore the punctuation in carrying out the grammatical analysis will of course depend on one's decision as to whether the punctuation in its specific form presented here (*ie* with periods inserted) is fundamental to the definition of the variety as a whole, or whether it is due to the idiosyncratic position of a specific editor. In this instance, the latter is the case (*cf p* 156): what is important is the breaking up of the text in some clear way – whether periods or semicolons are used to do this is not of primary importance. Consequently we may ignore the normal sentence-closing function of the period in this text, and treat the whole, up to MAN (57), as a single structure. (We could not continue this argument beyond this line, of course, as all editions would require a period here, there being an unambiguous major grammatical break at this point.) Having said this, we may now analyse the structure of the statement in **V** as follows:

S – P – C – conjunction C,

each C having substantial subordination within it. Here again then we see a basically simple structure, whose complexity is due to the accumulation of coordinated finite and non-finite structures at clause level (*cf* also the importance of coordination at group level noted below).[5]

Text **IV** on the other hand is a mixture of types, moving from statement through imperative back to statement again. The types are not kept clearly apart, however: consider, for example, the way in which the nominal groups in 32–4 could be grammatically related to either the preceding statement or the following imperative; or again, the way in which a vocative – normally used only with imperatives in prayers – is placed after a statement (43). As far as analysis at sentence level is concerned, **IV** is an interesting example of the way in which a single prayer may combine different types of structure, and not confine itself to one conventional type. **IV** is also different from the other texts in that it consists of a number of grammatically complete sentences, some extremely short. This is not fortuitous, however; in fact it suggests the influence of yet another modality of religious language, the litany: excluding the nominal groups in 32–4, and the break between 43 and 44, we find that the sentences are in clusters, displaying parallelism of structure and rhythm (27–31, 35–40, 41–3).

Apart from the frequency of imperative structures, we should also note the absence in these texts of questions of any kind. Questions may occur in the more rhetorical types of prayer, and in certain Scriptural quotations, but they are on the whole uncommon, and of course would not normally be followed by a direct verbal response of any kind.

Formal religious English is also characterised by a certain deviation from the expected order of elements within sentence and clause structure. There is nothing as deviant as the structures noted in the Authorised Version (*p* 152 above), but one does find a frequent positioning of adverbials in marked positions, such as the early placements in 13, 18, 26, and 54 (where two adverbials are coordinated), which is sometimes clearly a function of some desired rhetorical effect, such as antithesis (as in 26), sometimes of no obvious rhetorical relevance (as in 13); *cf* also 20. Unexpected reversals of elements occur in 3–4 (where the adverbial of manner would normally follow that of place in conversational English), and in 6 (where the normal direct–indirect object order is reversed). Adverbial displacement is especially common in texts of the **II/III** tradition. Also, one should note the way in which the s may be separated from the p by the interpolation of lengthy non-finite or other structures (as in 21 *ff*), a particularly odd phenomenon when there is a pronoun as s.

Moving now to the question of the exponence of elements of clause structure, the most important point which has to be made is in connection with the vocative. Here the following possibilities are to be found: the proper noun only, as in *God, grant* . . ., which is rare in formalised types of prayer; the proper noun preceded by *O* alone, which is common; the proper noun preceded by an adjective, as in *almighty God* (with or without a preceding *O*), which is also frequent; and the noun followed by a postmodifying structure of some kind, usually a relative clause (illustrated in 13). None of these structures is used productively elsewhere in English: the vocative, when it occurs, is always unmodified, other than in certain idioms (*eg Dear Sir*). The introduction of an appositional element into the vocative (*cf* 1, 13) is not of course restricted to this province (*cf John, old boy . . .*) but it is far more frequent here than elsewhere.

A central feature to note in the exponence of s and c (and also in certain types of adverbial) in this province is the frequent occurrence of coordinated structures. The linkage may take the form of a coordinating conjunction linking two (or occasionally more) nominal groups, especially when the second is governed partly by an item in the first (*cf* the absence of premodification before the second noun in 23, 24); but most often the linkage is appositional in character – see 1, 2–3, 9, 13, *etc*. These appositional structures are extremely common, and they are very interesting. There is a tendency to take the apposition as a single unit (the constituent nominal groups often not being separated by punctuation, especially in certain common phrases, as in 14, 22), and to choose items which have a clear antithetical balance (a feature explicable in the Book of Common Prayer by reference to the stylistic fashion of the sixteenth century; in **IV** and **V** largely accounted for by reference to the Latin originals). In **III**, one may find remnants of older appositional usages no longer common, for example, *of that his precious death* (19) or *these thy creatures* (21). Perhaps the most distinctive aspect of apposition, however, is the way in which appositional structures may extend to cover a large number of nominal groups in this province – a rare phenomenon in all but very formal varieties of English – see 22, 32–4.

There is little else to note as far as s or c is concerned. Personal pronouns are frequently exponents of either, though pronouns as s and c rarely occur together in the same clause. These pronouns can also be substantially postmodified – *cf* the type of structure in 35 *ff*, which is common, whereas structures of the type *You who've been . . .*, *He who . . .*, *etc*, are infrequent in other varieties. The morphological idiosyncrasies of certain parts of the pronominal system of religious English have been so frequently pointed out that we shall not dwell on them here: it is clear that *thou* (with its related forms) is probably intuitively the most dominant feature of this variety. What is never pointed out, however, is that other pronouns show restrictions also: the first person singular rarely occurs in formal prayer, even when only one person is speaking (as in all the texts above) – the plural form is regularly used; *they* is similarly infrequent. These points are of course largely due to the semantic and logical nature of the utterance, but they are a definite feature of the formal 'picture' of the variety, and so should not be ignored.

The complexity of the group structure of this variety is the main reason why the underlying simplicity of sentence and clause structure is not readily appreciated, and it is the case that the most noticeable features of religious English are normally noted as being contrasts operating at group level. Both nominal and verbal groups display distinctiveness here. Within the nominal group, we would single out the following points for special attention. This is one of those varieties where adjectives are allowed to follow the noun (*eg* 32, 47, 48). Adjectives as such are frequent: most nouns are modified by at least one (*cf holy Gospel . . . perpetual memory . . . precious death . . .*, *etc*, 18–19), and it is by no means uncommon to see sequences of three, though the present extracts display this only once (16). Adverbial modification of these adjectives is also common (note especially the use of *most* in its sense of *very*, which is a further indication of formality – 20, 24, 43). The majority of nouns are uncountable. Well over half the determiners are possessive pronouns. Postmodification is normally present, and all types of this are to be found. Relative clauses are perhaps the most common, especially after vocatives and personal pronouns as s, and one may find without difficulty sequences of relatives such as would never normally occur in, say, conversation (*eg* 13 *ff*). *Whom* is also the form used when a relative pronoun co-occurs with a s in the relative clause, and prepositions regularly occur before the pronouns (*through whom, to whom, etc*). There are also many postmodifying prepositional phrases, especially the genitive, which is rarely in premodifying position (but one should note that the preposition *of* following a noun is often used in the sense of *by means of*, as in *of the Virgin Mary* (56), or *of thy tender mercy* (13)). Non-finite structures as postmodification can be seen in 50 *ff*. In short, nominal group structure in religious English is quite long and complex: a particularly interesting example of this is in 16–17, where the three adjectives simultaneously premodify all three nouns, to produce a combination of nine distinct senses in one structure.

The verbal group displays an even clearer range of distinctiveness – so clear, that often these features are discussed as if they were the only indications of this variety. In fact, a relatively small number of variety markers are involved, though some of these occur with great frequency. The most noticeable is clearly the inflectional system, where the characteristics already noted in the Authorised Version are to a great extent preserved: the *-eth* and *-est* suffixes are regularly used with lexical verbs, though much more common in **II/III** than in **IV/V** (where the *-eth* is usually restricted to certain formulae, similar to that found in 10 *ff*). The auxiliary verbs display a similar type of inflectional pattern, though their precise morphophonological form varies a great deal (*eg art, hast, didst*). Not all the archaic inflectional forms are retained: there is little trace of older strong verbs (*eg spake*) as are to be found in the Authorised Version. But there are many other indications of archaicness in the verbal system, especially in **II** and **III**: there is the use of unstressed auxiliary *did* to indicate past time without any contrastive overtones (as in *didst give* (14), *did institute* (18), where these days the *did* form would always communicate emphasis); there is a greater use of subjunctive forms than is common in contemporary English (not well illustrated by the above extracts, but *cf Glory be* . . . (25)); and one finds the occasional occurrence of an old auxiliary usage, such as *is gone* (9). The formality of the extracts is clearly indicated in the verbal system by the absence of contracted forms in the auxiliaries, and by the use of such negative constructions as *leave us not* (5) (*cf don't leave us*). Religious English of the type presented in this chapter normally restricts itself to the use of the present tense, except when referring to specific historical events, when the normal range of past tenses may be used (apart from the pluperfect, which is exceptional). The use of any of the auxiliaries referring to future time (*shall* and *will* in particular) is also exceptional in this variety. Imperative forms of the verb are very frequent, as already implied in our review of sentence types; but here one should note that it is common to have the subject of the imperative expressed (and moreover postmodified), as in 35 *ff* (this is regularly found elsewhere only in (especially political) public speaking – *You who have found us faithful, vote now* . . .). Many of the imperatives are followed by quite complex c structures, particularly after certain verbs (*eg grant* (21)), but archaic or formal c structures are in evidence after other verbal forms also, such as *give* . . . *to suffer* (14), *send to us* (6). Finally, there is the frequency of coordinated verbal structures, a further instance of the tendency towards coordination seen in this variety as a whole, and which we have already pointed out in the nominal group and elsewhere. The semantic implications of this we shall discuss below; meanwhile, one should note such cases as *did institute...command* (18), *begotten...made* (52), and *liveth...reigneth* (10).

The vocabulary of religious English is extremely distinctive, and its analysis produces several very clear types. First, there are a number of archaisms. Humour and literature aside, religious and legal English are the only varieties which allow archaisms. But this term requires some definition, as it is usually used in a very loose way. To be helpful, we must define archaisms to include both words where the referents no longer have any correlate in contemporary experience ('have no direct synchronic relevance'), and words no longer in current usage, but where the referents still exist and where more widely used synonyms are available. On either count, religious English displays varying numbers of archaisms, depending on the extent to which the text tries to reflect contemporary English. The first kind of archaism is illustrated by such words as *Pharisee, denarius, centurion,* and so on, and would obviously be more common in Biblical translations. The second type is illustrated in the above texts by such words as *whither* (8), *unto* (4), and *creatures* (21) – though none of these texts displays the extreme kind of archaicness that is to be found in many hymns, such as *Yea, though I walk in death's dark vale/ Yet will I fear none ill:/ For thou art with me; and thy rod/ And staff me comfort still*, which is still used. Related to archaisms are those terms which take their meaning from a historical situation (such as a specific person, place or action) which existed at the time when the religious beliefs were first being formulated. These are not archaisms in the same sense as that already described, as they are words which do have a direct synchronic relevance, usually because the event or person has a central place in the framework of belief which is being maintained. Examples in the above would be *the cross* (14 – note the specificity of the article), *his death and passion* (23), and *Virgin Mary* (56).

Secondly, any religious text is bound to display a number of theological terms, the equivalent of the specialist terminology of science, which provide the verbal basis for the formulation of a person's beliefs. The interesting thing about the semantic structure of theological language is the way in which there is a clear linguistic centre to which all lexical items can ultimately be referred, namely, the term 'God'. Regardless of the purpose of the piece of religious language being examined – for example, whether it be a statement of belief, or a prayer of praise or supplication – it is the case that the meaning of the whole derives from, and can be determined only by reference to this concept of 'God'. This semantic dependence is always made quite explicit at or near the beginning of the religious utterance (cf 1, 13, 25, 46). It can be clearly seen if we take a prayer (text **IV**) a phrase at a time, and present the relationships as follows, to show first the terms relating to the word 'God', and second those which introduce, through the central semantic link of the Father–Son relation, another set of concepts, which are directly related, initially through the grammatical parallelism, to the 'God' concept:

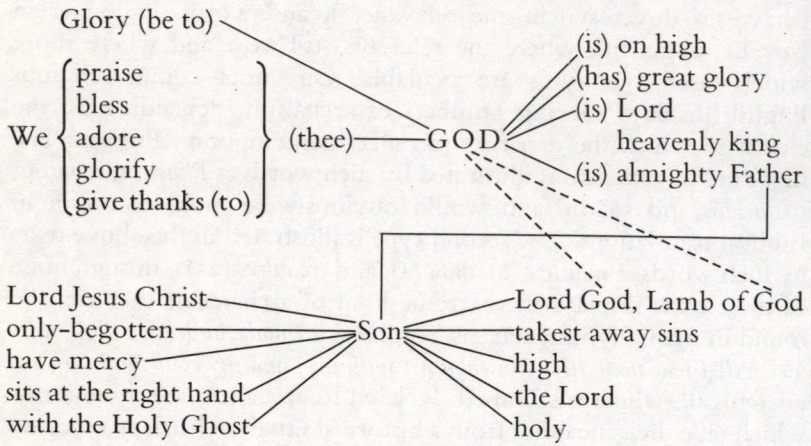

This leaves line 26, which is present mainly because of its occurrence as part of a Biblical quotation, but which can be incorporated into the above semantic structure through the word *peace* – what kind of 'peace' is involved?

This clear focal point is something which distinguishes religious language from other varieties. It may well be that the meaning of a scientific English text, let us say, can be explained only by referring the concepts within it to some fundamental notion, law, or set of laws, but from the linguistic point of view there is little parallel to religious English, as this dependence is rarely stated explicitly, and is in some cases extremely tenuous. In religious English, on the other hand, the link is always explicit, given a prominent position in the text, and referred to throughout. The most common method of doing this is through the appositional use of various figurative terms, some used as titles, some as epithets, where a human notion is taken and analogously applied to the term *God* (see 1, 13, 32–4, 51). These terms vary in their theological significance, and the extent to which they are capable of precise definition: some are simply epithets designed to provide a clearer imaginative picture of the 'God' concept, and are redundant in the sense that further theological exposition does not depend on them (*eg the King of Glory* (1), *Light from light* (51)); others are more central to the theological framework of the religion as a whole – for example, the specification of such divine attributes as omnipotence (*cf almighty* (13), *etc*), or the image of the Father and the Son (*eg* 13, 32 *ff*) – and would receive a more precise definition in any exposition. The centrality of the latter can be seen by the way in which further essential theological concepts derive from such basic notions: the identification of *Jesus Christ* (14) with all that this entails (*redemption* (15), *institution* (23), *consubstantial* (52), *salvation* (54), *incarnate* (56), *etc*). Elsewhere, other theologically important terms also occur, *eg sin* (17), *maker* (47), and *sacrifice, oblation, and satisfaction* (16).

Most of these terms work on two levels: on the one hand, they have a technical status as part of theological expression; on the other hand, they have a more general pragmatic status, in that they are terms which can be interpreted in an immediate albeit imprecise way by the average believer. For example, the full theological exposition of a term such as *almighty* is a complicated matter: a number of other metaphysical concepts have to be introduced and related, Scriptural reference has to be made, and apparent counter-examples have to be dealt with. The meaning of *almighty* to the non-theologian, however, is very different: it is conceived of in essentially human terms, as simply the maximum degree of 'might' that the believer can envisage, with all the implications of this. This is the main point about what is usually referred to as the 'analogical' nature of religious language: it is capable of being interpreted on two largely independent planes. Both planes can ultimately be conflated in the central notion 'God', but at any one time, either of the alternative modes of interpretation may be referred to. This inherent 'duality' is a distinctive feature of the character of religious theological vocabulary. It is not found elsewhere in English.

Thirdly, there are items of vocabulary which are not archaic, and which lack any direct theological status, but which are nonetheless very typical of religious utterance. Such terms as *exalt* (7), *perpetual* (19), *?hear* (20), *grant* (21), *receiving* (21), *remembrance* (23), *partakers* (24), *receive* (38), and *ages* (50) are cases in point: they are all of rare occurrence in English as a whole, being restricted to formal contexts, and usually entering into a specific and very restricted range of collocations in a particular variety (*eg partakers . . . Body and Blood*). There are many other such items: *praise*, *bless*, *adore*, *glorify*, and *give thanks*, for example (27–31). These items are interesting in that any full statement of their function must make reference to their variable connotative content. They are words which, in a sense, mean what one wants them to mean. The denotational meaning of a word like *adore* is very simple, specifying a particular attitude of mind and behaviour which the believer presents, usually profound and reverent admiration and devotion. But what one person means by 'profound and reverent' is liable to be very different from what another means. Such interpretative differences of course exist to a greater or lesser extent for all words: there are always idiosyncratic nuances. The point to be made here, though, is that in religious English a very high proportion of the words involved are quite unspecific, and would be empirically observable as being used with very great differences from one person to another. Normally, within a speech community, the response to a word is, on the whole, predictable: in religious language (as also in ethical language, which may or may not be distinguished, depending on one's philosophical position) uniformity of response is largely absent.

The collocational idiosyncrasies mentioned above provide a discussion-point in their own right for religious English. As in all varieties, certain high-frequency collocations occur, which form part of the distinctiveness – here one would note such cases as *kingdom-heaven*, *passion-death*, *body-blood*, *tender-mercy*, and *suffer-death-cross-redemption*. These are different from the collocations for these items normally found elsewhere. But what makes religious English so different is the way in which the expected collocability of one item is very often completely reversed from that expected in normal usage. For example, the term *death* in all varieties but this one has fairly predictable collocates. Here, however, the collocation is with *precious*, which superficially seems paradoxical, until placed within a theological perspective. It is often maintained in philosophical and other discussion of this area that the 'logic' of religious language is different from the 'logic' of other uses of language, such as scientific language. This word *logic* is rather unclear, but there does seem to be a good case for saying that the structural relationships between lexical items in religious English differ markedly from those in any other variety: the range of permissible synonyms, antonyms, and so on in religious language is very different from that found elsewhere. For further examples, consider the apparently paradoxical equations found in religious texts between such terms as *life* and *death*, or *kingship* and *service*, and the apparently uncivilised implications of *eat* and *body*, and *drink* and *blood*. The structural semantic approach would be of particular value in any study of the vocabulary of religious English, but so far it does not seem to have been used.

Further, one ought to mention the importance which formulae have in religious language. The majority of prayers are characterised by a restricted set of formulaic conclusions, such as is illustrated by lines 10–12. Prayers may also begin with a specific formula, and a very small number of formulaic interpolations are permitted within the prayer structure as a whole (*eg we beseech thee*). The language of public worship is thus characterised by a relatively fixed and traditional framework, upon which a large number of changes may be rung: the prayer for the Sunday after Ascension Day shares the same structural format as the prayer for the Sunday before, though what occurs between the opening and closing formulae is very different.

Finally, let us turn to the semantics of religious discourse as a whole. In the first place, the range of utterances in religious language reduces to a very limited set of types. For example, there is what might be called the 'statement of belief', illustrated by **V**; the 'prayer of supplication', illustrated by **II**; and so on. Each type displays its own 'favourite' grammatical and other structures, as we have already mentioned, and their semantic structure also varies. Compare the graphologically controlled point by point exposition of beliefs which characterises **V** with the single (although complex) point being made by **II** and **III**. Extract **IV** is a mixture: it has three parts, part one (25–31) being more a statement of certain facts than a prayer; part two (32–40) being a prayer of the 'supplication' type; and part three (41–5) being a prayer of praise. **IV** is perhaps abnormal in its conflation of these different categories; normally a religious utterance is semantically homogeneous, in the sense that a single point (or a series of very closely related points) is developed to a logical (or theological) conclusion.

The different texts, then, show a certain variety, though the total number of semantic types is few. Between types, however, there are certain unifying semantic features. We have already noted under the heading of vocabulary the way in which this variety makes use of a single concept, 'God', as a semantic cornerstone, this being primarily established through the meaning-relations operating between specific items of vocabulary in certain grammatical structures, especially apposition. We ought also to point to the rather abnormal semantic role played by some of the grammatical features. For example, the postmodified vocative mentioned above does not have a person-identifying role in religious English (as it would have in all other cases): the function of the postmodification is not to identify one particular aspect of the God-concept as opposed to others (*cf* O God, who . . . with *★O God who* . . .), but to provide a convenient means of accumulating relevant sense-associations in order to prepare the believer for the specific point which is the purpose of the prayer (such as the request element). This attempt to produce a summary of some aspect of the religion, with largely mnemonic value, as vividly as possible, also explains a number of other features about these texts, such as the repetition of certain familiar titles for God, which look at the same subject from different angles; the frequency of adjectives; and most aspects of the use of coordination at clause level (the semantic function of coordination at group level is very different, usually making an antithesis which has theological or pastoral relevance, such as *Body and Blood* (24), or *death and passion* (23)). Finally, there is the basic point that this is the only variety of English which is in whole or in part based on a translation. Extracts **IV** and **V** are completely translations; and **II** and **III** make use of the occasional phrase which has its origin in a Scriptural or related text (*eg world without end*). This is one very restricting pressure upon usage. The other is the presence of a usually explicitly defined historical or theological tradition which a text has to conform to. All these texts are sanctioned by a particular Church authority, and it is not possible to vary their form or content in any *ad hoc* way (except for phonological variation, and the type of vocabulary mentioned on *p* 150); the question of variation in singularity, in the sense described in Chapter 3 (*p* 76), therefore hardly ever arises.

It should be clear from all this that the variety we are here calling religious English is formally very different from all other varieties of the language. It is probably the most clearly marked variety of all, mainly because of its use of archaism, and its ability to go to extremes, as with such structures as *Give us to drink of very thee,/ And all we pray shall answered be* (hymn text). There seems no question that this should not be considered a variety, though the extent to which there are systematic stylistic variations within the variety is an aspect which has to be examined further. There is little variation in status, religious English usually being relatively formal (in such generally conservative texts, as those given above), with occasional informalities, depending on the extent to which reformers are prepared to go in approximating this kind of English to that used in everyday conversation. Modality differences certainly exist (for example, the distinction between **II/III** and **IV/V** already discussed, *p* 156), and it is possible that any general analysis into 'types' of utterance (such as statement of belief, prayer of supplication) might ultimately be best handled under this heading. But even in this introductory examination, the differences between the texts seem far outweighed by the similarities.

Exercises

1 It is frequently said in discussion about liturgical language reform that 'English has not got the capacity to produce a living liturgical language'. What do you think such a comment means? What does the evidence of this chapter suggest?

2 Certain bodies are trying to devise a single liturgical English which could be used in all English-speaking areas. What problems have to be faced in order to realise this aim?

3 It is generally felt that 'religious language should be intelligible to all'. How far is the aim of intelligibility compatible with such other desirable requirements as 'dignity' and 'euphony'?

4 How would you define a litany linguistically?

5 The following version of text **V** was in use in Great Britain in 1968. Identify the grammatical and lexical differences and suggest some reasons for the changes.
   . . . The almighty Father, maker of heaven and earth,
   Maker of all things, visible and invisible.
   I believe in one Lord, Jesus Christ, the only-begotten Son of God,
   Born of the Father before time began,
   God from God, Light from Light, true God from true God.

Begotten, not made, one in substance with the Father; and through him all things were made.

For us men and for our salvation he came down from heaven, Was incarnate of the virgin Mary by the power of the Holy Spirit, and was made man.

6 Compare the extract from the Authorised Version with more modern translations (*eg The New English Bible*), and account for the main linguistic differences.

Notes

1 *Cf* C. L. WRENN, *The English Language*, Methuen, 1949, *pp* 150 *ff*; also S. BROOK, *The Language of the Book of Common Prayer*, Deutsch, 1965.

2 *Cf* the notational innovations introduced by ORM into his *Ormulum* (c. 1200), for example; or the discussion of the relationship between intonation, punctuation, and plain chant in P. CLEMOES, *Liturgical Influence on Punctuation in Late Old English and Early Middle English Manuscripts*, Department of Anglo-Saxon Occasional Papers, No. 1, Cambridge, 1952.

3 *Cf* D. CRYSTAL, *Linguistics, Language and Religion*, Burns and Oates, 1964, *pp* 149 *ff*.

4 *Cf* BROOK, ibid., *p* 91.

5 Only *and* out of the whole range of coordinating conjunctions is at all common: a coordinator like *but* is very restricted in its use (for example, it may occur after a negated imperative, such as 'O God, do not X, but Y . . .'), and the others are hardly ever seen.

Chapter 7

The Language of Newspaper Reporting

'Journalese', like 'jargon', and a few other pseudo-descriptive terms, is a label which seems to have a clear-cut sense until we begin to look closely at the way it tends to be used. Then we see that it is never given any kind of precise linguistic definition, and that it is rarely more than a vague and (sometimes nastily) pejorative criticism of a way of writing that people feel is in some way typical of the press, or a particular paper. To what extent is it possible to define this kind of English more precisely? We can obtain a clearer picture of what is involved in this notion of 'journalese', but only if we delimit our field first. Obviously, everything that happens to be printed in a newspaper or magazine or written by a journalist is not going to be linguistically homogeneous – nor is there any reason for expecting it to be so. A newspaper is always very eclectic, from the stylistic point of view. Besides news-items, we find within its pages articles, reviews, imaginative writing of various kinds, advertising, competitions, and much more, which from the linguistic viewpoint would be dealt with under the heading of other kinds of English, or would be too idiosyncratic to allow generalisation. We have therefore restricted our attention to what is generally considered to be the central function of a newspaper, to inform, and consequently to the notion of newspaper *reporting*. What linguistic characteristics, if any, can be associated with this? As we shall see, while it is possible to make a few generalisations about the way language is used in this situation, it is impossible to be comprehensive or final in these statements. It seems that the concept of 'the language of newspaper reporting' is not as meaningful as is generally assumed. There is not one, but a number of 'journaleses' that can be found between the pages of the daily and weekly press; and while they do have a certain amount in common, their overall styles are very different. The pejorative use of the label 'journalese', moreover, seems to be restricted to one kind of newspaper-reporting language only, namely, that illustrated by extract **I** below.

We have chosen the extracts in this chapter so that they represent different extremes of journalistic writing; they are generally accepted as being at different poles, as far as the daily press is concerned, so, in discussing them, we should cover a large number of the devices found in newspaper reporting. We must not be put off by the fact that the kinds of English used are very different: the disparity can largely be explained by reference to the very different audiences envisaged by the two papers concerned. We shall in fact be concentrating as much on these linguistic differences as on the similarities, to clarify the idea that 'journalese' – and it is a handy word – is not a single thing, but rather a composite, a blend of what is characteristic of a number of different kinds of journalistic material. If nothing else, the exercise will show the danger of making generalisations of too facile a kind about uses of language, and point the need for adequate descriptive preparation. But the language of **I** and **II** (which follow on *pp* 175–7) does not differ in every respect, as we shall see; the two texts share some important linguistic features that are not generally found outside newspaper reporting; and the amount they have in common suggests that putting them together in one chapter may not be too misleading, but may, rather, prove illuminating.

One point which the two extracts clearly share is that their underlying aims are identical: they are both concerned to present a certain number of facts in as interesting a manner as possible to audiences whose constitution they are fairly clear about. Also, the general pressures working on the authors are the same – the need for compression of the information into a limited space, the need for clarity, the avoidance of ambiguity, and so on. **I** and **II** are two treatments of the same story by different papers, which appeared on the same day. By keeping the subject matter constant, we feel that the different stylistic colouring which each paper throws over the story may be more clearly seen.

Graphetic and graphological variation is of great importance in defining the distinctiveness of this kind of English: between the beginning and end of an article one always finds different sizes and shapes of type juxtaposed – the most noticeable device being of course the graphetic highlighting of the headline. The function of headlining is complex: headlines have to contain a clear, succinct and if possible intriguing message, to kindle a spark of interest in the potential reader, who, on average, is a person whose eye moves swiftly down a page and stops when something catches his attention; and the chief

I

If the weather's bad...

BLAME THE COMPUTER IN FUTURE

THAT big black cloud for ever hanging over the heads of Britain's weathermen has vanished.

Those "Yah, ha-ha-got-it-wrong-again" remarks from the weather-conscious public won't trouble them too much any more.

For should that "continuing dry" forecast develop into a depressing downpour they can blame the new member of the staff: Mr. Comet.

Mr. Comet—a £500,000 computer, joined the ranks of the Meteorological Office, Bracknell, Berkshire, yesterday.

He can scan half a million weather reports from all over the world—and come up with the answers in one and a half hours: Blow, blaze, or below freezing.

He requires an operating staff of three and another 50 processers to feed in weather statistics. But he can cope with 1 million calculations a second. And he is hardly ever wrong.

Much faster

The introduction from today of regular computered charts for weather forecasters was welcomed by the Meteorological Office's new director-general, 42-year-old Dr. John Mason, who took over a month ago.

He described Mr. Comet as "a great stride forward." For he admitted that the humble, human weatherman poring over his charts and figures can "sometimes be wrong."

Whereas Mr. Comet, flashing and clicking away in his sunshine room at the top of the Meteorological Office, does the job just as well "if not better" and almost five times as quickly.

... ...

Up to now Mr. Comet's generalised weather charts have been compared each day with charts produced by the seven-to-ten-hour human process. The results are almost identical.

In a few more months Mr. Comet will be such a trusted member of the staff that his charts will be accepted without a qualm. The forecasters will use them as the basis for the detailed bulletins.

Said Dr. Mason: "It will relieve the staff of a lot of donkey work."

Already the Meteorological Office is thinking of a big brother for Mr. Comet, who has a memory bank of a mere 50,000 words.

A bigger computer would cope with a hoped-for expansion in the number of world-wide weather stations and a bigger communications centre to handle more and faster-arriving information.

One of the Bracknell experts glanced at Mr. Comet's current prediction of the weather to come. By the side of the computered chart was another produced by human hands.

He said: "They both say the same thing, I'm afraid—cold winds and the first real frost of the winter."

II

Weather Forecasting by Numbers

From Our Science Correspondent

Revolutions can begin quietly. One began yesterday at the Meteorological Office headquarters at Bracknell. For the first time in routine procedure an electronic computer contributed to the forecast chart published today on this page. To look at there is nothing special about the chart. The change for the forecaster was only that an extra aid was given him. As well as preparing his own forecast chart of pressure distribution—always the first step in forecasting—he received a second chart drawn from the computer-made calculations. For the issued chart he could make use of either or both as he pleased.

The second stage—the translation of forecast pressure distribution into forecast weather—was entirely his own. Why, then, the excitement?

Meteorologists have long hoped to make the transition from assessment and judgment to calculation, from forecasting to prediction. The forecaster's job, as it has persisted up to the present time, is summed up in two sentences from a 1950 publication: "By studying the sequence of charts it is possible to see how the various pressure systems and fronts are moving and developing. The art of forecasting consists in making a correct assessment of the movements and developments during the period covered by the forecast."

The now accepted goal of "numerical weather prediction" owes its name to a book published by an Englishman, Dr. L. F. Richardson, as long ago as 1921. The goal will have been reached when weather, as well as pressure distribution, is calculated numerically and when the greater precision suggested by the term "prediction" is attained regularly in practice.

EQUATIONS OF MOTION

Requirements, like the goal, have been clear for a long time. Weather is the result of air movements on an immense scale. Air is a compressible fluid and a first requirement is that the motion of compressible fluids should be understood quantitatively. The equations of motion for such a fluid—assumed to be of uniform composition—were written down more than 100 years ago by Louis Navier in France and by Sir George Stokes and Lord Kelvin in Britain.

A second requirement is that the state of the air should be known well enough over a big enough area for the use of would-be exact methods to be profitable. No computer—human or electronic—can do better than the data available permit. For the purposes of the Meteorological Office—which include forecasts for air routes and shipping as well as for the British Isles—this means knowing about air movements above an area extending from the American Middle West to beyond Moscow, and from beyond the North Pole to well down in Africa; and in altitude from sea or ground level to a height of more than seven miles. The contribution made by reports from ships on the North Atlantic has been, and remains, vital. The needs of air pilots have led to a rapid expansion in upper air observations: in the northern hemisphere they are made twice daily by radio-sounding balloons from about 600 places. But only a few—from weather ships—are made from sea areas.

. . .   .

THE COMPUTER'S JOB

The job of the computer, known as "Comet", has been made as nearly automatic as possible. Its first task is to select data. Every day there pour into Bracknell a little under half a million five-figure numbers—all meteorological information in code. It is quicker to give the lot to the computer than to attempt to arrange the data by hand. The computer is programmed to pick out all stations that make observations of wind and temperature at high levels, to take all observations from ships at sea, to reject observations of visibility, cloud and so on which do not concern it, and, for the rest, to select.

The next stage is one of analysis. From the information at its disposal the computer arrives, by interpolation, at values of sea-level pressure, or of heights of pressure surfaces, at an even network of grid points. It applies checks of consistency—but a few cases, such as the retention or rejection of a vital isolated report, are reserved to human judgment. All is now ready for the numerical forecast. This is carried forward step by step, looking only an hour ahead, or less, in any one step. This is being continued at present for 48 hours.

. . .   .

How will forecasts be affected? No dramatic change should be looked for. Too many needs have first to be met, each reacting on the others. One is for more information about high-level conditions above the Atlantic as a whole, the tropics, and surprisingly (from a British standpoint) the southern hemisphere. A second need is for research. Air, for example, is not a uniform fluid, but differs from place to place, and from time to time, in humidity. The relevant facts need to be included in the basic computation—not merely injected at the end, as an aid to "putting weather into the forecast". More, too, needs to be known about the working of the atmosphere as a whole. A third need is for more or bigger computers—not only to handle the increased amount of information but for research to enable information to be better used. Weather forecasting, so long an art based on science, is in process of becoming a branch of applied mathematics.

means of producing 'eye-catching' effects is by making use of the full range of graphetic contrasts. These contrasts will of course vary from one publication to another; they form part of the consistent, visual house-style which any newspaper tries to maintain. The graphetic distinction between the headline types of **I** and **II** is shown above, reduced a little in size, but it may be helpful to describe the salient differences. In **I**, the headlines were bold, the first line being printed in 19 mm high, heavy, lower case italic letters, the remainder being in 6 mm high italic capitals. The first words extended most of the way across the top of the page, continuing away from the article over an accompanying photograph. In the case of **II**, we find a quieter, 10 mm high roman lettering, extending over the two columns in which the article was printed, and no more.

Apart from the headlines, the most obvious visual feature of the extracts is the paragraphing, the way in which the narrative as a whole is split into smaller units. The use of subheadings in the centre of the column of print is of course the main distinctive feature shared by all newspaper reports of any length. Apart from this, **I** and **II** are very different. **I** breaks up the text into very short paragraphs, of a few lines each; **II** tends to keep the paragraphs long. We shall be discussing the grammatical and semantic consequences of this shortly. Meanwhile, it is clear that one result of the difference is to make **I** very much more easy to read than **II**. The latter is relatively monotonous; there are few obvious resting-places for the eye; and the reader has to concentrate for longer periods. An additional aid to readability in **I** (again, not fully reproducible here) is the variation in type-size used throughout: the first word is in capitals; the first paragraph is printed in a noticeably larger type than the remainder; the second is slightly smaller than the first; the next portion (up to 52) is in a smaller size again; and the rest is in the smallest size of all. The most likely reason for this procedure is that it facilitates reading at the beginning of the article – a psycholinguistic hypothesis which would have to be tested before being taken for granted, but which does seem a reasonable explanation for the variety of visual stimuli which accumulate at the beginning of **I**. (A further small, but psychologically important feature is the initial *T* of the first paragraph, which is twice the size of the other capitals, and extends downwards to take up almost two lines of space – a kind of visual 'bridge' between headlines and story.[1] Whatever the function this graphetic variation has (could one conclude that **I** is written for an audience which wants to have the job of reading made as easy as possible?), it is clear that **II** makes no such concessions: here, there is the same, small type-size throughout.

There is little that is distinctive about the punctuation of the two extracts. Commas are absent from many places where they would normally be expected; for example, there is a tendency to omit them after initially placed adverbials (53, 58, 90), between coordinations (129, 137), or between sequences of adjectives. The reason is probably to avoid disturbing the tempo of reading more than is necessary. In such places, the grammar gives sufficient indication of where the break between structures comes, and consequently it is not essential to have an additional indication, in the form of a punctuation mark, particularly when this mark would carry with it on most occasions the expectation of a pause. And whereas under-use of punctuation will undoubtedly cause structural ambiguity, it is equally important to avoid breaking up the text unduly, and adding difficulties to the reader's attempts to assimilate fairly long stretches of text at a time. If one tries reading any of the above examples with commas introduced, this point quickly becomes clear.

Frequent use is made of inverted commas, and moreover in a variety of functions. One finds them used for direct quotation, for indirect quotation (*eg* 13), or to spotlight terms for particular attention because they are being used in a new or technical way (131). This double-function of attention-drawing and actual quotation sometimes produces ambiguity – for example, *putting weather into the forecast* (221) could be an unacknowledged quote, or a reference to a well-known saying in the field, or simply a remark of the author's which he wants to give special prominence to. It is also worth noting how the use of quotation gives a strong impression of verisimilitude and immediacy to the articles, as well as adding extra interest and variety. This is particularly true of **I**. To assess the effect, contrast *He described Mr Comet as 'a great stride forward'* with *He described Mr Comet as a great stride forward.*

The use of dashes is also interesting, and characteristic of this kind of writing. In both texts they are used, quite normally, to mark a parenthesis (*eg* 171), though other styles of writing might well have substituted commas here. The effect of putting dashes rather than commas is to give the parenthetic phrase a greater independence (not necessarily a longer pause), as can be seen from a comparison of the following pair of sentences:

But only a few – from weather ships – are made from sea areas (171).
But only a few, from weather ships, are made from sea areas.

Apart from this, we see, especially in **I**, the 'informal' use of the dash, to link expansions of thought or afterthoughts with the main part of the sentence – a usage which is at its most frequent in informal letter-writing, where we find dashes used to replace almost any punctuation mark. Consider, for example, *They both say the same thing, I'm afraid – cold winds and the first real frost of the winter* (81), where a colon would produce an impression of care and premeditation in the speech (*They both say the same thing, I'm afraid: cold winds and the first real frost of the winter*). This use of the dash is particularly common in writing which tries to give a general impression of informality and chattiness to a piece of written utterance. I evidently finds this very desirable: *He can scan half a million weather reports from all over the world – and come up with the answers in one and a half hours.* Compare this sentence with the dash replaced by a comma or semicolon, and then with it omitted. There is a significant difference in tone.

The phonology which underlies the written form of newspaper reporting is not normally stylistically significant, presumably because this is language written to be read, rarely read aloud. But certain auditory effects can be found, which presumably reverberate mentally. I seems to favour alliteration to give added zest to the story, as in *depressing downpour* (14), *Blow, blaze, or below freezing* (26), *humble, human* (43). II on the other hand goes in for more complex rhythmical effects, using balanced phrases and antitheses (as in *when the greater precision suggested by the term 'prediction' is attained regularly in practice* (130). Needless to say, in I, the comparatively simple phonological structure of the words and the relatively uncomplicated rhythm units between punctuation marks, add a great deal to its readability.

There is most to be said about these extracts at the grammatical level. Headlines of course are a separate study in themselves, being radically different from the rest of newspaper reporting language. We do not have space to make a separate examination of the techniques of headline-writing here, but any such study would have to begin by considering the kinds of word which tend to be omitted, to gain the desired compression (as in *Man finds gun on beach*), the types of ambiguity which may arise from leaving out important structural cues (as in *Giant waves down funnel*), and the very restricted range of sentence-types which may occur as headlines, which amongst other things are idiosyncratic to this kind of English.[2] As far as the rest of reporting language is concerned, there seem to be two main areas of stylistic importance – sentence structure, and group structure.

As a perspective for any study of sentence structure, we should immediately note the contrast between I and II from the point of view of paragraph structure. Take the simple measure of the number of sentences composing each paragraph: I has sixteen paragraphs, of which eleven are composed of one sentence, four of two, and one of three. II on the other hand has nine paragraphs, of which two are composed of two sentences, two of four, one of five, two of six, one of seven, and one of ten. In the case of I, there are no paragraphs with more than three sentences; in **II**, there are no paragraphs at all of a single sentence, the majority being over three sentences long. And when we consider that the average length of sentence in **II** (measured quite simply in terms of number of words from capital letter to full-stop) is much greater than in **I**, we begin to see the extent ʻof the difference in organisation between the two extracts. Of course, length by itself is not of very great interest to the linguist. How long your sentence is depends as much on *what* you want to say as on *how* you decide to say it (that is, the content rather than the style). What is linguistically much more interesting is the type of sentence used, defined by reference to its internal structure, and the ways in which the sentences link up with each other within and between paragraphs. And here, the two extracts, while not by any means being identical, have a great deal in common.

In both **I** and **II**, sentence-types are largely statements (as one might expect), with the normal order of elements, SPC. Occasionally in the language of reporting we will find a question which is not in inverted commas, and of course these must be either questions which do not expect an answer, or questions which the writer answers himself, and which he has introduced to keep the pace of the article from dragging. There are two questions in **II** (107, 206), and their function is worth studying from this point of view. Occasionally, also, we will find an imperative, almost always with a complement of some kind – the headline in **I**, for example. And we may even find minor sentences, particularly functioning as exclamations, and often with more than one exclamation mark, in the style exemplified by **I**; but usually these appear only in headlines.

The three most significant features within the broad category of statement-type sentences concern the position of the subject in relation to the verb; the position of adverbials within the clause; and the types of phrase and clause structure which may occur within any given sentence. The first phenomenon, distinctive subject position, is exemplified only once (64), but its importance is considerable in this kind of English as a whole: the normal SP word-order becomes PS – *Said Dr Mason* . . . . This deviation is restricted in its occurrence to verbs of that large class to do with speaking, *eg declare*, *explain*, or *laugh* (in the sense 'said laughingly', as in *Laughed the Prime Minister:* '*I really think* . . .'). It does not imply any general permission for word-order flexibility, and *Went Dr Mason* . . . is as impossible in this context as it is anywhere else.

Adverbials are extremely common in newspaper reporting (as one would expect from the need to be explicit as to the place and time of activities); but their positioning is also very interesting. Apart from that small group of adverbs which have a fixed or relatively fixed position before the verb (such as *just*), adverbials tend to come towards the end of a clause, either after the verb, or at the very end, when everything else has been said. The stylistic point to be made is that when an adverbial whose normal position is post-verbal is brought forward from this position, and put anywhere near the beginning of the clause, then it fulfils a strongly emphatic function. This is usually reinforced by the intonational nucleus, which also moves forward from its usual place near the end of the clause, and stays with the adverbial. The contrast that can be made, then, in its simplest form, is between normal, unemphatic position and its opposite; and of course there may be different degrees of emphasis involved. Now in conversation, when the emphatic position is used, the extra-linguistic context regularly provides us with a reason for the change: if someone says

|outside the ↑cìnema I 'said we'd 'meet them|,

(referring to where a meeting was going to take place), instead of

I |said we'd 'meet them 'outside the cìnema|,

then we can be sure that the preceding context was someone doubting what had already been said once, asking for a repeat, or something similar. In newspaper reporting, however, not only is beginning-position very common for adverbials, but one regularly finds that no reliance can be made on the preceding context to explain why initial positioning has been selected. The distinction in position seems to be made purely for the sake of varying the emphasis within a given sentence, and no more. We may compare the normal placement of *yesterday* (21), *in one and a half hours* (25), and *a month ago* (39), for example, where the reporting is factual and devoid of any special prominence; and the following, where the items are brought right into the forefront of our attention: *up to now* (53), *in a few more months* (58), *already* (66), *for the first time in routine procedure* (89), *for the issued chart* (101), *for the purposes of the Meteorological Office* (153), and so on. If one tries placing any of these towards the end of the sentence, one finds that the interest and impetus of the narrative is greatly reduced.

Thirdly, the two extracts illustrate very well the kind of changes which may be rung on the basic theme of spc by introducing various types of coordination, subordination, and parenthesis. **II** is much more complex than **I** in all these respects. **I** has hardly any coordination at clause level (*He can scan . . . and come up with*, 22), though there is more at group level (27, 44, 71, 82, and the adverbial linkage in 51). This may be contrasted with **II**, which has substantial coordination. We see it between main clauses (138, 197, and *cf* 216), between various types of dependent clause (96, 129), and very frequently between groups (102, 109, 128, 144, *etc*). Moreover, there is complex coordination of adverbials, of the kind exemplified by 155 *ff*; and coordination using such linking devices as *not only . . . but* (225) and the comparative (181). Lists, of which a good – if complex – example occurs in 184–190, are common in this kind of English as a whole, though poorly represented in the above (*cf* 184, and in **I**, 26). This relates to the use of other coordinating devices, such as apposition (104), parallelism (109), and the use of punctuation to make a graphological coordination (as with the use of the colon in 168, or the frequent use of the dash, as in 219, 225).

The variety of coordinating devices is thus a feature of the structure of **II** which is almost entirely absent from **I**. Similarly, **II** shows a greater use of features of grammatical subordination: adverbial clauses are not much used (but see 102, 112, 128), but there are cases of noun clauses (as in 138, 147) and a great deal of subordination within the nominal group (*eg* the non-finite clauses in 92, 100, 121, 125, 130, 142, *etc*, largely using *-ed* forms). Dependent clauses of any kind tend to be less frequent in the kind of English represented by **I** (13, 58), and while there is as much subordination within nominal group structure in **I** as in **II**, it is worth noting that the former tends to rely more on non-finite clauses using *-ing* (6, 44, 47) and relative clauses (39, 68).

In all this, the tendency, hinted at in **I**, marked in **II**, to 'think in pairs', providing alternatives or lists of descriptive terms, stands out very clearly. It is one way of packing a large amount of information into a fairly simple grammatical structure. Another way, frequently used in newspaper reporting, is through the introduction of a parenthetic phrase, clause or group into a larger structure, as in – *a £500,000 computer* (18). This device is common in **II**, as in 98, 142, 151, and it provides a useful alternative to more lengthy and possibly more awkward kinds of coordination. Parentheses of course tend to be fairly short and simple, in view of the danger of losing the train of thought begun in the superordinate structure.

There is thus a greater diversity of structural types in **II** than in **I**, but in neither do we go very far towards a complexity which could produce obscurity or unintelligibility. In **II**, for example, the more complex sentences do not follow each other in a string; they tend to be distributed among the shorter sentences, which aids both readability and comprehension. And in both **I** and **II** the more complex sentences tend to be avoided at the beginning of the articles. But there is another reason for the overall clarity of both these extracts, namely, that the connectedness of the discourse is well organised and clearly defined. There is no disjointedness. Particularly in **I**, it is important that the story, once begun, should carry the reader through to the end. And while the text has been split up visually into separate units, one should note how these units are bound very closely together in grammar, so that the whole text forms a closely knit passage, which reads extremely smoothly. We have already noted the lack of intra-sentence coordination in **I**, which results from a tendency to split the text up into small paragraphs with fairly short sentences; now we can see that the balance is restored, as it were, by the presence of a significant amount of inter-sentence (and inter-paragraph) coordination, which is particularly characteristic of this style.

The first important type of sentence-linkage occurs frequently in **I**, less often in **II**. The device is to begin a sentence with a conjunction of some kind, which then acts as a 'bridge' between the sentence following and the one preceding. They cannot be taken as one sentence, because both retain their individual graphic identity. For examples, see the sentences beginning on lines 13, 29, 42, and 47. Sometimes this usage produces a sentence which would rarely exist in isolation, and would probably be considered unacceptable if heard on its own by most native speakers. In all these cases, the sentences could have been joined by a semi-colon or a colon, producing further coordination of the kind discussed above; or the conjunctions could have been omitted without leaving structures which were ungrammatical. But to do this would have detracted from the overall effect of the article. We have already discussed the value of the paragraphing technique used by **I** (*p* 178). To retain this paragraphing, but to omit the conjunctions, would produce a narrative which was extremely disjointed; to lose the paragraphing, by running sentences together, would cause a lot of the pace of the narrative to be lost, as well as much of the drama, for the main effect of having short, snappy, and loosely coordinated sentences of this kind is to produce an echo of the rhythms of colloquial speech, along with a sense of urgency as item after item is thrust at the reader. These links are of course essential in story-telling of any kind; consequently they are of great importance in this kind of English. In **II**, on the other hand, there is less story and more discussion; consequently the conjunction-type of linkage is rare (*cf* 171), and this extract relies on other techniques of reference between sentences. These other techniques have already been outlined in Chapter 2 (*p* 44): amongst other things, they involve the use of the definite article, the demonstratives and personal pronouns, lexical repetition, 'prop' words (such as *one*) and certain kinds of adverbial. To show the importance of such features for the establishment of meaning, all one has to do is take some sentences which display these features, and quote them in isolation: they will be seen to be very obscure: *One began yesterday at the Meteorological Office . . .* (87); *This is being continued at present for 48 hours* (204); *And he is hardly ever wrong* (31).

This is the normal use of these structural features – as a means of backward-reference to something which has just been mentioned. And in both texts constant use is made of these features in this quite normal way. But occasionally in the language of newspaper reporting (and also in literature), special stylistic effects can be gained by using them abnormally. Ordinarily, as we have just seen, there has to be something for such features to refer back to, otherwise we get near-nonsense. We cannot *begin* an utterance with the words *He left at seven o'clock*, for example, unless the *he* is clearly defined from some previous utterance, or is unambiguously implicit in the extra-linguistic context. But we may find the use of such features initially in a written English utterance as a deliberate stylistic device, and it occurs here. In **I**, we find a sequence of opening sentences using the demonstratives: *That big black cloud . . .*, *Those 'Yah, ha-ha . . .'*, *That 'continuing dry' forecast . . . .* Now the writer can only get away with this if he can be sure (as in this case he can) that we have a good idea which cloud, remarks and forecast are being referred to. He has not told us this in his article: what he is doing is relying on our national consciousness about these things to fill the gap. And in this case, of course, he can be fairly certain that this is acute, in view of the British mania for discussing the weather, particularly at the beginning of conversations, where it acts as a kind of 'ice-breaker' or prelude to further conversation. We, the public, are well aware of the legends associated with the weather and forecasting. The author knows we know. Consequently, by assuming this knowledge, he immediately puts himself in an intimate relationship with us. He is on our side: and this accounts for the tone of familiarity which we feel in these opening sentences. The note of 'mutual interest' is there, and we are prompted to read on. To test this explanation, all one has to do is substitute *A* for *That* in line 5, and so on, and examine the effect: the tone is instantly more impersonal; we do not feel implicated any more. Devices of this kind are very common in the more informal styles of newspaper-reporting English.

Apart from the features operating at sentence level and between sentences, we should note certain distinctive characteristics operating within the nominal and verbal group. Let us take the nominal group first. Here, the most noteworthy feature is the presence of much more complex pre- and postmodification than we normally hear or write. It is noticeable (especially in **I**) how few nouns function on their own, without some form of adjective or other modification. There is a particularly strong tendency to introduce adjectives wherever possible, to add detail and colour to a story. Thus we find, not just *a computer* but *a £500,000 computer*, and so on. To express this via a dependent clause would of course be possible but cumbersome, particularly if used often. Moreover in **I** we do not find just single adjectives, or adjectives with adverbial modification, both of which are to be found in any kind of English, but the coining of new and sometimes outlandish adjectival formations, such as *weather-conscious* (11), *continuing dry* (13), *seven-to-ten-hour* (56), *hoped-for* (71), *faster-arriving* (74), *computer-made* (100), and of course *Yah, ha-ha-got-it-wrong-again* (9). Then there are many sequences of adjectives, such as *big, black* (5), *humble, human* (43), *seven-to-ten-hour human* (56), *more and faster-arriving* (74), and such a construction as *42-year-old Dr John Mason* (38), which is getting very close to the oft-parodied style of such American magazines as *Time – said tall, grey-haired, blue-eyed, 32-year-old ship's carpenter Andrew Jones . . .*

In **II**, the emphasis on nominal modification is still there, but it takes different forms: vivid description is replaced by more technical terms as adjectives. Many of these adjective-plus-noun groups function almost as compound nouns, *eg routine procedure* (90), *electronic computer* (91), *forecast chart* (92), *pressure distribution* (97). This contributes a great deal towards the descriptive precision of the article. In addition there are a fairly large number of unmodified nouns (largely abstract terms, grammatically uncountable) such as *weather*

(135), which is technical in this usage, *assessment* (109), and *calculation* (110). This could be contrasted with the particularising, concrete tendency of the nouns in **I** (note that *a qualm* is used in 61, where *qualm* could have been used). There is nonetheless a balance in nominal group modification between the two extracts, through the greater use of postmodification in **II**, as we have already seen.

There is only a hint in these extracts (37) of the use of the pre-modifying genitive where it would not normally go – as in *The University of London's James Smith said . . .* – a feature which is common in the American press; and we have space only to point to the characteristic way of listing the whole of a title within one structure, *the Meteorological Office, Bracknell, Berkshire* being a case in point (19). As far as the verbal group is concerned, there is an expected bias towards the use of certain tense-forms (though this is not as marked here as is normal for this kind of English): the simple past tense (*eg walked, was walking*) is usually the dominant form, but here there is an above-average proportion of present tense forms, due to the scientific nature of **II** (*cf p* 252). Other tense-forms tend not to occur (except, of course, in quotations, reported speech, *etc*), but modal verbs are frequently used. The tendency in the popular press is to use the active voice rather than the passive – **II** again gives a false impression here, containing nearly thirty passives (as opposed to three in **I**), the effect being to give the same impression of neutral, objective, factual reporting as occurs in scientific language (see Chapter 9). The passives here, however, are different from those in scientific English in two main respects: they display a wider range of forms; and a larger number of verbs are involved. Contracted forms also occur, in the more informal passages (*cf* the beginning of **I**).

Turning now to the vocabulary of the two passages, the most striking feature is clearly the word-formation in **I**, where there is a greater inventiveness in compounding than is normally seen in English: only a minority of the hyphenated words (*eg world-wide*, 72) are common. Phrases tend to be used as words (*cf* 9, 13). In **II**, the dominant lexical feature is the technical terminology, most of which is taken for granted as not requiring explanation – such phrases as *by interpolation* (193), for example. Such technicalities are noticeably lacking in **I**, where simpler words are used (*eg computered*, 79). The nearest we get to specialist usage is *generalised* (53), *processers* (28), *memory bank* (68), and perhaps *communications centre* (73).

We have already noted the dramatic qualities of the headlines in

I, which result from their graphetic prominence, the intriguing nature of the title, and the force of the imperative. The vocabulary of the remainder of the text is also deliberately emphatic, as is clear from the use of such 'extreme' or 'absolute' words and phrases as *big black, vanished, blaze, blow* . . ., and *downpour*. And this relates to the very important differences of status between the two passages. There is a certain amount of informality in **II** (*cf give the lot* . . . (182), *Why, then* . . . (107), but in **I** this is the tone throughout. We notice colloquialisms such as *won't* (11), *weather's* (1), *Yah, ha–ha* . . . (9); and idioms such as *joined the ranks of* (19), *come up with* (24), *too much* (12), *took over* (39); and *in the nick of time* (occurs in the omitted section). The actual conversations quoted also retain the informal characteristics of colloquial speech to a great extent (*donkey work*, 65, *I'm afraid*, 82). Then there is the overall jocular tone of the article, which again fosters greater informality. The computer is personified throughout (*Mr* Comet, compared with the sober *known as Comet* in **II**, 175), but this theme is not restricted to the use of the *Mr* form. Pronouns referring to the computer are masculine; it is referred to in human terms (*member of the staff*, 16), has human relationships (*big brother*, 67), and does human things (by being used with verbs which normally take only human animate subjects, such as *cope*, 30, *join ranks*, 19). There is a tendency to word–play (*eg cloud*, 5); and in the omitted section, *forecasters* is glossed in brackets as *human*.

In **II**, on the other hand, the tone is much more formal and restrained, as the use of such 'careful' terms as *contributed* (91), *persisted* (112), and *attained* (131) shows; for all of these, less formal equivalents could have been used. Phrases like *up to the present time* (112), *assessment and judgment* (109), *retention or rejection* (198), and *relevant facts* (218) have an official ring about them; and the formality is marked in the grammar by such careful phraseology as *and, for the rest, to select* (190), *has been, and remains, vital* (165), *have long hoped* (108), and such parallelisms as *from* . . . *from* . . . (109). A good example of the technically normal (but nonetheless formal) agreement using a plural verb is found in *data* . . . *permit* (152), where informal speech would tend to substitute the singular. The absence of vivid, dramatic vocabulary in **II** is consistent with the writer's purpose, which he makes explicit twice in the above extract – *revolutions can begin quietly* (87), and *no dramatic change should be looked for* (206).

But such comments are already bound up with points that are really to do with the semantics of the two passages. The basic aim of the two extracts, to report the facts, may be the same, but their interpretations are very different. The two papers take very different lines as to what are the relevant facts – that is, the facts which their audiences would find interesting. Not only is different language necessary to suit the different temperaments of their respective audiences, but a different type of information is also given. If we compare the actual information given in the two texts, we can see how the same basic story is interpreted very differently. In **I**, we are given the human, personal angle: there is a photograph; we are told about Dr Mason, given his age, told when he took over, and what he feels about the situation; we are told how many staff there are to work the machine; we are given the forecasters' feelings; continual reference is made to our own (the readers') communal everyday interest in the weather; we are told how much the computer has cost (very human!); there is the tone of witty informality already discussed; the text is larded with snippets of relevant conversation; there is the overall sense of drama (and note here how facts tend to be presented, in round, dramatic figures, *eg 1 million calculations a second* (30), memory of *50,000* (69), *five times as quickly* (51)); and, in short, a general impression of great goings-on. And truly, a subject which might well have been dull for many, may now have become interesting, through the addition of these human details and sidelines.

In **II**, however, we get none of this *at all*. Instead of human details, we get research details, and the scientific and historical background; there is greater precision (*cf* **I** *half a million* (22) with **II** *a little under . . .* (179), the mention of the Meteorological Office's *headquarters* at Bracknell (89), and the important mention in **II** that this is the first time in *routine* procedure (90)); there is a concern for accuracy via the use of moderately technical terms; and the tone is restrained, one of routine reporting, aiming to present facts without drawing too dramatic a conclusion (*cf* **I** *vanished* (8) with **II** *no dramatic change . . .* (206)) – the only hint of humour is in *human or electronic* (151). It is worth pointing out that apart from mentioning the name of the machine, where it is, when it began working, and what the data are, the only other shared information in the extracts is that both mention the need for bigger computers and the time of Comet's activity (**I** one and a half hours, **II** (in the omitted portion) 70–75 minutes). There is little else semantically in common. Both extracts try to commence, in their respective ways, with a lively introduction: there is a sharp switch in style between 32 and 33 in **I**, and between 107 and 108 in **II**, the introductory sections containing shorter and less complex sentences, and relatively more vivid and dramatic information. The routine details are left till later. When **I** does get down to factual detail, indeed, its language approximates very closely to **II** – the third paragraph from the end in **I** could have been used by **II** with little change. Finally, the thought progression in **II** is not necessarily 'better' organised than **I** on account of all this, but it *is* more complex and involves a greater and more explicit degree of control: consequently, points to be discussed are listed, summaries are given, there are clear topic sentences in paragraphs (usually at the beginning); and so on. In **I** the thought progresses in jumps, with very little development of individual points being made – a technique which is invaluable for getting the gist of a story over.

It should be clear from all this how different these two types of reporting language are, despite the many points of similarity which have emerged; and these are but two texts chosen from a wide range (*cf* questions 8 and 9 below). On this basis, 'the language of newspaper reporting' is evidently a very general label which should be used with great care. There are certain linguistic features which tend to occur only in a journalistic context, but – parodies aside – it is unlikely that all or the majority of these would occur in any given newspaper report. It is better to consider 'journalese' as a range of usage which may be tapped when necessary, to a greater or lesser extent. Only in this way can one allow for the overlap of many kinds of news reporting with other varieties of English (such as scientific language), and for the introduction of a great deal of idiosyncrasy on the part of an individual journalist.

It is not a question, of course, of calling one of these articles linguistically 'better' or 'worse' than the other. We cannot use such terms except in relation to the overall aims and success of both – did the articles succeed in what their authors set out to do? The issue which every reader is faced with is first and foremost to decide how the information he has been presented with is to be interpreted, which means being aware that what he has been given is very much a *selection* of all the facts available. This may not be so important in the case of the above extracts, where the subject matter is not of world-shattering importance. But in other matters, such as politics or religion, we can see that, using similar techniques, a topic can be presented to the public in very different lights; and it is up to us to judge to what extent this colouring is obscuring the truth of a situation. There is always the danger of bias (conscious or otherwise) in any writing: the attitudes of the writer towards his subject tend to creep in. But by paying careful attention to the language vehicle he uses for these attitudes, we can take care that we are not easily fooled.

Exercises

1 The following sentences are both from the above articles (in the sections omitted). How unambiguously can they be identified with one or the other?

> Forecast pressures on contour heights at the chosen grid points can be printed out automatically at any stage.
> For Dr Mason said yesterday that his human staff had 'just about' reached the limit where their minds just couldn't absorb any more information.

2 Write a report in the style of either **I** or **II** on an event which you witnessed recently. Give it a headline, and try and bring in features which you think are consistent with each other.

3 Rewrite the first paragraph in **II** in the short paragraphs of **I** (eg the second paragraph beginning at *For the first . . .*). Discuss the effects produced.

4 What devices to produce emphasis can you find in the extracts, apart from those already mentioned? In what other ways could *By the side of the . . .* (78) have been said? Compare the effects.

5 To determine the extent of the sequence signals in extracts of newspaper reporting, select a text and cut it up into its separate paragraphs, then mix them up, and see if you can sort them out into their correct order without any difficulty. Try this with sentences within a paragraph also.

6 Collect all the cases of numbers which occur in the two extracts. Some of these are logograms (as in *500,000*), others are written in full (*seven-to-ten-hour*), and others are a mixture (*1 million*). Can you see any pattern behind the differences?

7 Subheadings exist in both extracts. Examine their relation to the body of the text, and see where the editor gets them from. What do you think their function is?

8 A typical news item is the short one-sentence report, of the type:
Three people were hurt when a fire-engine crashed into a wall at the

junction of Smith Road and Clover Street during the rush-hour yesterday.
Occasionally there will be a 'follow-up', *eg It was returning from a
false alarm* . . . Discuss the important features of this type of reporting. Look in your own daily paper, and see what variations on this
basic theme exist.

9 There is often a very obscure boundary between what is news and
what is discussion in a report. Examine a number of reports to see
to what extent this poses a descriptive problem.

Notes

1 *Cf* the comment on initial capitalisation in legal language, *p* 198.
2 *Cf* H. STRAUMANN, *Newspaper Headlines*, London, 1935. For similarities between
this and other kinds of English, see G. N. LEECH, *English in Advertising*, Longmans,
1966, *pp* 90 *ff.*

Chapter 8

The Language of Legal Documents

The law includes many different activities, from the drawing up of statutes to the contracting of agreements between individuals, all of which need to be recorded in a written form. In spite of their diversity, it is perhaps not too far from the truth to say that each of these activities is in some way connected with the imposition of obligations and the conferring of rights. And from time to time, of course, someone or other is sure to become morbidly curious about his obligations, and even scrutinise them closely to see if they may possibly be wriggled out of! Similarly, rights occasionally come in for the kind of examination that has as its main aim stretching them to a credible limit and, if possible, even further. Consequently, whoever composes a legal document must take the greatest pains to ensure that it says exactly what he wants it to say and at the same time gives no opportunities for misinterpretation. The word 'say' is important in this context, because when a document is under scrutiny in a court of law, attention will be paid only to what, as a piece of natural language, it appears actually to declare: any *intentions* of the composer which fail to emerge clearly are not usually considered in arriving at what the document means,[1] and if the composer happens to have used language which can be taken to mean something other than he intended, he has failed in his job.

But to externalise intentions in this way is not easy. Natural language being such a breeding ground for ambiguity, to communicate just one set of meanings while excluding many others is often impossible; but the lawyer must at least make the effort, and legal language has many oddities that are clear evidence of the kinds of effort that have been made.

To speak of legal language as communicating meaning is in itself rather misleading. Of all uses of language it is perhaps the least communicative, in that it is designed not so much to enlighten language-users at large as to allow one expert to register information for scrutiny by another. This is another factor which has provided opportunities for unusualness. Legal writers, pushed into oddity by their attempts to be unambiguous, are pulled as it were in the same direction by the knowledge that since their productions are for the benefit of someone as familiar with the jargon as themselves, they have no need to bother too much about the simpler needs of a general public.

But we should again be somewhat misled to think of the lawyer – or his legal draftsman for that matter – as sitting down to think up the contents of a document from scratch. Lawyers have been doing basically the same things – conveyancing property, drawing up wills, and so on – for a long time, and for each species of transaction there has developed a linguistic formula – or rather collections of such formulae – which are known to do the job adequately, having been subjected to long and thorough testing before the courts. There is a strong motivation for any lawyer to turn to a form of words that he knows he can rely on rather than take a chance on concocting something entirely new which may turn out to have unsuspected deficiencies. Therefore, much legal writing is by no means spontaneous but is copied directly from 'form books', as they are called, in which established formulae are collected. Quite apart from the question of reliability, however, there is another reason for turning to a model: the complexities of legal English are so unlike normal discourse that they are not easily generated, even by experts. It is a form of language which is about as far removed as possible from informal spontaneous conversation. It is essentially visual language, meant to be scrutinised in silence: it is, in fact, largely unspeakable at first sight, and anyone who tries to produce a spoken version is likely to have to go through a process of repeated and careful scanning in order to sort out the grammatical relationships which give the necessary clues to adequate phrasing.

The reliance on forms which were established in the past and the reluctance to take risks by adopting new and untested modes of expression contribute to the extreme linguistic conservatism of legal English. This conservatism is one reason that has led us in this chapter, as, for similar reasons we have also done in Chapter 6, which deals with religious English, to pay a certain amount of attention to history; but it seemed worth while to give some historical background so as to admit relevant information that we would otherwise have been compelled to ignore. Another reason for dabbling in linguistic history is that during the course of its development legal English has had to rub shoulders with, and sometimes give way to, both French and Latin. As a result of these contacts, it has acquired a number of distinctive characteristics, especially of the kind mentioned later in this chapter in the discussion of vocabulary.

As we said at the outset, legal language covers a wide range of activities, and like any other variety it becomes blurred at the edges and changes imperceptibly into something else – consider, for instance, the legal flavour of the excerpt of Civil Service language which we include in Chapter 9 – but we have chosen two examples that we felt to be reasonably central in a linguistic sense, and also among the most likely to be met by the average person. **I** is from an endowment assurance policy, and **II** from a hire purchase agreement.

I

Whereas a proposal to effect with the Society an assurance on the Life Insured named in the Schedule hereto has been duly made and signed as a basis of such assurance and a declaration has been made agreeing that this policy shall be subject to the Society's Registered Rules (which shall   5 be deemed to form part of this policy) to the Table of Insurance printed hereon and to the terms and conditions of the said Table and that the date of entrance stated hereon shall be deemed to be the date of this contract AND such proposal has been accepted by the Society on the conditions   10 as set forth in the proposal

NOW this policy issued by the Society on payment of the first premium stated in the Schedule hereto subject to the Registered Rules of the Society

WITNESSETH that if the Life Insured shall pay or cause to   15 be paid to the Society or to the duly authorised Agent or Collector thereof every subsequent premium at the due date thereof the funds of the Society shall on the expiration of the

term of years specified in the Schedule hereto or on the previous death of the Life Insured become and be liable to pay   20
to him/her or to his/her personal representative or next-of-
kin or assigns as the case may be the sum due and payable
hereunder in accordance with the Table of Insurance printed
hereon and the terms and conditions of the said Table
(including any sum which may have accrued by way of   25
reversionary bonus) subject to any authorised endorsement
appearing hereon and to the production of this policy
premium receipts and such other evidence of title as may be
required

IF UPON THE DEATH OF THE LIFE INSURED there   30
shall be no duly constituted personal representative or
nominee or assignee of the Life Insured able and willing to
give a valid receipt for the sum payable such sum may in the
discretion of the Committee of Management be paid to one
or more of the next-of-kin of the Life Insured whose receipt   35
shall effectually discharge the Society from all liability under
this policy

IN WITNESS WHEREOF we the Secretary and two of the
Committee of Management of the Society have hereunto
attached our signatures   40

II

7. Notwithstanding the termination of the hiring under Clause 6 the
Hirer shall pay all rent accrued due in respect of the hiring up to the date
of such termination and shall be or remain liable in respect of any damage
caused to the Owner by reason of any breach by the Hirer of any stipulation
herein contained and on the part of the Hirer to be performed or observed.   45

8. At any time before the Owner shall have recovered possession of
the goods and before the Hirer shall have terminated the hiring under
Section 4 of the Hire-Purchase Act 1938 (as amended) the Hirer may on
the payment to the Owner of the total amount of any instalments then
remaining unpaid of the rent hereinbefore reserved and agreed to be paid   50

during the term and the further sum of ten shillings purchase the goods:

Provided that such payment as aforesaid shall be a condition precedent to the exercise of the option to purchase so conferred (this agreement
not being an undertaking by the Owner to sell the goods on credit or without such payment as aforesaid being first made) and accordingly any   55
notice unaccompanied by such payment as aforesaid of an intention to
exercise the said option shall be void and shall not constitute a binding
agreement to purchase or sell the goods.

Early legal documents made few concessions to the convenience of
the reader as far as layout was concerned.[2] Their contents were usually
set down as a solid block of script whose long lines extended from
margin to margin across the parchment on which they were written,
and there were no patterns of spacing or indentation to indicate either
the sections of which a document was made up or the relationships
between them. Various reasons have been suggested for this unbroken
format, including economy in the use of parchment and an intention
to defeat fraudulent deletions (by providing no tradition for spaces)
and additions (by leaving no space into which they might be
squeezed). The part played by these and other pressures in establishing
the practice is a matter of guesswork, but there can be little doubt that
the mass of script which resulted did not make any easier the task of
deciphering a kind of language which was already specialised and,
at least for any layman who happened to be confronted by it, extremely difficult. The sentences which went to make up a document
were usually long; and in fact it was quite common for draftsmen to
compose an entire document in the form of a single sentence. When
it came to understanding these lengthy structures (lengthy in a
physical as well as a linguistic sense, since pieces of parchment might
measure a couple of feet from side to side) there was not much help
from punctuation, which, if it was not completely absent, tended to
be sketchy and haphazard.

When legal documents came to be printed, compositors, influenced
by practices that were already well established, helped to confirm the
tradition that legal language, in keeping with the 'unbroken' nature
of its grammar, should have a visual coherence interrupted as little
as possible by features that could be regarded as not forming an
essential part of the language itself. The effects of the tradition are
still to be seen in the characteristic appearance of much written legal
English. Even today, documents that have been drafted without
paragraph divisions are occasionally to be found, and long, thinly
punctuated sentences are the rule rather than the exception. But this

is not to say that legal English any longer consists of undifferentiated masses of print. In general there has been a tendency to make more and more use of layout and other graphetic and graphological devices as a means of revealing structure, content and logical progression. The beginnings of this process were evident even in the old manuscript deeds, where the occasional important word might be picked out by capitalisation, underlining or a different style of script; and gradually the potentialities of arrangement were exploited. This happened particularly with statutes, which often contain a large number of separate provisions that have both to be set out in an orderly manner and also made readily available for reference. In order to meet these needs a visual arrangement which attempted to reflect the logical progression of ideas was adopted, along with the appropriate lettering and numbering of sections and subsections, and the practice spread to include numerous kinds of business documents, of which our second extract may be taken as an example. There are, however, still many areas of legal writing – and in this instance extract **I** is typical – in which draftsmen make use of layout to reveal the structure of a document but decline to go in for lettering or numbering of the sections.

Thus legal English, at least from a graphetic and graphological point of view, has something in common with many other varieties in which clear logical sequence is essential. As in technical handbooks, collections of instructions, and much Civil Service language, blocks of print are arranged so as to reveal the sections into which the content is organised, the relationships between them, and their relative importance (*cf* sections 4 and 5 in Chapter 9). But the process often goes further than this and draftsmen are in the habit of emphasising, by visual means, a whole collection of bits and pieces considered for one reason or another to merit special attention. In extract **I**, the use of Gothic characters for the initial *Whereas*, and the capitals for the words or phrases with which all the other sections of the document begin is perhaps partly a feature of arrangement, to be compared to the use of indentation for similar purposes in **II**. Perhaps also it owes something to the decorative tradition, going back to the illustrated manuscripts of the Middle Ages, in which initial words or letters were given distinctive visual emphasis. But clearly the process is not restricted to arrangement and decoration. It is no accident, for instance, that *Witnesseth* (15), which is the main verb of the first and most important sentence, is printed in capitals; and, in line 9, although it is apparently not intended to be regarded as beginning a new section, the word *AND* is capitalised, presumably as a means of giving increased emphasis to the clause it introduces.

The contents of **I** are also spaced to show the divisions between the three sentences, which end on lines 29, 37, and 40 respectively. But in addition to this, the long first sentence is itself broken up by line spaces to make more obvious certain important subdivisions within it. The main verb, as we have already mentioned, is picked out in capitals, and it introduces the very complex predicate, which is printed as a separate block in lines 15–29. Preceding this, in lines 12–14, there is another section made up of an adverbial, *Now*, and a long nominal group which is obviously entitled to be regarded with some awe, since, as subject of *Witnesseth*, it is the subject of the main clause. And as a preamble to the meat of the sentence there is the section from lines 1–11, made up of the mass of dependent clauses, or 'recitals' as they are called by lawyers, which is introduced by *Whereas*. It can be seen from all this that the legal draftsman is prepared to call attention by graphetic and graphological means to any grammatical unit or combination of units in order to point more effectively the meaning of the whole document. The process is also at work in **II**, where the complex of conditional clauses introduced by *Provided that* (52) is separated by indentation and spacing from the first part of the sentence. As we have already mentioned, **II**, unlike **I**, uses numbers to identify its sections. Some legal instruments combine both types of layout by attaching a set of numbered provisions – often in the 'small print' that laymen never bother to read – at the end of a section which deals with the fundamental rights and obligations to which the separate provisions relate.

Both extracts contain plenty of examples of the initial capitalisation which is used to dignify certain lexical items. It seems that sometimes a principle is applied whereby capitalisation is used only for words that have been given a precise definition in a document, but where no definitions are involved, as is the case with both of our extracts, it may be difficult to see on exactly what basis some words have been chosen for capitalisation and others ignored. (Why, for instance, *Schedule* in 2, but *policy* in 4, *etc*?) Once the words have been chosen, however, the treatment of them seems to be quite consistent; and, also, a few roughly definable categories emerge. These include various personalia referred to, such as *Life Insured* (2, *etc*), *Agent or Collector* (16), *Secretary* (38), *Hirer* (42, *etc*), *Owner* (44, *etc*); parts of the document itself, or of attachments to it: *Schedule* (2, *etc*), *Registered Rules* (5), *Table of Insurance* (6), *Clause 6* (41); and what may be loosely called institutions, of one kind or another, some of which may be so close to names as to qualify for a capital in their own right: *Society* (1, *etc*), *Committee of Management* (39).

Unless parentheses are counted, extract **I** is completely unpunctuated, and the punctuation in **II** is restricted to final periods and a colon. This dearth of punctuation is perhaps one of the first things that springs to mind in connection with printed legal language, no doubt because most people at some time have experienced the difficulty of picking their way, without even the help of an occasional comma, through the already complex grammar of a lease or an insurance policy. An explanation reminiscent of that referred to earlier in relation to the lack of spaces in old documents is sometimes put forward to account for the rarity of punctuation marks. It is suggested that since they may so easily be added or deleted by anyone intent upon achieving ends less commendable than ease of reading it was felt better to do without punctuation altogether, so removing an opportunity for relatively simple forgery. The pictures conjured up make this an engaging theory; but a more likely explanation is to be found if the nature and evolution of punctuation itself are taken into account.[3] It seems that punctuation originated as a largely prosodic device or an aid to phrasing: that is, it attempted to do no more than show in a crude way the points in a piece of written language at which anyone reading it aloud ought to pause, or give some indication of a break. As such it was quite unequal to the task of revealing features of the grammatical or logical structure of written language, and remained until the eighteenth century little more than a prop to oral reading. A public performance which would necessitate accurate reading aloud, of course, was about the last thing likely to happen to those legal documents – probably the majority – whose chief function was to serve as written records, and hence the thinness of their punctuation. It is not true that legal language was always entirely punctuationless, and in fact the occasional specimens which were intended for oral presentation – proclamations, for instance – were quite fully punctuated. The idea of totally unpunctuated legal English is a later development, perhaps started by early compositors who, looking for something to guide their own rather shaky ideas in this area, consulted manuscript documents and concluded that the punctuation was so sparse and erratic that it could not have been put there intentionally in the first place. By degrees the tradition grew up that commas, periods and so on had no part to play in legal writing, and some authorities went so far as to say that when they did occur they were to be accorded no recognition in the interpretation of meaning – something that could be got only from the words themselves. This extreme point of view, however, never gained complete acceptance in the courts and the tendency nowadays is to recognise the usefulness of punctuation as a guide to grammatical structure – provided, of course, that it is used systematically. But it should be noted that only a limited range of punctuation marks is allowable in legal English, and the occurrences are few by normal standards. Extract **II** gives a reasonable idea of this, while **I** is a reminder that the tradition of non-punctuation is still operative.

If as a starting-point for looking at the grammar of legal language we take the way in which its sentences are linked together, we immediately find a point that needs to be considered, because of the implications that it has for distinctiveness. In the first place, in those documents which have been composed as one very long sentence, the question of sentence linkage does not arise – and features that would elsewhere operate as sentence connectors can be considered only for the part they play in joining together clauses. The same holds true, to a considerable extent, for most written legal language, since even in documents which are divided into sentences the sentences tend to be extremely long. It is a characteristic legal habit to conflate, by means of an array of subordinating devices, sections of language which would elsewhere be much more likely to appear as separate sentences. As a result, legal sentences are usually self-contained units which convey all the sense that has to be conveyed at any particular point and do not need to be linked closely either to what follows or to what has gone before. It seems that many types of discourse – especially conversation – prefer to convey connected information in a series of short sentences which need linking devices to show their continuity, while legal English moves in the opposite direction by putting all such sequences into the form of very complex sentences capable of standing alone. It can be argued that the process is at work in a great deal of written language – that in fact it gives rise to some of the chief distinctions between written and spoken grammar – but in legal language it goes to greater lengths than anywhere else.

The variety is remarkable for the fact that, apart from occasional introductory adverbials like, for instance, *IN WITNESS WHEREOF*

(38), almost the only formal linkage to be found between the long and self-sufficient sentences is the repetition of lexical items – and of this there is a good deal. The habit is to be expected in a variety which is so much concerned with exactness of reference. In almost all other varieties too much repetition is regarded as tiresome. It is often reduced by the use of anaphora, in which a substitute word – for instance, one of the pronouns *he*, *she*, *it* or *they* – replaces, or, to put it another way, refers back to a lexical item that would otherwise have needed repeating. Some anaphoric devices, such as forms of the verb *do*, may substitute for stretches of language larger than a single lexical item, replacing whole clauses, or sections of clauses, and some, notably the demonstratives *this* and *that*, are commonly used to refer to considerable stretches of language, perhaps comprising a number of sentences. The trouble with substitutes of this kind, however, is that they can often look as though they are referring back to an item other than that which the writer had in mind, producing ambiguities and confusions which would be of very little consequence in conversation – or even in a good deal of written language – but quite intolerable in a legal document.

Consequently, draftsmen never use anaphoric links between sentences, and are prepared to put up with the repetitiveness that results. But the matter goes further than sentence connection, and legal English is in fact notable for the extreme scarcity, even within sentence structure, of the pronoun reference and anaphora which are used so extensively in most other varieties. In the extracts, there is only one instance of reference being made by a pronoun, when *him/her*, in 21, is used to point back to *the Life Insured*. This, of course, is a case in which there is almost no possibility of confusion, although a wildly improbable interpretation might just manage to see *him/her* referring ambiguously to the *Agent or Collector* of line 16. But it is not simply that referential pronouns are avoided only where their use could raise genuine confusion; they seem to be eschewed as a species. And in environments in which even the most bizarre misreading would be unlikely to find an undesirable meaning, the lexical item is solemnly repeated, as, for instance, in 48, where there would seem to be little objection, at least on grounds of sense, to substituting *he* for *Hirer*. Perhaps the most notable omission is *it*. This is an extremely common cross-referencing item in many varieties, but in written legal language the pronoun turns up only in constructions such as *It is agreed as follows*, where in any case the *it* is perhaps best seen as a filler of the subject position rather than as a substitute for anything that might be identified as an antecedent.

Legal English contains only complete major sentences. Both the incomplete sentences which help to characterise conversation and also the minor sentences which are so notable a feature of commentary and by no means rare even in some written varieties are entirely lacking – which is not surprising, in view of the kind of context in which all legal language originates. Most of these complete sentences are in the form of statements, with no questions and only an occasional command; but the statements are very often of a characteristic type which is reflected in equally characteristic sentence structure. Reduced to a minimal formula, the great majority of legal sentences have an underlying logical structure which says something like 'if X, then Z shall be Y' or, alternatively 'if X, then Z shall do Y'. There are of course many possible variations on this basic theme, but in nearly all of them the 'if X' component is an essential: every action or requirement, from a legal point of view, is hedged around with, and even depends upon, a set of conditions which must be satisfied before anything at all can happen.[4]

In terms of sentence structure, 'if X' is most likely to be accommodated by means of adverbial clauses – very often of the kind that are sometimes called conditional or concessive – and since such clauses expound the A element in sentence structure, legal sentences are, almost without exception, complex. It is perhaps the adverbials which contribute most to the distinctive quality of the sentences. The first twenty-nine lines give a good impression of the kind of sentence structure that is common in legal documents, and the following breakdown into component elements (of which all except the shortest have been abbreviated) may provide a convenient guide to this particular example:

A *Whereas* a proposal . . . has been duly made . . .

A and a declaration has been made . . .

A AND such proposal has been accepted . . .

A NOW

S this policy . . .

P WITNESSETH

C that . . . the funds of the Society . . . shall . . . become and be liable to pay . . . the sum due . . .

This arrangement emphasises the way in which adverbials tend typically to cluster at the beginning of the sentence, although they are not confined to that position; and a quick glance at the extract will show the length and complexity of the three initial clauses, and especially of the second. Following another adverbial – the word *NOW* – comes the long nominal group which constitutes the subject, and then, introduced by the main verb *WITNESSETH*, there is the very long *that* clause which functions as complement.

In the clause structure, as in the sentence structure, there is a tendency to length and complexity. The elements s and c are very rarely expounded by pronouns, and all clauses, both finite and non-finite, are very likely to contain adverbials. It is perhaps the frequency of these adverbial elements that is the most notable feature; but almost equal in importance is the variety of positions that they adopt. Legal draftsmen take full advantage of adverbial mobility, but always as a means of clarifying meaning and avoiding ambiguity: they seldom seem to move adverbials around, as is done in some written varieties, simply as a means of achieving greater elegance of expression. The result of this primary concern with meaning is that adverbials are put in positions which seem unusual by more normal standards. In line 1, for instance, *a proposal to effect with the Society an assurance . . .* might look a little more ordinary if the order were *a proposal to effect an assurance with the Society*, but no doubt the idea is to get *with the Society* next to the verb it modifies in order to avoid a possible ambiguity. Similar examples are to be seen also in 15–17, *shall pay . . . to the Society . . . every subsequent premium*, and in 20–22, *pay to him/ her . . . the sum*. In 45, *on the part of the Hirer to be performed or observed*, reverses what would seem to be the expected order. There may be some considerations of clarity or logic at work in this particular instance, but perhaps the connection is rather with the preference that **II** seems to show, at a number of points, for the distinctive order A + participle – compare *herein contained* (45), and *hereinbefore reserved* (50), for instance, with *printed hereon* and *stated hereon*, both from **I**, which adopt the more usual sequence of participle + A.

The adverbial elements are very often coordinated: *on the expiration . . . or on the previous death . . .* (18–20); *subject to any authorised endorsement . . . and to the production . . .* (26–7); *on credit or without such payment . . .* (54–5), and so on. And it is convenient at this point to mention that coordination at all levels, and of all kinds of structures is extremely common in legal English, as may be gathered from the instances – too numerous to need exemplifying – found throughout the extracts.

One of the most striking characteristics of written legal English is that it is so highly nominal; that is, many of the features in any given stretch are operating within nominal group structure, and the long complicated nominals that result are noticeable by contrast with the verbal groups, which are relatively few, and selected from a restricted set of possibilities. There is a very marked preference for postmodification in the nominal groups, and the kind of complexity that develops is clearly seen, for instance, in the group found in 49–51, which may be broken down as follows, so as to show more clearly the relationships which hold between its component parts:

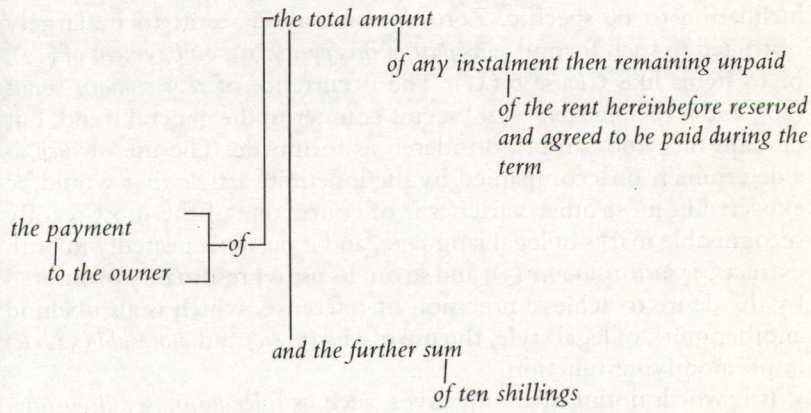

Much of the special flavour of such groups, and indeed, of legal language generally, results from a fondness for using non-finite clauses, which in many other varieties would probably be replaced by finite clauses, as postmodifiers of nominal elements: *any instalment then remaining unpaid*; the rent *hereinbefore reserved and agreed to be paid during the term.*

Another source of oddity is the insertion of postmodifying elements at precisely those points in a group at which they will most clearly give the required sense. The need to achieve precision or avoid ambiguity always takes precedence over considerations of elegance, and unusual sequences are as a result common: note, for instance, in the example above, *the payment* TO THE OWNER *of the total amount*; and *any instalments* THEN REMAINING UNPAID *of the rent.* Notice also the effect of placing *the further sum of ten shillings* at the end of the much longer construction with which it is coordinate (*ie of the total amount . . . during the term*): the tendency on reading this part of the document for the first time is to see *the further sum . . .* as being coordinated with the nominal which immediately precedes it, that is, *the term.* Several scannings are necessary, in the absence of punctuation, before the structure at this point becomes clear. This instance is typical of the way in which the concern for logical structure makes a reader's task more difficult, and that of anyone attempting to 'sight read' such passages (as in reading aloud) almost impossible.

By contrast with postmodification, premodification is restrained, although it has to be remembered that the determiner position in almost every nominal is filled, no doubt in keeping with the general inclination to be specific. Zero determination seems to be largely restricted to such formulae as *part of this policy* (6), *on payment of* (12), or to items like *Clause 6* (41). The occurrence of *reversionary bonus* (26), and *premium receipts* (28) seems counter to the general trend, but perhaps they too can be considered as formulaic. The use of *such* as a determiner, unaccompanied by the indefinite article that would be expected in most other varieties is of course one of the most readily recognisable marks of legal language, and it occurs repeatedly in both extracts, *eg such assurance* (3), and so on. Its use is presumably prompted by the desire to achieve precision of reference, which is also behind another quirk of legal style, the use of *said* (8, *etc*) and *aforesaid* (52, *etc*) in premodifying function.

It is worth noting that adjectives, such as *splendid, wise, disgusting,* and *happy* are much less frequent than in many other varieties, and that intensifying adverbs like *very* and *rather* – extremely common elsewhere – are completely absent.

Many of the nouns which are modified by the structures of pre- and postmodification that we have been discussing are themselves either 'abstract' in the narrow sense or at least are not primarily to be taken as referring to some physical object; for instance, *proposal* (1, *etc*), *declaration* (4), *conditions* (7), *termination* (41), *stipulation* (44), *possession* (46), and so on.

The verbal groups used in legal language are notable for the high proportion of non-finites and for the number of finites that are of the type *modal auxiliary* (usually *shall*) + BE + past participle. *Shall* is invariably used to express what is to be the obligatory consequence of a legal decision, and not simply as a marker of future tense, which is its main function in other varieties. Between the auxiliary and the lexical verb there is sometimes a quite remarkable degree of separation: for instance, the very long group that we used a short time ago to illustrate nominal group structure is part of a prepositional phrase which separates the auxiliary *may* (48) from its lexical verb *purchase* (51).

Verbs seem very often to be selected from one or other of a fairly small number of lexical sets which are rather difficult to define with any precision, but which are hinted at by such items, chosen at random from both extracts, as *deem, accept, require, agree, issue, state, specify, constitute, perform or observe, exercise*, and so on.

The range of vocabulary that may be met in legal language is extremely wide, since almost anything – whether a collection of objects, a set of circumstances or a network of personal relationships – may become the subject of legislation or legal tabulation in some way or other; and a statute regulating the importation of sheep and pigs will obviously differ greatly from a mortgage deed. But lawyers have developed marked preferences in their choice of words, and some very clear characteristics emerge. It is especially noticeable that any passage of legal English is usually well studded with archaic words and phrases of a kind that could be used by no one else but lawyers. It seems likely that these words give the man in the street his most reliable guide for identifying the language of a legal document. They may be less immediately obvious, from a visual point of view, than the graphetic and graphological devices we have mentioned, but most people, when asked to imitate or parody the language of lawyers, will probably not get very far before throwing in a 'witnesseth' and adding a sprinkling of 'aforesaids' and 'hereinbefores'. The first of these – *witnesseth* (15) – is interesting in that it shows the preservation of an -*eth* ending for the third person singular present tense form of the verb. The usage is quite isolated: it seems that lawyers are attached to *witnesseth* simply as a matter of tradition; *witnesses* would be a perfectly acceptable alternative. Elsewhere, the modern ending is used, and something like *hath been duly made* (*cf* 3) would be just as unusual in a legal document as in English generally. This state of affairs contrasts with some varieties of religious English, where the -*eth* form is used consistently in place of its modern equivalent. Both of our extracts hint at the frequency and variety of those words which consist of an adverbial word or place to which a preposition-like word has been suffixed: *hereto* (2, *etc*), *hereon* (7, *etc*), *hereunder* (23), *hereunto*

(39), *herein* (45), *hereinbefore* (50), *thereof* (17), and *whereof* (38). All these are useful for the kind of precise references – especially to the document or its parts, and to the contracting parties – which lawyers find it so necessary to make; but again it seems possible to see in the almost ritualistic repetitiveness more than a little reverence for tradition.

Archaisms nearly always seem to add a touch of formality to the language in which they occur, and in this respect those found in legal documents complement the extremely large proportion of words which, even though in current use, seem highly formal in their effect. *Duly* (3, *etc*), *deemed* (6, *etc*), *expiration* (18), and *terminated* (47) are just a few that may be taken as representative. If collocations are taken account of, in addition to separate words, then of course the tendency becomes even more noticeable, and combinations such as *term of years* (19), *upon the death of* (30), and so on, show a degree of formality that none of the constituents possesses in isolation.

Some of the most characteristic collocations are those in which synonyms, or near-synonyms, are coordinated, sometimes in quite extensive lists, but more usually in pairs: *made and signed* (3), *terms and conditions* (7), *able and willing* (32). Draftsmen got into the habit of using these pairs at a time when there were in the language both native English and borrowed French terms for the same referent. In this situation there was often a certain amount of doubt as to whether such 'synonyms' meant exactly the same thing, and there developed a tendency to write in each alternative and rely on inclusiveness as a compensation for lack of precision. The result was the large number of couplings of the 'breaking and entering' and 'goods and chattels' type 'in which an English word is complemented by its French equivalent.

As we mentioned earlier in this chapter, the French element in legal vocabulary is of course extremely large – a consequence of the wealth of French legal terminology that was conveniently borrowable after the Conquest. Some impression of this may be gained by looking at the words contained in the opening lines of **I**. If we ignore the words used primarily to signal grammatical relationships, which are mainly descended direct from Old English, we find that *proposal, effect, society, assurance, insured, schedule, duly, signed, agreeing, policy, subject, rules, form, terms, conditions, date, entrance, contract*, and *accepted* are all from French, and *printed* may be from the same source. Nearly all the French originals derive of course from Latin; but in legal English there is in addition a large number of terms which have come directly from Latin. The first few lines of **I**, taken again as a source of examples, give the direct borrowings *basis* and *table*, and also *declaration, registered, stated,* and *part,* which have various types and degrees of direct connection with Latin. This leaves us with only *life, named, made, deemed,* and *said* as representatives of Old English: a similarly high proportion of Romance to Germanic words would probably be found in most specimens of legal English, and would be equalled by only a few other varieties.

All the words we have been discussing, whatever their origins, became English words when they were adopted into the language, and many of them are in general use; but there is still a relatively small collection of both French and Latin legal terms which have lingered on in their original forms, even though their pronunciation has been modified to suit native habits, from the days when legal business was carried on in these languages. These words and phrases of Law French and Law Latin, respectively, have never become 'naturalised' in the manner of other loan-words. They are used much less frequently than was once the custom, but quite a number of those that still survive play an important role as technical terms and so constitute an active and highly distinctive part of the legal vocabulary. Law French includes such items as *estoppel, fee simple, laches,* and *quash,* and among the terms of Law Latin are *alias, amicus curiae, nolle prosequi,* and *res judicata.* Locutions of this kind have remained largely the property of lawyers, but a few (*cf quash* and *alias* above) have made their way into everyday use.

Many of the words that have been used for illustration in the course of this section belong to the technical vocabulary that the law, in common with all other specialist occupations, has built up for itself. Just as cricketers need their *off cutters* and *backward short legs* to cope with the difficult business of being specific about niceties on the field, so lawyers find it convenient to have at their disposal terms which will be immediately and economically meaningful to anyone acquainted with them. There is a tremendous amount of stylistic information to be gained from a knowledge of what words are used as technicalities in any given area of language. This is true, in a very obvious sense, of words which are unique to a variety: the great stylistic importance of *hereon* or *tort* is that they positively identify any specimen of language in which they occur as having been produced by some sort of legal situation – even if it was only someone being funny about the linguistic peculiarities of lawyers. It is also true of those common words which a province takes over and converts into technical terms by using them in a special way – often by allowing them to keep only one of a range of meanings they may have elsewhere. There are plenty of these in both extracts: *proposal* (1, *etc*), *life* (2, *etc*), *provided* (52), and so on. The same effect may also come about by the reverse process, as it were, when, as with *liable* (20, *etc*), a technicality is allowed to slip out into general use, widening its range of meanings in the process, but kept strictly to heel within the discipline concerned.

It is usual to regard as technical terms only those words which appear to have a very precise reference, and often what are believed to be less exact items are classified under such headings as 'argot', 'slang', 'cant', and 'jargon'. But 'exactness' of meaning is a tricky thing to calculate, and since this kind of classification tends to bring in value judgments as well it is probably best avoided for stylistic purposes, where the points at issue are whether a word is unique to a province, or, if not unique, whether it is used there in a special way. This makes it unnecessary to deal with the awkward problem of exactness of meaning, and allows both the words which are confined to a certain variety and those which adopt in it a meaning which is different from or very much narrower than normal to be lumped together as being 'variety-specific' – that is, they give an observer clues for confident statements about the origin of any passage in which he finds them.

Even though there is no stylistic information to be got directly from a knowledge of the exactness or otherwise of items of vocabulary used in a variety, in legal language this question of precision is worth considering simply because it is one about which lawyers have always been deeply concerned and often highly articulate. The technical terminology or special vocabulary of the law is remarkable not for the fact that it contains a mixture of words, some with exact and some with less exact meanings, but because in many instances the degree of exactness is the subject of a kind of tacit agreement between lawyers. This is especially noteworthy in the case of what are known in the trade as 'terms of art'. Terms of art are those words and phrases about whose meaning lawyers have decided there can be no argument. Their application within different legal contexts may be disputed, but when terms like *tort*, which we mentioned above, are used, lawyers are quite certain what is meant. And so they are about many other terms which, unlike *tort*, put in an appearance in everyday usage: *alibi*, *appeal*, *bail*, *defendant*, *landlord*, *plaintiff*, and *prayer* all mean something far more precise in law then they do to those men in the street who ever get round to using them. There is no consolidated list of such terms. Many of them have achieved their status through legislation, in which terms that were presumably rather too evasive for comfort have been pegged down in some statute or other. Many more may be pointed to in the written records of judgments, where successive opinions have whittled down possibilities of interpretation. But a large number seem to owe their exactitude to some function of the collective unconscious of the legal profession by which all lawyers – or at least all expert lawyers – can sense the sharpness of the words available to them. They can, it seems, sense bluntness too. Much of their special vocabulary, without being vague, lacks the precision of terms of art, and is accordingly handled by them in a different way and for different purposes. Thus, while *liable* (20, 43) means the same thing to all lawyers, words like *valid* (33) and *damage* (43) are not exact enough to qualify as terms of art. And then there are many words and phrases which are useful in law simply because they are so general. Lawyers are not exclusively devoted to the pursuit of precision, and on the frequent occasions on which some part of a document needs to leave room for the meaning to stretch a little, then in will come terms like *adequate*, *and/or*, *due care*, *intention*, and *malice*; but here, of course, in many instances such items are in no way distinctive of legal language, having the range of meaning and kind of distribution that characterise them in general use.

As we have said earlier, a knowledge of the narrowness or breadth of meaning in individual lexical items provides us with little stylistic information. It is possible, however, that the pressures to be precise or vague, in a purely terminological way, are stronger in law than almost anywhere else and will vary quite distinctly according to types of document and situation, and even according to the sections of a document and the stages of a situation. If this is so, there will be corresponding fluctuations in the kind of term selected. Lawyers are not only conscious of the necessity for precision and the benefits of judicious vagueness: they are also aware, perhaps uniquely, of the potentialities their trade lexicon gives them for securing these qualities. Any adequate lexico-semantic treatment of legal language would have to take account of this linguistic consciousness, and attempt to assess its consequences on the distribution of specialist vocabulary.

But the concern with meaning affects more than the choice of terminology. Lawyers know that anything they write, and much of what they say, is likely to be examined with an acuity that is seldom focused on other forms of language. It is as if the products of their linguistic activity become objects to be dissected and probed – often in a purely destructive way. Consequently, much care is called for in the construction of these 'objects'. When so much depends on the results of interpretation, the lawyer must go to great lengths to ensure that a document says exactly what he wants it to say, that it is precise or vague in just the right parts and just the right proportions, and that it contains nothing that will allow a hostile interpreter to find in it a meaning different from that intended.

It is impossible to read any line of the extracts without getting an impression of the care with which words and constructions have been manipulated to produce the effect that the drafter wanted. To develop this point, we shall take a closer look at the opening paragraph of **II**, a convenient passage from which to illustrate. Here we see the habit of making absolutely clear who or what is being referred to by repeating the noun in question rather than allowing in pronouns with their hint of vagueness. *Termination*, *hiring*, and *Hirer* all get this treatment. There are the characteristic coordinations – in this case with *or* – by which opportunities for misinterpretation are reduced. The hirer *shall be or remain* liable: presumably this is to call attention to the continuation of any liabilities incurred already, and to avoid the risk that *shall be*, if unaccompanied by *remain*, might be taken as implying futurity and allow the interpretation that the hirer's responsibilities start only after he has terminated the agreement. Similarly, by *performed or observed* the hirer is expected not only to have done certain things, but to have kept to provisions that did not involve *doing* things in a physical sense at all. These are devices for ensuring precision, but it is interesting that nearly all the precision is aimed at the hirer, while the owner tends to get the benefits of any vaguenesses that are going. Note that the hirer is *liable* – a term already mentioned as being extremely exact in meaning – but liable in respect of *damage* – which is a term we used to exemplify flexibility. And not just damage, but *any* damage, caused by *any breach* of *any stipulation*! It would be difficult to be more inclusive than that, and such calculated imprecision is obviously an important component of the meaning of the document as a whole.

It is because this concern with meaning is so constant and inescapable in legal contexts that the semantic aspect of legal language is in many ways the most important for stylistic study. Fréquent stylistic insights are to be gained at this level for the simple reason that so many of the most distinctive variety markers to be observed at the other levels clearly relate directly to the lawyer's attempts to meet the demands imposed on him by the special brand of meaning he is called on to produce. There are, for instance, the features of layout by which attention is directed towards parts of a document which are crucial to meaning; then there are grammatical characteristics such as the chain-like nature of some of the constructions, and the restriction on the use of pronouns, both of which are connected with the need to avoid ambiguity; and in vocabulary there is the studied interplay of precise with flexible terminology.

Similarly, a number of the more general characteristics of legal language – those which arise from the interaction of features and contribute to its special stylistic 'flavour' – are products of the semantic framework that lawyers have always had to work in. The most notable of these is the extreme conservatism of the variety: its preservation at all levels of forms which have long since been abandoned elsewhere. Some of this no doubt stems from the ceremonial element in legal contexts; and perhaps some deliberate archaisms begin to lose their linguistic character and become features comparable to the extra-linguistic realia which are usually involved in the performance of ceremonies of any kind: *hereons* become directly equatable with wigs, as it were. But most of the conservatism is nothing more than reliance on forms of language that have proved effective in achieving certain objects. The principle is that what has been tested and found adequate is best not altered. It is for this reason that lawyers turn to some form of precedent before going into print themselves; and however repugnant they may find many of the linguistic complexities they require their clerks to copy out they are reluctant to alter formulae which have always been known to work before. Lawyers subscribe more than most people to the beliefs that it is impossible to alter form without in some way changing content.

In spite of this conservatism, however, legal language has changed, even if slowly. Some of the changes have resulted from changes in the fashion of drafting documents, but many others have followed changes in the law itself. Nowadays points may be found in legal documents at which the language is considerably simpler than was once the case, perhaps allowing a single term to stand in place of a whole string of synonyms, or a simple phrase to indicate a series of legal operations that once needed several lines to set out in full. Very often such economies have been made possible by provisions in statutes to say that the shortened version is legally acceptable and that lawyers will no longer run the risks they may have incurred formerly by failing to repeat the rigmarole in full. This points to another characteristic of legal language that sets it apart from most varieties: it is a form of language that must always behave in conformity with the body of rules – the law – of which it is the vehicle. Certain things must be said in certain ways for fear of seeming to misrepresent the law, and before they may be said differently the law itself must often consent.

Faced with such a series of constraints – the need to avoid ambiguity, to be precise or vague in just the right way, to evade the possibilities of misinterpretation and to conform to the linguistic dictates of the law – lawyers, as we said, became and have remained in their use of language, cautious, conservative, ingenious, and self-aware. There are on record many of the wrangles into which they enter over particularly knotty points of meaning and interpretation. No other section of the community can ever have been concerned so agonisingly about the possibilities raised by the form *and/or*, or the precise nature of what permutations of meaning are allowable among a string of adjectives, joined by *and*, which premodify the same nominal head.[5] There have even grown up a number of semantic principles which are well known to lawyers, and to which they are careful to subscribe when arranging information. Amongst these are the *ejusdem generis* principle, by which general words which follow specific words are taken to apply only to persons or things of the same class as already mentioned, so that in 'house, office, room, or other place' the final item is not allowed to refer to an uncovered enclosure, even though this may be a 'place'. Complementing this is the principle of *expressio unius est exclusio alterius*, which ensures that if a list of specific words is not followed by a general term, then the provisions being made apply only to the things mentioned, all other things being implicitly excluded. Then there is the *noscitur sociis* principle, which asserts the importance of allowing the verbal context in which any word appears to enter into the definition of its meaning. Perhaps the most important of all these rules is the Golden Rule of interpretation. This rule states that whatever the intention behind a legal document, when it is being interpreted 'the grammatical and ordinary sense of the words is to be adhered to unless that would lead to some absurdity or some repugnance or inconsistency with the rest of the instrument, in which case the grammatical and ordinary sense of the words may be modified so as to avoid that absurdity and inconsistency, but no further'.[6] Whatever the status such principles might have in any linguistically-orientated semantic theory, the fact that they are widely recognised by lawyers means that a full treatment of legal semantics would have to take them into account, and identify the effects they may have on the semantic structure of legal documents.

Exercises

1 (a) Punctuate extract **I** and add any extra punctuation to **II** that you consider necessary. Some of your insertions would no doubt be obligatory by normal standards of punctuation; others would be optional – perhaps of the kind that is sometimes regarded as an aid to 'phrasing'. How far is it possible to distinguish the two? (You may find a good deal of enlightenment on this point by trying the next part of this question.)

(b) Using the system of notation explained in Chapter 2, write out a version of each extract which shows one of the ways in which it could be read aloud. Relate each of the punctuation features you added under (a) to the corresponding phonological feature or features you now suggest.

2 Attempt to replace some of the archaic and highly formal vocabulary with more modern, less formal substitutes. Note the kind of difficulties you run into, and any consequential changes you are forced to make. (You might also try reshaping some of the grammatical constructions along similar lines.)

3 Note any points in the extracts where a certain amount of ambiguity remains, in spite of efforts that have been made to avoid it. Do the same with a few passages of similar length chosen from some other varieties of written English and compare the results.

4 Precision and freedom from ambiguity are aims of legal language that may conflict with the aims of simplicity and intelligibility. Suggest ways of minimising the conflict, and also the priorities you think should be applied when conflict is unavoidable.

5 Mention was made in this chapter of the fact that legal English has changed considerably in the course of time. What further changes would you advocate?

6 Let us assume that your local authority wants to stop parking in the main street during busy periods, but does not wish to prevent wholesalers delivering goods to the shops by such a ban. Attempt a draft of a by-law that will achieve these objectives with clarity and precision, and ask a friend to try and find flaws in it.

7 The following royal warrant has a number of similarities to legal English. There are also some important differences. Try to identify both the similarities and the differences.

ELIZABETH R.

ELIZABETH THE SECOND, *by the Grace of God of the United Kingdom of Great Britain and Northern Ireland and of Our other Realms and Territories* QUEEN, *Head of the Commonwealth, Defender of the Faith, to Our Trusty and Well-beloved Graham Malcolm Wilson, Esquire,*

Greeting!

WHEREAS *by Warrant under the Royal Sign Manual bearing the date the sixth day of August, 1965, We appointed a Commission, to be called the Royal Commission on Medical Education:*

NOW KNOW YE *that We, reposing great trust and confidence in your knowledge and ability do by these Presents appoint you the said Graham Malcolm Wilson, to be a member of the said Commission, in the room of Our Trusty and Well-beloved John Rupert Squire, Esquire, deceased.*

Given at Our Court at Saint James's the fifth day of April, 1966.
In the Fifteenth Year of our Reign.

By Her Majesty's Command.

Notes

1 For the exceptions to this rule, see what is said about interpretation when we deal with semantics, p 215.

2 Cf E. L. PIESSE and J. GILCHRIST SMITH, *The Elements of Drafting*, Stevens and Sons, 3rd edn, 1965, pp 23 ff.

3 For a fuller treatment of the history of legal punctuation, and the ways in which both usage and attitudes have changed, see D. MELLINKOFF, *The Language of the Law*, Little, Brown and Co, 1963, especially pp 152 ff.

4 Lawyers have long been concerned about what is called 'the legal sentence'. In 1843, George Coode wrote a memorandum 'On Legislative Expression' in which he came to the conclusion that legal sentences in statutes consisted of four parts, which he listed as follows (implying by his ordering that this was the best possible arrangement):

'1. the *case* or circumstances with respect to which or the occasion on which the sentence is to take effect;

2. the *condition*, what is to be done to make the sentence operative;

3. the *legal subject*, the person enabled or commanded to act; and

4. the *legal action*, that which the subject is enabled or commanded to do.'

(Cited by E. L. PIESSE and J. GILCHRIST SMITH, *op cit, pp* 13–14.)

It is clear that Coode was thinking mainly of the logical rather than the grammatical structure of the sentences with which he was concerned, and there is of course no necessary one-to-one relationship between his four parts and any one set of grammatical divisions; but there are nevertheless likely to be far-reaching effects on the syntax used by anyone who has to conform to the constraints imposed by some such logical or semantic framework.

5 For instance, in one case 'charitable and benevolent institutions' was declared to mean 'institutions that are both charitable and benevolent', while in another it was decided that 'religious, charitable and philanthropic objects' could refer to (a) religious objects only, or (b) charitable objects only, or (c) philanthropic objects only, or (d) objects that are religious and charitable and philanthropic. (Cited in E. L. PIESSE and J. GILCHRIST SMITH, *op cit, pp* 69–71.)

6 LORD MACMILLAN, 'Law and Language', in *Voices in Court*, ed W. H. DAVENPORT, Macmillan Co, 1958, *p* 115.

Chapter 9

Suggestions for Further Analysis

We hope that Chapters 4 to 8 have illustrated our analytic procedure sufficiently to allow others to make use of it. However, there still remains one other area of practical difficulty, which the present chapter tries to anticipate, namely, the problem of selecting and obtaining useful material – particularly of a spoken kind – on which to practise further analysis. We have therefore brought together in the following pages a selection of spoken and written texts representing distinctive kinds of English not so far discussed in this book. The selection by no means displays the complete range of varieties available, but it should give a clearer picture of the kinds of difference and distinctiveness which exist. We have preceded each text by a few introductory notes, intended as a perspective and guide for analysis; the questions by no means cover all that is of interest in a text, but simply indicate some important points that we feel ought to be considered in carrying out an analysis.

1 THE LANGUAGE OF TELEVISION ADVERTISING

This is a kind of English which is becoming more and more familiar these days, and an attempt at a linguistic description has already been made (in different terms from those outlined in this book): see G. Leech's book in this series, *English in Advertising*. We may examine this use of language in the first instance without reference to its visual correlates on the screen, as there is a great deal which is formally distinctive in the phonetics, phonology, grammar, and vocabulary. (A full statement of the semantics would not of course be possible without visual information.) But one ought to bear in mind the implications of placing all of this kind of language in a visual context – to what extent is linguistic continuity affected by visual linkage? (Consider the types of sentence used, and the system of pause, in particular.) Television advertising language is written language being recited, often by professional actors, but in any case after a great deal of rehearsal. What effect does this have on the language? Leech's book concentrates almost exclusively on a description of the grammar and vocabulary of this kind of English: to what extent do you feel, from examining the texts below, that the dominant area of stylistic distinctiveness is in fact the non-segmental phonology? To what extent do different kinds of advertisement correlate with different types of presentation (for example, using specific sets of non-segmental features, or certain types of adjective or sentence? Also listen for specific kinds of voice quality and regional dialect used in advertisements – though these are not indicated in the transcription below). On the other hand, what have all these texts got in common? Finally, what differentiates this kind of advertising from the press advertising described below? (Consider, for example, whether there are phonetic and phonological correlates here for everything that is of graphetic and graphological importance in press advertising, and *vice versa*, and whether there is as much deviation from linguistic norms.)

I

'creak'	|fresh as a 'brēēze through '⌄ʙʟòssom|' –
	|ʟèмon 'blossom| – |nēw̄ · ↑lemon
'breathy'	'bouQuèт|' – |nèw| '|lighter' ғʀàgrance|
'breathy'	in your |body mist sPRÀY| – |ₕ"sPRÀY| ·
'breathy'	|spray on nēw̄ '↑tangy' ↓ғʀÈsнness| – –
'lento low creak'	'ef|ғɛ̄cтive 'freshness| 'that |lasts
	and ʟàsтs|' – |ₕbody mist de↓òdorant| ·
'breathy'	|now in ↑two 'ex'citing' ↓ғʀàgrances| –
'narrow'	'|new ↑lemon bou'quet in the ↑ʏɛ̄ʟʟow
	'pack|' – |perfume you кnòw| in 'the
'low tense'	|màuve 'pack| – – '|"bòdy mist|'

II

'breathy'	|it will ↑нàppen| |ány dày ' 'now|' –
'breathy'	you'll |be 'on 'нòʟiday|' – |yóu| · |and

'alleg' "low"   ⁺your HÀIR| – – – |YÔU 'know| · ' "you've
|used ↑SÉA 'witch|" – but you |don't
let ↑ÒN|' – – you |don't let ↗ÒN| that
you've |NÒticed| – that |THÊY have

'alleg'   'noticed| 'that there is |something
a↑"BÒUT you this 'summer|' – which |wasn't

'piano'   there be↗FÔRE| – – '|SÈA 'witch|' – – it's
su|PPŎSED to be| · |just a ↑HÀIR

'piano'   'colourant| – – 'but |WHÓ KNÒWS|' –

'lento' 'forte   '|S̄ĒA 'witch|' – – – 'there are |FÓURteen
tense'   ↙SHÀDES| "at ⁺your |CHÈMist|" – |"ŎNE| ·

"alleg"   is for |"YÒU|'

III

'lento' "husky"   at the |ₕend of a '↗s̲pecially "'hard" DÀY|'

'lentiss'   – – – |ₕyou desÉRVE| a '|lon͞g hot̄ "↗sòna|" '
"breathy" |tonic ↓BÀTH| · 'it |ᵢ"does you the
"WÒRLD of 'good| – – |ₕwhen you've been
'working HÀRD| – a |lon͞g hot̄ ↗sòna|
|tonic ↓BÀTH| – |you de↗SÈRVE it|

IV

|after ↑forty YÉARS| of |medical re↙SÉARCH|

'narrow'   you |"still 'cannot BÚY| a more ef|fective
↑PÀIN relÍEver| · than the |active
⁺in 'GRÉdient|' ⁺in ⁺this̄ · |ᵢÀspro
'tablet| – but |ₕNÓW| · its |form has
been ↙CHÀNGED| in |"NÈW| |MÌcrofined
'aspro| – |ₕmicrofined ↙MÈANS| · that

'low' 'high'
"alleg"

'low spiky´'

'breathy' 'low'

'forte'
'cresc'

'low piano'

the |ₙạspro in↓GRÈdient| has been
|ₙsuper ↓PÒwdered| a|'bout' · ' ' "↑thirty
times| ↓finer than be↑FÒRE| " – |₁some
↓one hundred and ↑fifty ↑↑MÌLLion| of
|₁these ↑microfined ↑ₙPÁRTicles| –
'go |into each' ↑TÀBlet| – |ₙWHÝ| –
·|"no PÀIN re'liever| can be|"gin to ₙWÓRK|
'until 'it |gets into the ↓BLÒODstream| –
the |ₙstomach ↓WÀLL| is an ab|sorption
'↓BÀRRier|' – be|'cause' ↑new aspro is
↑M̄Ĭcrofinedǀǀ· it |spreads its ↑pain
relieving PÓWER| |more QÙICKly|
through the ab|sorption ↑ₙBÁRRier| ·
and |"concentrates it in the ↓BLŌODstream| ·
|₁ready with re↓LÌEF| – '|new ÀSpro| –
|M̄Ĭcrofined|' 'to |beat the ab↑sorption
↓barrier ↑FÀSTer|'

V

|only ↑HÒOver| |gets out ↑GRÌT| |like
↑THÌS| – 'be|cause ↑only HÓOver| |has
this ↑built in ↓CÀRpet 'beater|' ·
|only ↑HÒOver| |gets out ↑DÚST| –
|"FLÚFF| – |"ĂND| |damaging ↓GRÌT| – –
and |here's the ↑PRÔOF| – |see how
'dust and FLÚFF| |float 'on TÒP| ·
|while the ↑GRÌT 'sinks to the BÓTTom| –
there's |grit like ↑that in ↑"YÒUR 'carpet
[|NÒW]| – |unless ↑YÒU'VE GÓT| a |ₙHÒOver|
– |ₙHÒOver| – with the |built in
↓CÀRpet beater|

VI

|"ȯʀdinary ↓DÚSTɪng| |doesn't re↑MȮVE|
|sticky ↓MÀRKS| – |now ↑"PLÈDGE| – –

'high' |ₕturns your ↓duster ↑ₙɪ̀Nto| – – 'a
|MÀGnet|' for |d̪ust and MÀRKS| – with
|PLÈDGE| · |just a "WĬPE| |picks up
↑ₙDÚST| and |sticky MÀRKS| – |leaves a
↑reaꞀ 'wax sHÌNE| · |"ɪ̈Nstantly| – |ₕso
when ↑"you DÙST| – |turn your ↓duster
↑ɪ̀Nto| a |"MÀGnet| for |dust and MÀRKS| ·
|"with ↑"PLÈDGE| – |worth ↑"È̄Ʋery "penny| ·

'gliss''   be|cause it ↑CLÉANS| · '|and' ↑sHĬNES| ·
|as you ↑DÙST| – |"PLÈDGE| · |₁from
↑"JȮHNsons|

2 THE LANGUAGE OF PRESS ADVERTISING

This covers a very wide area, though usually the notion of 'advertising' is identified by reference to commercial consumer advertising
only. Advertisements are easy to get hold of, consequently we have
illustrated only a few here, to indicate something of the range which
would be covered by the term. Is there a linguistic case for taking the
kind of advertisement shown in **I** as separate from all other written
advertising? Do you think it is likely that all commercial advertisements have certain features in common: is it the case, for example,
that an advertisement is always set in more than one kind of type? In
order to examine the possibilities, compare the kind of advertisement
appearing in, say, *The Times, The Daily Mirror*, a woman's magazine,
and a specialist journal. Is it true to say that the intention of advertising
is not so much to please the eye as to catch it? What linguistic features
affect this issue? What linguistic devices do advertising men use to
get you to remember their product? How do they praise their
products? Advertising needs both to inform and to persuade: is there
a clear distinction in the language between these functions? Categorise
and discuss the kinds of deviation from normal usage which occur;
for example, graphological (as in *Beanz Meanz Heinz*, or in such

I

COLLIER ROW, Romford. S/d. Nash hse. 3 beds., lnge., kit./diner. Gge., own dr. Fhld. £4650 o.n.o. LON 5074/Billericay 394 evgs.

CUCKFIELD, SUSSEX. A rare opportunity to buy a period farmhouse of character. Recently modernised. Leaded light windows, oak doors, etc. 3 beds., 3 recs. Gge. Gdns. £6975 Freehold. Adjoining paddock and outbuildings also available. LETTS BROS., 340 RICHMOND-RD., E. TWICKENHAM. POP 9032.

...   ...

KNIGHTSBRIDGE ESTATES, 10 Beaucham-place, S.W.3. KNI 9779 & KEN 0608. Unfurn. Prince of Wales-drive, S.W.11. 1st fl. 2 rec. 3 bed., k. & b. 6½ yrs. £515 inc. Furn. Lansdowne-cres., W.11. Gdn flat, c.h., c.h.w. 1 rec., k. & b. 20 gns. p.w. Also 1st fl. flat, c.h., c.h.w. 1 rec., k. & b. 15 gns. p.w. Furn. Kensington, S.W.7. 4th fl., c.h., c.h.w., ptge. 4 bed., 2 rec., k. & b. 45 gns. p.w.

LEINSTER TOWERS. De luxe service apartments. Phone AMB 4591.

LUX, furn. flat, Kensington. 60 gns. p.w. Cooper, Sibson. PAD 0727

MARYLEBONE HIGH-ST. Sgle. mod. furn. b-sit., ckr. unit. Tel. £5 10s. p.w. BIS 8172.

MAYFAIR Bond-st. Furn. house. 2 bdrms., recep. 20 gns. p.w. KNI 7552 bef. 6 p.m.

II

CAN'T SLEEP?

Could it be your after-dinner coffee that keeps you awake at night? Perhaps you are one of those people who simply can't take coffee in the evening, because the caffeine in it stimulates your mind and nerves. Coffee containing caffeine *does* make some people restless, just when they want to feel relaxed. So, before you rush to the doctor for "something to make you sleep," change over to H.A.G. Caffeine-free Coffee—blended and roasted to perfection for the supreme pleasure that drinking good coffee gives, but *without the after effects.* H.A.G. is the coffee that continental people, who are such great coffee drinkers, have been taking in the evenings for over 50 years. Take your choice of H.A.G. Decaffeinated Beans, Ground Beans or Instant Coffee—enjoy Good Coffee and Good Sleep. Delicatessens, Health Food Stores and most Grocers have H.A.G. Coffee. If any difficulty send (with retailer's name) for free sample from THE A.A. SUPPLY CO. LTD., Dept. P, 31/33 Priory Park Road, London, N.W.6.

III

The absolute end
of memorable meals
CHARTREUSE

Houses Hospitals Schools

The Nation's priorities.
And the Guardian
cares about all of them.
If you do too—buy the
Guardian tomorrow

The Guardian gets to the heart of things

One of a series of advertisements issued by *The Guardian* and printed
in *The Observer* during the Autumn 1965.

V

How can you create the big impression without seeming to show off? Drive an Austin 1800. The big impression is built in.

The big impression (or if you prefer, the grand impression) isn't something you have to work at in the Austin 1800. It's a fact.

Officially, the 1800 is a five-seater. But to use up all the seating space, your passengers would have to be giants.

Ordinary-sized people don't ever have to squeeze in: the doors are so big they just drift in.

Inside, the effect is amazing. With the front seats pushed back to their fullest extent, a six-footer in the back could put on an extra six inches and still have plenty of room for his knees.

Is there a simple explanation? No. But the basis of it is the same inspired idea that won greatness for the Mini and the 1100: an engine turned sideways. Add to this front-wheel drive, Hydrolastic® Suspension, extensive sound-damping, superb fresh-air ventilation and a score of other features that have nothing to do with size, everything to do with *results*, and you have a possible world-beater.

The 1800 was acclaimed by the press from the beginning. Today it grips the public imagination as firmly as it holds the road.

Creating the big impression is a speciality of the Austin 1800. Take a test-drive and see what we mean!

brand-names as *Chilprufe*); phonological (as in the use of alliteration – *Piccadilly pack a promise*, metrical rhythm – *Drinka pinta milka day*, conversational rhythm (*cf* **V**), and so on); syntactic (*cf* such usages as *the now cigarette, They moved mountain – tamed desert – and stunned the world* (cinema advertisement), or *Why do you think we make Nuttall's Mintoes such a devilishly smooth cool creamy minty chewy round slow velvety fresh clean solid buttery taste*); and lexical/semantic (as in *happiness is egg-shaped*, the use of catch-phrases, and of metaphorical language in general). How important to this kind of English is word-play (*cf* the pun in **II**)? How would you explain the effects of such advertisements as *A small deposit secures any article* (the product being glue)? What linguistic correlates, if any, can you find to substantiate the popular accusation that advertising is 'propaganda'? Have you noticed advertising language having any (*a*) temporary, or (*b*) permanent effect on the use of language elsewhere? (Consider the usage of such coinages as *pinta*. To what extent is it significant that a BBC television news reporter, referring to a political event, recently talked of a *Stork from butter situation*?)

3 THE LANGUAGE OF PUBLIC SPEAKING

This again is a very broad label, which covers a variety of types, distinguishable partly on the basis of the occupation of the language-user, partly on the purpose of the language. We illustrate the range of uses which might be subsumed under this heading by taking our extracts from a sermon (no notes were used, though the sermon was probably rehearsed, and may have been given before), a lecture (where notes were used), a radio discussion (a spontaneous answer to a question, no notes being used), and a formal speech (which was written out in full). What influence does the written language have on the speakers' usage? These extracts clearly share certain linguistic features – what are they? (Consider in particular the part non-segmental phonological contrasts play in the success or otherwise of a public oration of any kind; also note the function of coordination, especially between sentences.) Take each extract on its own, to see to what extent it displays features not shared by the other three. **I** naturally shares many of the linguistic characteristics of the religious language described in Chapter 6 – how great an overlap is there? What evidence is there in the transcription for the so-called 'parsonical' tone of voice? What is the function of the illustrative story in a sermon? How archaic is the language (*cf p* 165)? What rhetorical devices does the preacher use? **II** represents one kind of lecturing, at the more 'academic' end of a scale (at the other end of which one would find the oratorical performances often designed to entertain rather than inform). What are the linguistic correlates of the lecturer's attempts to get his meaning across clearly? (Note the well-defined progression of ideas, and his use of paraphrase.) To what extent is the speaker trying to obtain a balance between formality and informality? **III** is an extract from a rather artificial discussion situation (the convention being that the speaker is not normally interrupted until he has finished his introductory speech). What evidence is there here of the speaker's attempt to keep the discussion at a relatively informal level? What are the linguistic correlates of the speaker's desire to persuade his listeners of the merits of his case? **IV** is one of the most formal kinds of language to be found in English: what are the indications of this? How could one tell clearly that this was written English read aloud (*cf* the pause and speed systems in particular)? Examine in detail the way in which the pitch-range system is used almost to the exclusion of other non-segmental contrasts. Compare this extract with other examples of written English read aloud, such as the broadcast news in section 7 below: identify and account for the differences.

I

'high narrow'	the '|book of the 'prophet isÁɪah| –
'high prec'	|thirtieth' '„CHÁP'ter|' – 'the
'narrow dim'	
"prec"	|fifteenth 'verse of the "CHÀP'ter|"' –
'narrow'	i'|sÁɪah|' |chapter ↑thirty 'verse
'trem' 'reson'	fif'TÈEN|' – – – in re'|"turning' and
	"RÈ̄ST| – ye |shall be sÁ̄VED| – – in
	|quietneš̄s · and in ↑cÒNfidence| –
'piano' 'alleg	shall |be your '↓STRÈNGTH|' – 'in
dimin'	re|turning and 'rest ye shall be'
'dimin trem'	'„sÁ̄VED|' in |quietness and 'in
'piano'	„cÒNfidence| – |shall be ↑your'
'pianiss' 'alleg'	'↓STRÈNGTH|' – – – '|this is a "'story
"gliss'"	of a 'man" who was in a "↑"ḫÙrry|"' –
"tense"	

'tense'	(and) who |travelled · too 'FÀST|' –
'forte'	(he was) a '|white MÁN| · |TRÉKKing|'
'dimin' 'alleg'	in a '|wild part of ÀF̄rica|' – – 'and
	he was |having TRÓuble|' · with his
'dimin'	'|af̄rican ↓CÀRRiers|' – – – |eve'ry
'tense'	now and THÉN| |they – would 'in↑sist'
	on · ↑STÔPPing| – – and |laying
'reson'	'"down' their ↓LŌADS| – and |sitting
'trem' 'tense'	DÓWN| by the '|side' of the '↓T̲RÀCK|' – – –
'alleg'	'|he was in a HÚrry| to get |ÔN| ·
	bùt' · |no ₙÁRguments| · |no ₙTHRÉATS| ·
'trem'	|no 'promises of 'rewÁRD|' would
'tense' 'trem'	in '|"duce' them to 'MŌVE|' they just
'lento' 'alleg'	'|s̄at 'there ↓SÒLidly|' – – 'but at
"reson"	"|"last" with 'great DÍFFiculty|' he
'low'	|drāgged out the ↑RÈAson '['for ↑all
	|ₙTHÌS\]|' – – – the |head 'man of the
'trem'	'carriers ex'PLÁINED| – – (that)
'reson'	they'd '|"travelled so FĀR|' and |walked
'reson'	so 'FÀST|' – – that they'd |"left their
'trem'	'↑sōuls' be↓HÌND| – – and |nōw they
'piano'	mùst – 'sit 'down and 'wait 'for
'dimin' 'tense'	↑them to' '↓catch ÙP|' – – – the '|"PÀCE|'
'tense' 'low	– had |been · ↑too 'MÙCH' – '[|FÒR
piano'	them]|' – – – |ₙWÈLL of 'course| ·
	|one would ↑not at↑TÈMPT| – – – to
'narrow'	de|fine the 'reLĀtionship|' · which
'narrow trem'	the un|tutored 'african con'CÉIVED|'
'narrow' 'dimin'	as ex'|"ÌSTing'| between '|body and
	↓SÒUL|' – – but |from this ÍNCIDENT| ·
'piano prec'	|one 'thing is 'CLÈAR|' – – |that
	↑african · HÉAD 'man| · in his |ōwn

'tense' 'trem'	''graphic' '„ìDiom|' – – was de|picting
'lento' ''narrow''	the 'con ''↑Dītion''| – – of the ''|people
''dimin''	of the 'we͞stern 'wōrld to↓DÀY|'' ' – –
'alleg' ''forte''	'he was ''|acting as un↟witting''
''narrow'' ''dimin''	in ''↟TÈRpreter|'' to a ''|''whōle' generÀtion|''
'narrow'	– – – in that |''quaint expla'NÁtion
	of 'his|' · he |LÁID| his |finger on
'tense' 'monot'	the '↟RÒOT|' – – – '(of) |many of our
'piano'	'present' – ↑TRŌubles| – – 'and
'narrow'	'mis|GÌvings|' – – |this gene'RÀtion'|
	has |travelled ↑so FÀST| – – – (that)
'tense' 'trem'	it's '|''left' its '↟s̄oul' beHÌND| – – –
	and un|less we „PА̄USE| and |wait ·
'alleg'	for our ↑s̄oul to 'catch ÙP| – – '|who
'tense'	shall 'say what' '↑''perils' and
'narrow' 'dimin'	dis'ÀSters'| · '|lie beFÒRE us|'
'alleg forte gliss''	'the |pace of 'life toDÁY| is
'alleg'	|proving' '↑''too „''MŬCH 'for us| – –
''forte''	and it's ''|time we ↟sat' DÒWN for a
	WHÍLE| and |laid asíDE| our |[„BÙRden]''
'tense'	of CÀRE| – – |took '↑STŌCK|' of our
'dimin'	'|situÀtion|' – – – |somewhere
	LŌNGfellow sÁYS| that the |sabbath
'rhythmic'	is 'like a '↟s̄tile be'tween the
''trem'' 'lento'	'fields of ''↟TŌIL|'' ' – – – '|where we
''rhythmic''	can ''↑kneel and PRĀY| and |sit'' and
''dimin'' 'piano'	''med'i↓TÀTE|'' ' – – – 'and |„HĒRE| – – –
''trem''	this |quiet 'sabbath '' MÓRNing|'' –
	in this |peaceful ↓„CHÙRCH|' – – –
	with a '|comforting SĒN͞SE|' – – that
	we are |compassed aBÒUT| · with a
'alleg'	|great cloud of „WÌTnesses| – 'who

"lax"	|through the " 'ringing 'groves" of
'tense' 'accel dimin'	ₙCHÀNGE|' · have '|steadfastly' '↓kept
'piano'	the ↓FÀITH|' – – '|here we can ↓SÌT| – –
'alleg'	and|medi↓TÀTE|' – – |always with the
'trem'	wórds| of our |lord him '↑"sèlf| at
'alleg' 'accel'	the |back of our' 'MÌND|' – – |what
'reson'	shall it '↑profit a MÀN|' – – – 'if
'alleg piano'	he |gain the 'whole' 'WōRLD|' – – –
	'and |lose his 'own ↑SÒUL|'

II

'high' "alleg"	' "well |NŌW|" · I'd |like to ↑turn' 'now
	to as↑SÈSSMENT| – and I |ₙhope you
	won't MÍND| if I |use this oppor↑TŬNity|
	to |ₙtry to give ↑some indi↓CÁtion| ·
	|of · əm – – ↑a · ↑more ↑ₙMÒDErn| –
	more |RÈcent| · ap|PRÓACH| |TÒ the
'low'	as'sessment ↓PRÓBlem| · '|thañ per↑haps
	'I my'self was 'brought · 'brought ↑ÙP
'alleg'	on|' – 'and I |WÀNT|' · |very ÀRBitrarily
	if I MÁY| to di|VÌDE this| into |THRÈE
	HÉADings| – |and to ↑ask · ɔː · ↑three · 'three
	↓QUÈStions| · as|sessment ↑"WHȲ| –
	as|sessment of ↑WHÀT| – and ↑as|sessment ·
	"HÒW| · so |this really · MÉANS| I |want
'gliss`'	to 'talk a'bout · '↑first of all' the
	↑"PÙRposes of assÉssment| what |"WHȲ we
	are as'sessing| at |"ĂLL| – ɔːm |SÈcondly|
	the |kind of ↓FÙNctions| and |processes
'rhythmic'	that are ↑"BÈing assÉssed| – '↑and

|thirdly I want to 'talk about

'alleg'   techNÌQUES| ' – 'and I shall · I

shall |have to 'go 'through THÍS| '

|FÀIRly RÁPidly| · and I |HÒPE| ·

that |if it's ↑TÒO RÁPid| you'll

'dimin'   '|pick me up ˚in 'question time

'high'   ↑ÀFTerwards| ' – – 'well |first of

all' the ↑PÙRpose of as'sessment| – – –

'high'   nòw · 'I |think' there are FÓUR|

|RÒUGHly SPÉAKing| |FÒUR PÚRpo'ses| –

'low'   ə: 'which · I |want to dis'cuss ↑very

BRÌEFly| ' – – the |ₙFÌRST 'purpose

'narrow'   of as↑'SÉssment' | · |ĭs| – |if I may

↑use a de↑RÒGatory ₙTÉRM| · |purely

ad↓MÌNistrative| · nòw · I |don't

want to 'cause any of↑FÈNCE ↓HÉRE| ·

but I |must ↓make it ↑quite ↓CLÉAR| ·

'descend'   that I |THÌNK| 'that we |HÁVE| in this

|CŌUNtry| and |elsewhere ₙSTÍLL| ' ·

|ₙmuch too MÙCH| |psychological

'narrow'   TĔSTing| · |much too much as'SÉssment' | ·

'precise'   the |purpose of '`which is' ad↓MÌNistrative|

'narrow'   – ə: and |BŶ ad↑'MÍNistrative'| I |ₙMÉAN| –

ə: the |children are ↑TÈSTed| in |order

to 'make a de↑cĭsion| · a|"bout the

↑kind of edu↑CĀtion| ˚that |they ˚should

HÀVE| – and |GĔNerally| · əm thē

as|sessments are ↑ₙDÓNE| – in |ÒRDer to

'gliss'   decÍDE| |whether 'children' ÁRE| · as

the |TÈRM now ↑ₙÍS| |suitable for

e˚du'cation in ↓SCHÒOL| – so |ÒBviously|

|these · ↑ₙCHÍLdren| · whose · in|TÈLLigence

is in ↗QUÉStion| · as to |whether they

↑should · ↙GÓ| · to thē · ə |MÀINstream

of edu↗CÁtion| which in|CLÙDES of 'course|

'low narrow'   '|schools for the e s ↗Ń|'[1] · or |whether

they should 'go to ↗junior ↑TRÀINing

CÉNtres| · and |be deCLĀRED| |unsuitable

'alleg'   for educÀtion| 'it |used to be ↗called

in↑ĚDucable|' · but |now we 'use this

deli de↑licious ↗EŬPHemism| ·

'accel'   '|un|suitable for edu↗cation at ↗SCHǑOL|

"breathy"   and |everyone's busily "↑"PÀTTing"

themselves on the 'back| a'bout'

'alleg' |HÓW en↑LÌGHTened we 'are| – 'it

makes |very little 'difference to the

'low'   ↗PÀrents' 'it 'seems to 'me|' – –

III

you |can't have in↗formed O↗PÌNion| ·

|on this ↑VÌtal MÁTTer| · with|out

being kept ↑VÈRy much up to DÁTE| ·

'narrow'   with the |LÁtest FÀCTS [of de|'FÈNCE']| –

now |what "ÌS WRÓNG| with a |coalition

GÒVernment| – of |course you ↑"NÈED a

coalition GÓVernment| in |time of

CRÍsis| – but the |dreadful "PÀRT of

a 'coalition 'government you ↗KNÓW| ·

'high gliss''   is that to |'keep it' a"LÍVE| · you

|have to go in for ↑one ₙCÓMpromise|

'lento dimin   '|after aNÒTHer|' – you |have you see

precise'   'people ↗sitting RÓUND| the |CÁBinet

'room| · with |different ↙VÍEWS| · and

[1] Educationally sub-normal.

	un|less there ↓can be a ↑shifting of
	opínion| · to|wards ↑some ↑fòrm of
'accel'	cómpromise| 'be|tween those ↓different
	↑víews|' · the |coalition 'government
	fálls| · and |we be'come · a'nother
'rall'	frànce| – 'now |I ↑dò belíeve| that the
"narrow"	|whole quèstion [of de|" fènce "]| – 'the
'lento'	|whole 'question of a ↓stand upon
	'summit tàlks| · the |whole re'action
	as to ↓whether 'britain ought to ↓take
	a ↓lèad| in this |question of the h̄
'high'	bomb|' – 'as to |whether we 'ought to –
"forte" 'alleg'	"↓have that ↑"mòral|" ' · '|léadership|
'high'	and |give that ↑moral exámple|' · '|by
	↑saying ↑"nòt|' · we |unilaterally ·
	↓disàrm| – |that 'I've "néver 'said| ·
	and |that many 'members of my ↓own
	↑párty| · |"mòst 'members of my ↓own
'piano'	↑párty| '|have ↑never belìeved in|' –
	|what we ↑"dò say at this móment [as the
'high forte'	|oppo↑sítion]| |is thìs| · 'for |hêaven's
'forte'	'sake|' |give a lèad| – and · '|"trý and
"lento"	[|bréak][|dówn]| · this "|dreadful
	sui↓cidal wáll|" where |no one will
"high"	↓yield an ↓ìnch| – "|say that you" ' 'do
	↓not in 'fact intènd| |over the ↑next
'low narrow'	↑six '↓mŏnths · if you ↓líke|' · to |have
'reson'	any more tèsts| – '|ʰsay · "sòmething|' that
	can |start the dis↓armament talks gòing| ·
'alleg'	'now |if 'you "fìrmly believe in thát|' ·
	|"don't go in for a coalìtion| · be|càuse
	as I've ↓sáid| · |that's a ↑very ·

↑"vìtal contri'bution I be↓LÍEVE| ·
to|wards the ↑peace of the ↓WÓRLD| and

'dimin breathy'   to|wards our ↑town de↑fence 'PÒLicy|' ·
and |"don't go in for sŏMEthing| · which
|might mean a cÒMpromise| · but |"do
by ↑"ÀLL 'means [|sÈE]| · that the

'narrow' |opposition is kept ↑PRÒperly in 'FÓRMED '|
'dimin' "low"   'as they |SHŎULD 'be| · "of de|fence
'measures for the ↓CÒUNtry|" ' – – –
(applause)

IV

'high'   '|my ↑GŌVernment|' · |re'af'firm
            their su'PPÓRT '| · for the de|"fence
'narrow'
            of the ↓free ↓ₙWÓRLD| – 'the
'low' |basic ₙCÒNcept| · of the at|lantic
            al"LÌance|' – – – and |they will
            con↑tinue to 'play their ↑full
            PÁRT| – in the |north at'lantic
'narrow'   ↓TRÈAty organi'sÁtion '| – and in
'low' |other ↑organisÁtions| 'for col|lective
            de↓FÈNCE '| – – |they will re↑view
            de'fence ₙPÓLicy| – 'to 'en|SÚRE|
'rhythmic' by re'|LÁting| our com|MÍTments|' · and
'high' |our resŌUrces| – that '|my ↑armed '
'narrow'   ↓FŌRces| · are |able to ↑dis'CHÁRGE '|
'low'   their |many TĀSKS| '|oversĒAs|' – with
            'the |greatest 'ef'fective'ness · and
'high'   e↓CÒNomy| – – – '|in 'parTĬcular|' –
            |they will 'make con↑structive
            pro↓PŌsals| – .for re|NĒWing| the
'narrow' |interde'PÉNDence '| of the at|lantic

'narrow'	a 'LLÍance'| – in re|lation to
	'nuclear WÈAPons| – |in an en↑deavour
	to prevēnt| |dupli'cation of ↓ÈFFort| –
'low'	'and the dis|semination of ↑ₙWÈAPons| ·
'high'	of |mass desTRÙCtion| – – – '|new
	ar'rangements have ↓been' ₙMÁDE| ·
'narrow'	to |ₙÁID ['and 'en'|CÓUrage']| the
'narrow'	|e'co'nomic and ↑sòcial ad'VÁNCE'| ·
	of the de|veloping ↓NÀtions| –
'rhythmic'	in'|cluding the re'maining 'de'pendent
'high'	↓TÈRRitories|' – – – 'my |ministers will
"narrow"	↑also en"DÉAvour"| – to pro|mote the
	ex↓pansion of' TRÀDE [to |this ÈND]|
	and |they will ₙSÉEK| in co|opeRĀtion|
	with |other ₙCÓUNtries| · and the
'low'	u|nited ₙNÀtions| 'and its |ₙÀgencies'| –
	to |stimulate ↑fresh ₙÁCtion| · 'to
	're|duce the ↓growing disPĀrities| of
'narrow'	|WĒALTH| and |oppor'TÚnity'| · be|TWÈEN
'low creak'	[the |PÈOples]| 'of the |WÒRLD'| – – –
'high'	'|my ↑ₙMÍNisters|' will |have a
'narrow'	↑SPÈCial ['re'|GÀRD']| · for the
	u|nique RŌLE| of 'the |CÒMMonwealth| –
'narrow'	'|which it↑self reFLĒCTS| so |many
	of the ↓ₙCHÀLLenges'| · and |op'por'tunities
'low'	'of the ↓WÒRLD'| – – – |they will ↑foster
	the 'commonwealth 'CONNĒCtion| on a
'narrow'	|basis of ↑racial e'QUÁLity'| · and
	|close consul↓TÀtion| be|tween ↑member
	GÒvernments| – – and |will pro↑mote
	'commonwealth col'laboRÁtion| in
'narrow'	|TRÁDE| · |e'conomic de'VÉLopment'| ·

|edu↑cĀtional| · |scienTĪFic| and
|cÙLtural ₙCÓNtacts| · |and in 'other
'high'   ↓WÀYS| – – – '|my 'government ↑will
conTÌNue| to |play a ↑full' PĀRT| in
'narrow'   the |european 'organi'sÀtions'| · of
|which · ↑this 'country is a ₙMÉMber| – –
and will |seek to proMŌTE| |closer
euro'pean co operÀtion| – – – a
|BĪLL| will be |intro↑DÚCED| to
pro|vide for the 'inde'pendence of
'high'   ↑GÀMbia| – – – '|MÉMbers| of the '
|house of CÓMMons| – |Éstimates [for
'low'   the |public ₙSÉRvices]| 'will 'be
'piano' |laid 'befÒRE you|' – – – 'my |LŌRDS| ·
and |members of the ↑house of ₙCÒMMons|'
'rhythmic'   – – 'at |HǑME| – '|my ↑government's
"narrow"   ↑first con"↓CÉRN"|' · will |be to
main↑tain the 'strength of ↑STĚRling| ·
by |dealing with the ↑short 'term
'balance of ↑payments ↑DÌFFiculties| –
and |by i'nitiating the ↑longer 'term
'narrow'   ↑structural 'changes in ↑our e'CÒNomy'| –
which |will ensÚRE| |PÚRposeful|
'narrow'   ex'|PÀNsion'| – |rising ₙÈXports| · and
a |healthy 'balance of ↑PÀYments| – – –

4 THE LANGUAGE OF WRITTEN INSTRUCTIONS

There are certain central criteria governing the formulation of any set of instructions, such as the paramount need to organise the information into a series of clearly defined stages, to avoid ambiguity, and to bear the level of one's audience clearly in mind. What linguistic evidence do you find in the following texts to suggest that these criteria have been followed? (The graphetic and graphological levels are particularly important for imposing organisation, but also note the use of sentence-connecting devices.) Is there linguistic evidence that a non-specialist audience is clearly envisaged for the following texts? (How much information is assumed by the writer to be understood by the reader? Could **IV** and **V** be legitimately considered as instances of technical English?) What alternative grammatical methods of instructing people are there, apart from the use of imperatives? Compare the language of these texts with section 5 below, which is also a set of instructions, though couched in very different terms – how much is there in common?

I

(1) Move the machine into position, remove the tabletop and wash tub lid.

(2) Check that the telescopic outlet pipe is in the position shown in the illustration on p. 1 – with its end fitting into the rubber socket behind the glass panel. This is the "Suds Saving" position.

(3) Check that all controls are OFF as shown in the illustration above.

(4) Plug into the power point. The machine is "dead" until the Master Switch is turned to HEATER or MOTOR.

(5) Turn the Master Switch to Heater.

(6) Leave the Temperature Control in the OFF position. If, by mistake, you turn the temperature control on when there is no water in the tub then the heater element will get very hot – but no harm will be done because an automatic cut-out operates. Just switch off and let the element cool.

(7) Turn the Master Switch to MOTOR. The motor will run but the agitator and spinner remain still.

(8) Turn the Wash Time control – say to 5 minutes. This starts the agitator working. The dial ticks gradually back to the OFF position, switching off the agitator automatically after the time you have selected. You can turn the dial back to OFF any time you wish, to stop the agitator.

(9) With the spinner lid closed turn the Spinner Control – say to 3 minutes. This starts the spinner and the control will switch off automatically after the time you have selected – but you can turn the control back to OFF at any time.

With the spinner running, open the spinner lid – note that the spinner is switched off automatically and is quickly brought to rest by an automatic brake.

Close the lid and the spinner will start again automatically. You can always stop and start the spinner by opening and closing the lid if you find this convenient.

II

PART 2

THE ROAD USER
ON WHEELS

*This Part includes rules applicable in general terms
to cyclists and those in charge of horses.*

Moving off

16. Before you move off, look round, even though you may have looked in your mirror, to see that no one is about to overtake you. Give the proper signal before moving out, and only move off when you can do so safely and without inconvenience to other road users. Give way to passing and overtaking vehicles.

Driving along

17. KEEP WELL TO THE LEFT, except when you intend to overtake or turn right. Do not hug the middle of the road.

18. Do not exceed the speed limits.

19. Never drive at such a speed that you cannot pull up well within the distance you can see to be clear, particularly having regard to the weather and the state of the road.

20. Where there is a double white line along the middle of the road, note whether the one nearer to you is continuous or broken and observe these rules:
—If the line nearer to you is continuous, keep to your own side of it and do not cross or straddle it.
—If the line nearer to you is broken, you may cross it, but only do so if you can complete your overtaking safely and before reaching a continuous white line on your side. A broken line does NOT mean that it is safe for you to overtake.

21. Never cross a single continuous or broken white line along the middle of the road unless you can see that the road well ahead is clear.

22. When following a vehicle on the open road, leave enough space in front of you for an overtaking vehicle.

The safety of pedestrians

23. When approaching ZEBRA CROSSINGS always be ready to slow down or stop so as to give way to pedestrians; *they have the right of way on these crossings.*

Signal to other drivers your intention to slow down or stop. Allow yourself more time to stop when the road is wet or icy.

DO NOT OVERTAKE when approaching a ZEBRA CROSSING.

24. At pedestrian crossings controlled by light signals or by the police, give way to pedestrians who are crossing when the signal to move is given.

25. Watch for the pedestrian who comes out suddenly from behind stationary vehicles and other obstructions. Be specially careful of this near schools and bus and tram stops.

26. When turning at a road junction, give way to pedestrians who are crossing.

27. On country roads watch out for pedestrians and give them plenty of room, especially on left-hand bends.

Lane discipline

28. Keep within lane markings and cross them only when moving into another lane. Do not switch from lane to lane. If you wish to move into another lane, do so only when you have given a signal and will not cause inconvenience or danger to other vehicles in it.

29. In traffic hold-ups do not "jump the queue".

30. Well before you reach a junction, make sure you are in the appropriate lane.

III

HOW TO MAKE
A CALL

First make sure you know the number

then consult your dialling code list if you have
one.

Lift the receiver

If you share a dial telephone press the button.
Should your partner be using the line, try
again later.

Listen for the dialling tone

The operator will demonstrate the tones if you
are uncertain.

Then dial:

For calls on your own exchange, the number.
For other dialled calls, the code and/or
number (*see your dialling code list*).
For all other calls, the operator.

If your telephone has no dial

just ask the operator for the number.

For enquiries or to report
service difficulties

consult your dialling code list or, if your telephone has no dial, ask for Enquiries.

IV

BANANAS AU RHUM

1 oz. butter
20 large bananas
9 tablespoons Demerara sugar
juice of three lemons
3 tablespoons water
3 sherry-glasses rum
1 gill double cream

Butter a large, shallow, fireproof dish. Cut the bananas lengthways and lay in dish. Sprinkle the sugar on top, then add lemon juice and water. Bake in a moderate oven – gas-mark 4 (350°F) – for 20 minutes or until brown. Add the rum 5 minutes before removing, except for 2 tablespoons which you add to the whipped cream, serving it in a separate dish.

SYLVABELLA
can be prepared the day before

6 oz. butter
5 oz. sugar
4 eggs, separated
4 oz. chocolate
2 tablespoons water
4 lumps sugar
$\frac{1}{4}$ cup water mixed with $\frac{1}{4}$ cup rum
21 sponge ladyfingers

Cream together butter, sugar and beaten yolks until smooth. Heat the chocolate and water in a bowl over boiling water, stirring to a creamy consistency. Add slowly to the first mixture, then fold in stiffly-beaten egg whites. Stir the lump sugar into some watered rum. Dip ladyfingers in this thin liquid and line a soufflé dish (5 in.–6 in.) with 18 of them. Pour chocolate into the middle and cover with the remaining ladyfingers, halved. Chill and serve with whipped cream and crystallized violets.

V

RIGHT FRONT

Using No. 7 needles, cast on 45 sts.
Work 6 rows in moss stitch (every row * K.1, P.1, rep. from * to last st., K.1).
Proceed in lace and moss stitch patt. with moss stitch border as follows:—
1st row—(K.1, P.1) twice, * K.1, w.f., K.3, w.f., sl.1, K.1, p.s.s.o., K.1, K.2 tog., w.f., K.3, w.f., (K.1, P.1) 4 times, rep. from * to last st., K.1.
2nd row—K.1, P.1, * (K.1, P.1) 3 times, P.16, rep. from * to last 3 sts., K.1, P.1, K.1.
3rd row—(K.1, P.1) twice, * K.1, w.f., sl.1, K.1, p.s.s.o., K.1, K.2 tog., w.f., sl.1, K.2 tog., p.s.s.o., w.f., sl.1, K.1, p.s.s.o., K.1, K.2 tog., w.f., (K.1, P.1) 4 times, rep. from * to last st., K.1.

5 CIVIL SERVICE LANGUAGE

The formulation and interpretation of rules and regulations applicable to the various individuals and groups constituting a complex society produces a number of different kinds of written language, of which the following extract represents one type. Official uses of language of this kind, which attempt to combine background information and instructions simultaneously, are frequently criticised for unintelligibility. Consider the linguistic structure of the text and decide whether this criticism is justified. What are the sources of difficulty? What alternative methods of presentation might improve matters?[1] To what extent is the pejorative use of the label 'officialese' justified in the following extract? Distinguish between technical terms which have no unambiguous brief alternative (such as *commission* or *emolument*) and those which have (such as *domiciled* or *purchase*). Is it necessary to develop a formal and impersonal kind of English for such matters? (Consider the function of such structures as the passive (including the explicit agent), the use of dependent clauses in order to express a series of alternatives, the use of modal verbs, the use of parentheses, and the function of such phrases as *in respect of* and *wear and tear*.) Is the relatively informal headline consistent with the way in which the text is written? How many familiar terms are given specialist senses here? What is the reason for such phrases as *the sale, etc, moneys*? Compare the use of the imperative here with the texts in section 4 above. Look at this extract in the light of what was said in Chapter 8 about the language of legal documents: have any features of legal language influenced the language of official instruction?

[1] *Cf* B. N. LEWIS, I. S. HORABIN, C. P. GANE, 'Flow Charts, Logical Trees and Algorithms for Rules and Regulations', *CAS Occasional Papers 2*, H.M.S.O., 1967.

HOW TO FILL UP YOUR RETURN

2.   Employment or Office

General. Enter the full earnings (including bonus, commission, casual fees, gratuities, etc.) for the year ended 5 April 1965.

Where your employer bears your Income Tax liability on some or all of your earnings instead of deducting it from your pay, the tax paid by him on your behalf counts as additional remuneration and must be included in the amount you return.

If:

(a) the whole of your duties (other than merely incidental duties) are performed outside the United Kingdom, or

(b) you are not resident or not ordinarily resident in the United Kingdom, and your duties are performed partly outside the United Kingdom, or

(c) your employer is not resident in the United Kingdom and you are not domiciled in the United Kingdom,

the basis on which your emoluments should be returned is different: the tax office will supply details on request.

...   .

Deductions from emoluments. You may claim:

...   .

(d) *Capital Allowances.* If a motor car is provided by you at your own expense and used only for the purposes of your office or employment, allowances may be claimed as follows:—

(i) if you purchased a car during the year ended 5 April 1965, an initial allowance of three-tenths of the cost of the car,

(ii) an annual allowance in respect of wear and tear,

(iii) a balancing allowance (following sale or the happening of some other event during the year ended 5 April 1965, giving rise to a balancing allowance) equal to the amount, if any, by which the expenditure on the car which has not been allowed for Income Tax purposes is greater than the sale, etc., moneys (or, in certain circumstances, open market price). If the sale, etc., moneys exceeded the difference between the cost of the car and the total allowances given for Income Tax purposes, tax will be charged, in certain circumstances, on the whole or part of the excess.

...   .

The amount to be entered in your return is the total deduction claimed for the year 1964–65, ended 5 April 1965. If you sold a car, etc., during that year, or permanently ceased to use a car, etc., for the purposes of your office or employment, particulars of the date of sale and sale price (or the date of cessation of use and open market price at that date), should be furnished on a separate sheet, unless they have already been given to the tax office. Particulars should similarly be furnished, if not already given, of the date of purchase, make and cost of any car, etc., acquired during the year.

(e) *Allowances to Clergyman.* If you are a clergyman or minister and live in a house from which to perform the duties of your office in circumstances such that the house is treated as occupied *otherwise than by you*, you may claim a deduction equal to one quarter of any expenditure borne by you in respect of maintenance, repairs, or insurance of the premises. If you pay a rent for the house and you use part of the premises mainly and substantially for the purposes of your duties, you may claim a deduction not exceeding one quarter of the rent for the year ended 5 April 1965.

6 SPOKEN LEGAL LANGUAGE

This extract was taken from a recording made in a courtroom. It differs from the original in that all personal references have been replaced by rhythmically equal words. Consider this text to see how far the language overlaps with Chapter 8. To what extent can one see the influence of the written form of legal language influencing the speech of the judge? What are the linguistic exponents of the judge's concern to be (a) precise, (b) impersonal, and (c) formal? What evidence is there that the judge is not reading his judgment from a script, but *is* using some written aids? What is the reason for such phrases as *that bicycle of the plaintiff's*? What is distinctive about the use of pronouns, coordination and adverbials? What is the evidence for regarding spoken legal language as essentially a fairly normal conversational English with fixed (and well-remembered) legal formulae embedded in it?

|this ÁCtion| · a|rises · 'out of a

↑MȪtor ÁCcident| – – |on · thi – – –

'low'   ↑road be'tween ↓HŌVE| 'and |BRȊGHton|' – –

at a|bout a ↑quarter to ↓TÉN| · on the

|ÉVEning| · of the |sixth of ↓ₙÁPril|

'high wide' |nineteen 'sixty ↓FÒUR| – – 'the

|PLÁINTiff|' |was ↓THÉN| · and |happily

'still ↓Ìs| – a |night WÀTCHman| ·

*em|PLÓYED| by the |well 'known

'very low'   ↓pharma↓ceutical ↓CHĔMists| '|messrs 'hall

↓JÄRvis|' – – |and he was ↑going on NÌGHT

DÚty| · at |that TÍME| and |on that ↓DÀY| –

|and he was ↑turning into the GÁTEs| of

'low' |hall ↑jarvis's FÀCTory| 'which |[lies just

'very low dimin' ÒFF]' 'thi ə ↑hove BRÌGHton [|RÒAD]|' – |when –

'alleg gliss`' his ↑BÍcycle| – |was 'when the |bicycle on

'lento' ↑which he was' ↓RÍding| – '|was ↑STRÚCK|' ·

'alleg low piano' 'to |use a ↑NÈUtral ex"PRÉSSion"| at |THÌS
"narrow" ₙSTÁGE|' · by a |MÒtorcycle| – |ridden 'by ·

'low' the deFÉNdant| 'mr |TÀYlor|' – 'who |HĀD| a
'descend' |young ↑ₙLÀdy| on his ↓PÌLLion|' – |and

'was pro↑CĒEDing| – [fr] in thi di|rection

'low' of ↓HŎVE| · |from ↑BRÌGHton| – '|as in↓DĒED| ·

was the |PLĂINTiff|' – – the |road at that

PÓINT| · was |twenty ÉIGHT 'foot| · |nine

'inches · ↓WÌDE| – at the |moment at 'which

the ↓accident 'took ↓PLÀCE| · |that

↑bi'cycle of the PLÁINTiff's| – and that

|mo'tor ↓bicycle of the de↓FÈNdant's| –

were the |only · 'two · véhicles| ·

|im · ↑MÈdiately| –|BȲ| · the po|sītion| ·

in |which the 'accident 'took ↓PLÀCE| – – –

the |sole ₙQUÉStion| |I 'have to

'very low' de'↓CÌDE| in |this CÀSE|' · is |who 'was

'respÒNsible| – the |PLĂINTiff| – |ÓR| ·

'creak' the de|FĚNdant| – – the |plaintiff 'SÁYS|' ·

that the de|fen'dant ↑came up from

beHÍND| · |notwith↑standing the wÁRNing| ·

'low' that |he the 'plaintiff · GÁVE| · 'that

he was a|bout to go a↓CRŌSS| from his

|own 'side of the ↓RÓAD| · to|wards the

'entrance to 'hall 'jarvis's FÀCTory|' ·

and |"struck the 'plaintiff's CȲcle| –

'rhythmic'   in |such a wāy| as to '|break the
               'plaintiff's ↓right ↓lèg|' – – the
               de|fendant sàys| – |that there ↑was
               and ↑hăd 'been| for |some 'time
               be↑fòre the áccident| |ei ↑mòtor car|
               a|hĕad of him| – |driving in the ↑same
               di'rection as ↓that in 'which the
               de'fendant was drìving| – – |and
               thát| – ə: thi · |that ↑mŏtor 'car| –
               |pulled 'out slíghtly| to |pàss|
               what |ₙpròved| to be the |plaintiff
               'on his cỳcle| – that the de|fendant ·
'dimin'   ↑fòllowed| the |mŏtor 'car| 'in |doing
               the ↓same ↓thìng|' – |and that ↑whén| ·
               the de|fèndant| was |some ↑thirty or
'alleg' 'low' ↓forty ↓yàrds| be|fòre| 'be|"hìnd|' 'the
               |pláintiff| |on his bícycle|' – the
'lento' |plaintiff ↑pùt out his hánd| · '|and
               with↑out ↑more a↓dó| – |pùlled| –
               a |cròs̄s̄ the 'main 'road| – |and ↑never
               ↓gáve| the de|féndant| a |chánce| of
               a|vòiding him|' – – |those are · the ↓rival
               ₙstóries| · and |I have to decíde| ·
'stac'   '|which · is · rìght|'

7 THE LANGUAGE OF
BROADCAST TALKS AND NEWS

The use of language over the radio imposes some very stringent
conditions on the user. It is normally written English being read
aloud, and there are important constraints on the writer of the language as well as on the speaker (who are often different persons). The
writer has to ensure that his material can be easily articulated, and
must avoid anything which would disturb overall fluency, such as

ambiguous structures (which could be read in any one of a number of ways – 'I'm sorry, I'll read that again . . .'), tongue-twisters, and so on. He must also ensure that his material can be readily understood: the listener cannot ask for a repeat of anything obscure; moreover, he is liable to lose the track if a sentence involves too complicated an internal structure or goes on for too long (such as by using a sequence of dependent clauses). Also, the absence of visual contact between speaker and hearer imposes important constraints on the kind of structures used (*cf p* 119). Examine the texts below for evidence that ease of articulation and reception is being carefully borne in mind. How do the speakers try to keep the listeners' interest? What evidence of informality is there? (Consider the pause system of **I**, in particular. Also, what aspects of the prosodic system would *not* be indicated in the punctuated script?) What must the speakers do to ensure that their speech will be comprehensible and pleasant? What must they not do? What are the linguistic exponents of the newsreader's 'neutral' position? Does he ever allow personal attitude to be introduced? Why is there so little figurative language in the news? Is there anything linguistically in common between the different topics being covered? (Consider the way in which each topic is given its own speech 'paragraph' (*cf p* 33), primarily through the use of prosodic features.) What does the popular notion of 'BBC English' mean, if anything? What are the main differences between **I** and **II** below?

I

the |"ₙJÛDGE| · in the |MÀIL 'train|
|RÒBBery TRÍal| at |ĂYLEsbury| has
'high' '|ordered · ↑round the' 'clock po↓lice
proTÈCtion| for the |families of the
'gliss`' ↑ₙJÙry| · |ÀLL MÉN| · |when they 're↑tire
to con↓sider their ↓VÈRdict|' – |when
'spiky`' mr '↑justice ↓edmund ↓davis ↓said this
in ↓court this' ↓MŎRNing| – he re|ferred
'alleg' to the FÁCT| that '|earlier this WĒEK| ·
|one of the júrors|' had re|ported an
'rhythmic' at'tempt at "BRÌbery| – the '|clerk of

the 'court had ↑ₙTÒLD him [he |SÃID]|' ·

'high'   'that the |JÚry|' were now |asking for

'alleg'   as↑sŭrances| 'that there would be' |no

'narrow'   'kind of 'interFÉrence|' with their

'low' |ₙFĂMilies| – '|while they were in
            re↑TÌREment|' – and he |SÃID| · so |far
            as it 'is with'in my PÓWers| |I di↑rect
            the po↑LÌCE [au|THÒRities]| that

'alleg'   pro|TÊCtion '[|will be provìded]| · for

'lento low' |twenty four' ↓hours of the DÀY| – 'and ·

"creak"   it |"will be ₙDÓNE| · |I am "sùrE|" '
            ·· ·· ·· ·· ·· ··

'high'   'the ex|ecutive of the' ↑PÒST office
            'workers ÚNion| has con|firmed ↑april the
            'sixTÈENTH| as the |day on 'which they
            will ↑hold their 'one day STRÌKE| – at a
            |meeting this MÓRNing| it was |also
            a'greed to ↑"ban 'all ↑Òvertime| in|cluding
            ↑SÙNday ₙDÚty| – for |two ↓WÈEKS| |from
            'april the ↑seven↓TÈENTH| – |april the
            ↑síx'teenth| |is · a THŬRsday| · |when
            there's heavy ↑FÒOTball 'pools [|PÒSTing]|
            ·· ·· ·· ·· ·· ·· ·· ·· ··

'high'   the u|'nited' STĀTES| has |warned the
            ↑RŬSsians| · that a |further de↑LÀY| in
            re|turning the ↑three a↑merican ↑ₙÀIRmen|
            |shot 'down 'over ↑east GÈRmany last
            WÉEK| – |ₙcould AFFÈCT| · |present
            'efforts to ex↑tend co'ope'ration
            be↑TWÈEN them| – a |note de↑livered in
            ↑moscow toDÁY| |says aGÁIN| that the

'narrow' |aircraft was ↑"NÒT| |on an in'↑TÈLLigence'

'stac' [|mīssion]| · '|and was 'unÀrmed|' · it
|sāys| that al|though an a↓mÈrican army
[|dòctor]| |hÀs been al'lowed| to |see
the ↑mÈmber of the crew| whō was
'narrow' |ĭnjured| · a|merican li'Àison
[|òfficers]|' · have been re|fùsed
per'mission| to |question the crēw| ·
'gliss`' to |fìnd [|òut]| · '|"why their ↓plane
went off ↓còurse|'

II

'high' 'his |work' as a ↓cărıcaturist| –
'spiky`' 'is |that in 'which he 'most
"breathy" "delìghted|" ' – it was |"nèver| a
|matter of 'formal ↑trăining| or |set
'spiky`' ↑pŭrpose with 'him| – ''it 'be|gan
with 'marginal' ₙskètches| in 'his
'spiky`' '|school and 'college' nòtebooks| – –
'husky' |when william ↓rŏthen'stein| 'e|rupted
into ↓ŏxford|' · to |do a ↓series of
↓portrait ↓dráwings| – 'he |gave
'en'couragement and ↑hèlp| – – it
'narrow' was |hè| 'who |taught máx| to |make
'gliss`' his ↑drăwings| – '|not 'mere 'personal'
↑cărıcatures| – 'but |decorative
desígns| 'with 'an 'aes|thetic
'alleg' 'ex'istence of their ↑òwn| – – 'and
we can |easily ↑tràce this 'process|' –
'narrow' if we |turn 'over a 'se↓lèction|' of
|max's ↑dráwings| 'in 'chrono|logical
↑òrder| – – the |èarly ónes| are
|ₙlively ↓cŏmments| on indi|vidual

↑personÁLities| – ˙in the |MÁNNer of|

'tense'   ˙|ʺÀPE| and |ʺSPỲ|˙' of |VÁNity ↑FÀIR| –

'piano' "alleg"   ˙and |they be˙long "↑MĂINly| ˙to ˙the
|world" ˙of ˙soCÍety| · |PÓLitics| and˙'
|SPÒRT| – – |ʺRŏTHenstein| |taught him
to ↑CÒLour his ₙDRÁWings| – and the
|delicate ˙water colour ↟MĂNNer| that
we as|SÒciate with ↟MÁX| · |was the
re↑ʺSÙLT| – – and |with THÍS| |came thĩ
re↑ʺLÈASE into his ↟WÓRK| · ˙of an
|ÉLement| ˙that was |ÁLways [|PRÉSent]|

'lento'   in ˙his |sen˙siBÌLity| – a · ˙|pre

"French   RÀPHaelite| · "|art nou↟VĔAU|" ' · |sense
pronunciation"
'rhythmic'   of ↟decorative desÌGN| – ˙a |taste for
'sinuous LÌNES|' · and wher|ever the
↟subject al↑LŎWED for it| · ˙for ˙a

'lento' |kind of ˙f̄ragile ↟PRÈTTiness|' – –
|women and ↟GÏRLS| · if they're |not
mere ↟figures of ↑FŬN| |like briʺTÁNNia|
or |mrs GRÚNdy| · are |GÈNerally
↟TRÉATed| ˙with |TÈNderness in

'piano'   ˙max's ₙDRÁWings| – ˙˙a |TÉNderness
that ˙goes ↑back to ↑burne ↓JÒNES| –
|sometimes ↑almost to ↑kate ↓GRÈENaway|'
– – |max said he↟LÒNGED| to the
|BÈARDsley ↟PÉriod| · but he has
|none of ˙beardsley's ˙cult · of the

'breathy'   ob˙scurely ˙SÌNister|' – ˙it's a
'piano' |GÈNTler ˙side| "of the |english
"narrow"   aes↟THÈTic MÓVEment| · that |left its
↟mark on ↑HĬM|" ' – – and in|stead of thĩ
hie↟ratic so↟LÈMnity| – of the |deep

DY̌ED| · |greenery ↑YÀLLery| ·

'high'   'ex|PÓnent|' – 'there 'is |wit · and

MÒCKery| – he |PÀRodies| |what 'he

'deLÍGHTS in| · what is a |part of

his 'own NÀture|

8 THE LANGUAGE OF SCIENCE

Compared with most of the varieties of English referred to in this book, scientific prose has been quite well studied, and a great deal of research into it is going on at present. One of the points which has still not been fully appreciated is the extent to which one may distinguish, within the general province of scientific language, a number of distinct uses, which for the most part we would account for in terms of our dimension of modality, *eg* the language used in reporting an experiment, in discussing a problem, in giving instructions as to how an experiment should be performed, in stating laws, or in defining concepts. For purposes of illustration, we have chosen two extracts from the same chapter relating to the first two uses just mentioned, which are probably the most frequently occurring and widely known kinds of scientific English. There are a number of specific issues which should be borne in mind in examining these extracts. It is generally agreed that the main problem for the scientist, as far as his use of language is concerned, is to define his subject matter precisely and to establish a clear and logical progression of ideas. What value has visual presentation in these matters (*cf* especially the typography, the use of subheadings and paragraphing)? What functions do the grammar and vocabulary have in carrying out this aim? The vocabulary of scientific English – probably its most obvious feature – has been pejoratively called 'jargon': is this justified? Scientists are themselves aware of the dangers of too much complexity, abstraction, and impersonality in their work, as the following quotation from the *Handbook for Chemical Society Authors*[1] shows: 'Sentences such as "Reduction of the ketone was effected catalytically" (which should read "Hydrogenation of the ketone gave") suffer from the abstract word and the passive voice ... Before the final typing every paper should be scrutinised to see whether it cannot be improved by eliminating abstract words and passive voices.' What is the significance of the fact that in this piece of advice the author

[1] Special publication No. 14, 2nd edn, The Chemical Society, 1961, *p* 13.

himself uses an abstract word and two passive constructions? What types of scientific vocabulary can in fact be distinguished in these extracts (*eg* the difference between everyday terms which have been given a specialist sense, and the morphologically complex constructs based on Latin or Greek elements). Why is the word *cleanest* in inverted commas? This kind of English has sometimes been called 'impersonal': what are the linguistic correlates of this? Is impersonality a desirable feature of scientific English? To what extent is grammatical complexity a function of the nominal group rather than of sentence structure (*cf* postmodification in the nominal group as evidence on this point)? Verbal groups are not normally complex, but they are nonetheless distinctive: what features do the extracts provide? What points should be made about the use of adverbials in the second extract? Most lay people – and perhaps many scientists – would hesitate over the pronunciation of the vocabulary of these extracts: what is the significance of this? What is meant by the so-called 'translatability' of scientific prose? Should the scientist ever attempt to write non-technical English, or would it be better for him to concentrate on developing a purely technical language in which he could address other scientists, and to abandon any effort to be intelligible to the layman?

I

The photolytic decomposition of phenylazotriphenylmethane in benzene apparently follows a similar course to the pyrolytic decomposition discussed above. It has been investigated by Horner and Naumann (1954) and Huisgen and Nakaten (1954), and was found to involve a primary dissociation into phenyl and triphenylmethyl radicals and nitrogen, in the manner indicated in equation (8). The phenyl radicals are capable of effecting arylation, and the arylation is inhibited by the presence of an excess of *p*-benzoquinone, which traps the radicals efficiently. Nitric oxide similarly prevents the formation of triphenylmethane by uniting with triphenylmethyl radicals, as also does iodine in the presence of ethanol.

3 ARYLATION WITH DIACYL PEROXIDES AND ANALOGOUS SUBSTANCES

(a) Preparative Use of Diacyl Peroxides

The thermal decomposition of diacyl peroxides provides what is undoubtedly the "cleanest", and, provided the required peroxide is readily available, most convenient source of aryl radicals for the arylation of aromatic substrates. The purified peroxide, which is generally crystalline, is added to the aromatic solvent, and the decomposition is effected by heating, usually to about 70–80°. Smaller quantities of tarry products are obtained, and the reported yields of diaryls are generally higher than with the diazo- and azo-compounds discussed above.

The products of the decomposition of diaroyl peroxides in various solvents (RH) were extensively studied by Gelissen and Hermans (1925, 1926), and Böeseken and Hermans (1935), who showed that the reaction obeyed their "RH scheme" [equation (9), cf equation (7) above], although the reaction mechanism was not at that time clearly defined.

$$(\text{Ar}'\text{CO}.\text{O})_2 + \text{RH} \quad \begin{array}{l} (a) \nearrow \text{Ar}'\text{H} + \text{CO}_2 + \text{Ar}'\text{CO}.\text{OR} \\[2em] (b) \searrow \text{Ar}'\text{R} + \text{CO}_2 + \text{Ar}'\text{CO}.\text{OH} \end{array} \qquad (9)$$

II

Thus stationary concentrations of both aroyloxy and aryl radicals are present in the reaction mixture at all times during the reaction, and, in principle, nuclear substitution in the aromatic substrate by either of these species may occur. Thus a certain quantity of a mixture of esters arising from substitution by aroyloxy radicals is always formed during an arylation reaction with a diaryl peroxide. Since aroyloxy radicals appear to be considerably less reactive entities than aryl radicals in aromatic substitution, the extent of aroyloxylation is generally small, and the phenolic esters formed thereby are easily removed by hydrolysis and extraction with alkali. Nevertheless, the process must be recognised and its products removed. Moreover, its extent must obviously increase with the reactivity of the aromatic substrate towards homolytic attack, and with more reactive compounds, such as naphthalene, aroyloxylation becomes a very important side-reaction.

Index

A **boldface** *number reference indicates a place*
where the meaning of the term is explained